ARCHITECTS AT CORSHAM COURT

The Picture Gallery, Corsham Court, designed by Lancelot Brown.

FREDERICK J. LADD

Architects at Corsham Court

A STUDY IN REVIVAL STYLE ARCHITECTURE AND LANDSCAPING, 1749–1849

MOONRAKER PRESS

© 1978 Frederick J. Ladd

FIRST PUBLISHED IN 1978 BY MOONRAKER PRESS
26 ST MARGARETS STREET, BRADFORD-ON-AVON, WILTSHIRE
SBN 239.00176.1
TEXT SET IN 12/14½ PT MONOTYPE TIMES NEW ROMAN
PRINTED BY LETTERPRESS AND BOUND IN GREAT BRITAIN
AT THE PITMAN PRESS, BATH

Contents

List of Illustrations

Frontispiece The Picture Gallery, Corsham Court; designed by Lancelot Brown 1760–63. (Photograph, Cooper-Bridgeman Library, courtesy Lord Methuen)

Portraits facing page 2 The Rt Hon. Sir Paul Methuen, K.B. (1672–1757) by Joseph Highmore; Paul Methuen (1723–95) by Thomas Gainsborough; Paul Cobb Methuen (1752–1816) by Thomas Gainsborough; Paul, 1st Lord Methuen (1779–1849) by John Linnell.

THE PLATES

References in the text to illustrations are denoted by the relevant number set in bold type in parentheses, thus (27).

Foreword

A systematic study of the architecture of Corsham Court has been long overdue. Articles and references have appeared from time to time in various historical surveys, journals and monographs, notably those of the late Mr Christopher Hussey. My research yields fresh material, clarifies some previous misattributions, and proposes a possible genesis for the design of the Elizabethan House. The last monograph devoted to the architecture of Corsham Court, with a catalogue of the picture collection, was John Britton's *An Historical Account of Corsham House*, published in 1806. It was the first of three special monographs by John Britton devoted to contemporary Revival Style houses that he admired, the others being Fonthill Abbey, Wiltshire, 1823, and Toddington Manor, Gloucestershire, 1840.

A series of admirable guide books to the house and its contents was edited by the late Paul Ayshford, Lord Methuen. Lord Anthony John Methuen has had published a third new revised edition in March of this year. At the moment of going to press, my attention has also been drawn to a study by Mr Leslie Harcourt, *Corsham Court: A Gothick Dream*, based upon aspects of John Nash's work at Corsham Court.

Much of the research made for this book at Corsham Court was carried out in 1970–71, during the occupancy of the late Paul Ayshford Methuen, RA, FSA, (1886–1974), the Fourth Baron. Lord Methuen inherited the title from his Father, Field Marshal Paul Sanford Methuen (1845–1932), the Third Baron. Since holding the title, and living at Corsham Court, Paul Ayshford Methuen patiently assembled the documents and drawings related to the house and its contents, and began the process of having them systematically catalogued. Much of our knowledge of Corsham Court today is due to his patronage of connoisseurs, preservationists and scholars who have studied and published upon various aspects of the house and its collection. They always found a most helpful, sympathetic and well-informed owner. Despite his wide variety of interests, and the many calls upon his time, Lord Methuen's most cherished project was the preservation of the house and its treasures. I owe a deep debt of gratitude to him for his interest in my research, and the helpful suggestions that he made. These were drawn from his recollections at a time when he was nearing the end of his long life, so intimately connected with Corsham Court.

Anthony Paul Methuen (1891–1975), the Fifth Baron, succeeded his brother to the title in 1974, only to hold it until the following year. Trained as an architect, and having worked with Sir Clough Williams-Ellis, Anthony Paul Methuen was responsible for saving the Picture Gallery Ceiling at Corsham Court, when one of the main beams broke during the 1914–18 war. I am most grateful to the present holder of the title, Anthony John Methuen, the Sixth Baron, who succeeded his Father in 1975, in graciously giving permission for the publication of this research.

The late Paul Ayshford Methuen had gathered around him a devoted staff who were most kind in their efforts to answer numerous questions and in locating research material. The record cannot pass without mentioning in particular the assistance received from Mrs Diana Bliss (née Kendall), private secretary; Miss Elmira Wade, OBE, the archivist; the late Mr Arthur Bowerings, the stone mason; Mr Richard Nolan, the principal guide, and other members of Lord Methuen's staff at that time. The advice of Mr Robert Blackmore, JP, a former Chairman of Hayward & Wooster, Bath, responsible for the restorations at Corsham Court, was invaluable.

I acknowledge the kindness of the following persons who replied to enquiries concerning my research; Their Graces, the late Duke of Argyll, and the Duke of Buccleugh, the Marquess of Bath, the Marquess of Lansdowne, Lord Boston, Sir George Trevelyn, Mr Antony Dale, Mr Allen David Francis; Mr G. F. Williams, Curator Coalbrookdale Museum; Miss Mary Delahoyd, Vassar College; Mr Willis Van Devanter, Paul Mellon's Librarian; The Royal Librarian, Windsor Castle, and the Croome Court Estate. I also acknowledge replies from the following institutions: Buckingham Record Office, Hampshire Record Office, Scottish Record Office, and the Wiltshire Record Office.

I wish to express my thanks to the following whose homes and institutions I visited: the late Lt. Col. H. N. Ingles, acting librarian for the Marquess of Bath, Longleat House; Mrs Katherine Burnett Brown, Lacock Abbey, Wiltshire; Mr A. E. Moulton, The Hall, Bradford-on-Avon, Wiltshire; Mr Barrington Brock, the custodian, Montacute House, Somerset; the Secretary, and Miss Constance Anne Parker, Assistant Librarian, The Royal Academy of Art; The Secretary, The Society of Antiquarians; Mr John Harris and the staff of the Royal

Institute of British Architects; the Secretary, The Courtauld Institute; the Staff of the British Museum; Mr Michael Holmes, the Victoria & Albert Museum; Mr J. Farrell and staff of the Bristol University Library; the Staff of the Bristol Municipal Library; Mr John Kite, Bath Public Library; Mr R. E. Sandell, The Wiltshire Archaeological & Natural History Society Museum, Devizes, Wiltshire; Mr John Scandrett, Bristol Museum & Art Gallery; The Principal, St Mary's Training College, Strawberry Hill; and the Keeper, The Muniment Room, Westminster Abbey.

The following persons very kindly made helpful suggestions upon problems related to my research: Dr Mark Girouard, Miss Dorothy Stroud, MBE, FSA, the Sir John Soane Museum; Dr Howard E. Stutchbury, City Architect of Bath, and Mr Kenneth Woodbridge, Freshford, Somerset.

I am also very grateful to my advisers at Ohio State University who sponsored this study, especially Dr William A. Gibson (now on the faculty of Idaho State University), whose guidance and suggestions immeasurably improved my research, and Dr Franklin M. Ludden, Chairman of my doctoral committee. I also extend my thanks to other members of the faculty who were involved with the project; Dr Glenn Patton (now on the faculty of Temple University), Dr Maurice Cope (now of the faculty of the University of Delaware), Dr Mark Morford, Dr Sadja Herzog and Dr Philip Poirier. The encouragement given by the late Rudolf Wittkower when I was first considering this topic should also be recorded. I am also very grateful to Mrs Claire Lenfest, my typist for the original manuscript, to Mr Michael Nimeroff for reading my early drafts, to Brother Brian Dybowski, CB, PhD, who helped to assemble the photographs, and finally to Mrs Jacqueline Sisson, the Fine Art Library, Ohio State University. It is hoped that this publication will contribute towards our knowledge of the complex history of Corsham Court.

Baltimore, Maryland.
June, 1977.

Acknowledgements

Publication of details from the Corsham Court Archives are with permission of the Trustees of the Late Field Marshal, Lord Methuen, and references to the Methuen Collection, the House and Grounds are with permission of the Lord Methuen. The method of cataloguing documents recommended by the National Buildings Record is used at Corsham. Blocks of numbers are allocated to specific items, such as personal correspondence, estate accounts, etc. Documents designated Corsham archives only, without a number, indicate they were not catalogued at the time of my research in 1970–71.

Acknowledgements of the Illustrations

I am grateful to the following persons, institutions and publishers who have graciously permitted me to reproduce their illustrations in this book.

The Lord Methuen for the drawings, plans and paintings from the Methuen Collection.

The Marquess of Bath, **12**.

Sir John Summerson, **3**.

Mr Prideaux-Brune, **8**.

Mr Chichester Constable, **90**.

Miss Dorothy Stroud, MBE, FSA, and Faber & Faber, **90**.

A. C. Cooper Ltd, **Portraits** of **Paul & Paul Cobb Methuen**.

Country Life Ltd, **42, 48, 49, 68 & 87**.

The Courtauld Institute of Art, the University of London, **Portraits of Sir Paul Methuen & Paul, 1st Lord Methuen.**

The National Monuments Record, **51 & 53**.

The National Trust—Attingham Park, **69**.

The City of Nottingham Natural History Museum, **20**.

Penguin Books Ltd, **3**.

The Royal Institute of British Architects, **58, 79, 80 & 84**.

The Trustees of the Sir John Soane Museum, **9**.

The Trustees of the Victoria & Albert Museum, **39, 46 & 83**.

The Wiltshire Archaeological & Natural History Society, **65**.

The Yale Center for British Art, Paul Mellon Collection, **66**.

Wilmarth Sheldon Lewis & the Trustees of the National Gallery, Washington D.C., **47**.

This book is dedicated to the memory of

PAUL AYSHFORD METHUEN, R.A., F.S.A.

(1886–1974), 4th Baron

AN APPRECIATION BY SIR JOHN BETJEMAN

Lord Methuen was a rare combination. He was a painter as well as a distinguished arboriculturist and horticulturist. The garden, trees and park at Corsham received his expert attention—so did the town of Corsham. He stood out against such modern horrors as concrete lamp-standards and sodium lighting. He was a man of few words, and all of them pertinent. He had delightful manners and his clothes and appearance were distinguished. He looked every inch the hereditary peer he was: he also looked like the artist he was.

London, January 1978

Introduction

Corsham Court is a country mansion situated in Wiltshire, England, ten miles from Bath on the London Road. The house stands adjacent to the village of Corsham on a slight rise in the ground surrounded by a 350-acre park. The main entrance is situated on the south side of the house. On the east side of the main entrance the parish church of St Bartholomew stands overlooking the park. The church forms the principal feature of the view from the south side of the house. The mansion is the home of Lord Anthony John Methuen. The centre part of the house and certain out-buildings have been leased to Bath Academy of Art since 1946.

The original part of the house is Elizabethan; an inscription on the south front suggests that it may have been completed in 1582. It was partly remodelled during the 17th century. Three major extensions were added to the house between 1749 and 1849; the park was also remodelled on two occasions. A succession of architects and landscape gardeners provided plans, and carried out the extensions to the house and layout of the grounds, including Nathaniel Ireson, Henry Keene, Lancelot Brown, James Wyatt, John Nash, Humphry Repton, and Thomas Bellamy. The principal object of the two extensions made in the 18th century by Brown and Nash was to provide suites of state rooms to house the picture collection assembled by Sir Paul Methuen (1672–1757). The third major extension in the mid-19th century replaced the work carried out by Nash half a century earlier.

This study will consider how each Revival architect who worked at Corsham solved two problems in the evolution of the house. The first was the preservation of the symmetrical Elizabethan plan, the second the incorporation of the Elizabethan south front into their designs for the north and east fronts of the house overlooking the park. The original Elizabethan-Renaissance style was a transitional style combining both Gothic and Renaissance elements. While a few Revival theorists recognised the dual nature of the Elizabethan style, most of them tended to emphasise either Gothic or Renaissance qualities to suit their particular point of view.

Each successive Revival movement brought with it a significant change of attitude towards the Elizabethan-Renaissance style. Each Revival architect re-modelled Corsham within the concepts of his Revival style architectural theory, and in doing so was confronted by two principal problems, a legacy of the design of the Elizabethan house that passed from one architect to another. The first was the symmetrical plan of the original house, itself a Renaissance feature introduced into English architecture during the Elizabethan period.

The second problem posed by the original house was to preserve its imposing and structurally sound south front. This front has survived intact with one major addition in the same style.

A secondary problem was the provision of two picture galleries, an important element of the designs for the extension of the house. The study will discuss the Palladian architects' concern for the size and symmetrical arrangement of the pictures as a part of the overall decorative scheme; and second, the significant changes in the design of the second gallery when the use of cast iron as a structural element made it possible to introduce sky lighting. This innovation caused a decisive break with the traditional concept of the picture gallery.

While the house was being enlarged Brown and Repton were commissioned to landscape the pleasure gardens and park. Brown created the park, and Repton enlarged it, adding a lake originally projected by Brown. Repton discussed the relationship of his landscape design to the Tudor-Gothic style that Nash and he had chosen to remodel the house. He also gave specific reasons for his choice of the Gothic style based upon the relationship of the house to the town, and formu-lated a general landscape theory for tree-planting, related to the architectural style of the house.

The stylistic influence of Longleat House, Wiltshire, on the Elizabethan house is evident in its symmetrical planning, the system of bay windows, chimney-piece designs, and architectural details in the porch. This influence may be attributed to the principal craftsmen who had worked at Longleat, Robert Smythson and Allen Maynard, who may also have been present at Corsham. Some of the work on Corsham derives from the Strand facade of Somerset House, London, perhaps the earliest Renaissance facade in England, while other influences at Corsham can be traced to Flemish and French architectural treatises the Longleat craftsmen used. The Elizabethan and Gothic Revival theorists cited Longleat as an important example of the Elizabethan style. Through its dependence upon Longleat, both

The Rt Hon. Sir Paul Methuen, K.B. (1672-1757), by Joseph Highmore (1692-1780)

Paul Methuen (1723-95) by Thomas Gainsborough, R.A. (1727-88)

Paul Cobb Methuen (1752-1816) by Thomas Gainsborough, R.A. (1727-88)

Paul, 1st Lord Methuen (1779-1849) by John Linnell (1792-1882)

for its symmetrical plan and the Renaissance character of the south front the style of Corsham can be readily identified as Elizabethan-Renaissance.

The Palladian Revival architects Ireson, Keene, and Brown faced the problem of integrating their designs into a house whose style they regarded as Gothic (the separate identity of the Elizabethan style had not been recognised at this time). All three architects did so while preserving the symmetry of the Elizabethan ground-plan, also a canon of Palladian design. The classicising of the north and east fronts of the house began with Ireson, who added the north front in 1749; his style can be traced to the influence of Colen Campbell. Keene, whose plans were rejected in 1759, submitted designs for a new library on the west side and a new picture gallery on the east side of the house. He proposed to double the existing wings to preserve the symmetry of the south front, a principle that Brown accepted. But Brown rejected Keene's proposal to classicise the south front, and faithfully repeated the extension in the Elizabethan style. Brown's solution for the picture-gallery design, while superior to Keene's, posed a problem for future architects by extending the picture gallery 27 ft beyond Ireson's north front. Although Brown's alterations have been hitherto considered as the first evidence of the Gothic Revival influence at Corsham, it will be shown that its influence was in fact introduced as early as 1754. Besides the Gothic, Brown's interior decoration shows the influence of Adamesque and Rococo styles, revealing the decline of Palladian interior decoration. Because Brown had control of both the architectural and landscape design, he was able to achieve an harmonious relationship between the house and the landscape. In all Brown's work at Corsham he was dependent upon the architectural and landscape style of William Kent.

By the time Wyatt, Nash, and Repton were consulted to remodel the house and grounds between 1795 and 1796, the Methuen family had shown a preference for the Gothic Revival style. James Wyatt submitted plans to Gothicise Corsham; though not accepted, they provided Nash with ideas that he evidently followed. The only surviving water-colour of Wyatt's design shows a castle-like extension to the north front. The east front was to be re-faced in a similar manner. Following Wyatt's dismissal, partly as a result of the newly-formed partnership between Nash and Repton, the latter jointly submitted an elegant design for the north front based upon Henry VII's Chapel, Westminster. Both Wyatt's and Nash's designs for the north front were classical solutions that preserved its symmetry although they used Gothic elements. While the Red Book Repton supplied for Corsham has been lost, sufficient information has survived to document Repton's Gothic Revival theories for remodelling the house and grounds. His theories provide a unique record of Picturesque Gothic Revival principles applied to the remodelling of a specific house. Repton was a serious student of 18th-century Gothic Revival architectural theory; his publications, in which he cites Corsham, contributed to the later work of Edward James Willson and Augustus Pugin. The technical importance of Nash's work lies in his innovative structural use of cast iron. The lighting in his picture gallery (music room) was pioneer work. Although it has not survived, its design formed the basis for his slightly later gallery at Attingham, and was adopted by subsequent architects as a structural principle for picture-gallery designs. His use of cast-iron brackets and girders at Corsham was a preliminary experience for the more imposing rooms he was to erect at Carlton House, Buckingham Palace, the Pavilion at Brighton and elsewhere. It was the poor quality of the materials and workmanship, and his own unfamiliarity with handling cast iron that led to the early demolition of his extension. Newly finished, his north front must have represented the ideal qualities of a Picturesque Gothic Revival House.

When Thomas Bellamy was consulted to remodel the north front in 1846, the theoretical principles of the Elizabethan Revival style had been established. The architectural theories of James Hakewill, James Dallaway, and Charles James Richardson in the 1830s had removed the Elizabethan style from its late Gothic classification that had been founded in part upon Repton's definition of the style as House Gothic. The Elizabethan style was popularised by the circulation of illustrated books, and the equivalent of Pugin's *Specimens*. Bellamy's second design provided for a new extension to the north front and an east front remodelled in the Elizabethan Revival style. Bellamy had none of the problems of the earlier Revival architects in incorporating the symmetrical ground plan, and the Renaissance motifs of the south front, into his design. In his design for the staircase hall and the corridors we see the influence of Italian Renaissance architectural planning, more logical and systematic than could be found in Elizabethan architecture. Bellamy's use of these Renaissance elements was influenced by Sir Charles Barry's Italian Renaissance Palace style, which the latter introduced into England in the 1820s. Thus Bellamy's extension incorporates both the Elizabethan and Italian Renaissance styles in the design.

From the time of the completion of the Elizabethan house in 1582, until the partial completion of Bellamy's extension in the Elizabethan Revival style in 1849, both Classical and Gothic Revival architects had attempted to remodel the house within the theoretical concepts of their movements. This was only possible because of the unique qualities of the Elizabethan style, which combined both Gothic and Renaissance elements. This combination also preserved the Elizabethan south front; its decoration was neither decidedly Gothic nor sufficiently Renaissance to justify its complete conversion into either style. The Palladian

Revival architects preserved the symmetry of the south front as they did the plan of the house, but regarded the south front as Gothic. The Picturesque Gothic Revival architects who had theoretically identified the Elizabethan style as 'House Gothic' ignored the Renaissance elements of the south front in order to remodel the house in a Tudor-Gothic style. They had to accept the Elizabethan or Classical symmetry of the plan as the best solution to remodel the north front left by Brown's projection of the picture gallery precisely when asymmetry was one of the cardinal principles of Gothic Revival planning. In his own reconstruction Bellamy was able to follow the principles of the Elizabethan Revivalists, and solve both of the principal problems that had existed throughout the architectural history of the house.

While Nash and Repton proved that the Gothic style was applicable to Corsham, the Elizabethan Revivalists emphasised the Renaissance qualities of the style, having mistakenly assumed a direct Italian influence. It was probably his wrong assumption that led Bellamy to introduce the Italian Renaissance features into his design for the corridor and staircase hall, since we know that he wished to be archaeologically correct in his treatment of the decorative detail. From the late 18th century onwards architectural theory played an increasingly important role in the assessment of the Elizabethan style, and architects remodelled the house after the theoretical principles to which their particular movement subscribed.

The history of Corsham Court reflects that of British architecture and architectural theory in the 18th and 19th centuries. The mansion as it stands today embodies three distinctly different styles, each one of which demonstrates the efforts of the architect to integrate his extension with the original Elizabethan plan.

Contributing greatly to this study are the correspondence and accounts for the work; unfortunately the surviving drawings for the alterations and additions are relatively few. But the correspondence and building-records are evidence of the influence of the patron's tastes and aesthetic principles, and add significantly to our specific knowledge of the architects responsible for the designs. The correspondence also clearly details the relationships among the patrons, architects, and craftsmen. The work executed by Lancelot Brown and Humphry Repton resulted in very cordial relations with the Methuen family, whereas the faulty work executed by John Nash created a strained relationship with Mr and Mrs Paul Cobb Methuen; the high cost of Bellamy's extension resulted in a family lawsuit.

The Methuen's architectural taste was partially influenced by the improvements their neighbours in Wiltshire were making to their properties. Social connections with the Court and London society provided a second formative influence. These ties developed by Sir Paul Methuen's long residence in London and his personal connections with the Royal Family were maintained by succeeding generations. For this reason they employed, with the exception of Ireson, architects with a national rather than a provincial reputation who brought to Corsham the latest metropolitan influences and designs fashionable at Court.

CHAPTER ONE

Corsham Court

SECTION ONE—THE ELIZABETHAN HOUSE

The architectural history of Corsham Court begins with Sir Christopher Hatton's lease of the Corsham Estate on 9 July 1572.[1] Previously, the medieval house lay derelict, as John Leland noted in 1541:

I left Chippinham a mile on the lifte hand, and so went to Alington village about a mile of, and thens 3 miles to Cosham, good uplandish town, wher be ruines of an old maner place; and therby a park wont to yn dowage to the Quenes of Englande. Mr. Bayton, yn Quene Anne's dayes, pullid down by licens a peace of this house sumwhat to help his buildinges at Bromeham. Old Mr. Bonhome told me that Cosham apperteinid to the erldom of Cornwalle, and that Cosham was a mansion place longging to it where sumtyme they lay.[2]

---

[1] Corsham Court, according to the medieval historian William of Malmesbury, occupies the reputed site of the summer palace of Ethelred the Unready, King of Wessex from 978 to 1017. The manor and park passed into the possession of William the Conqueror in 1066. Subsequently, it was held by various members of the Royal Family and their favourites until 1325, when it became the property of royal princesses and later formed part of the dower of the Queens of England. For a detailed account of the history of Corsham Manor, see Lord Methuen's brochure of Corsham Court published in 1958, and revised in 1965. Also, see Harold Brakespear, 'Corsham,' *Wiltshire Archaeological and Natural History Society*, **43** (1927), 511–39.

[2] Quene Anne 'is' Queen Anne Boleyn, mother of Elizabeth I, who had been executed in 1536. The Baytons succeeded to the Bromham Estate in 1508. 'Old Mr Bonhome' was probably the owner of the Manor of Haselbyry, which was erected by his father who descended from an old Wiltshire family. J. E. Jackson, ed., *Leland's Journey Through Wiltshire A.D. 1540–42* (Devizes: H. Bull, 1875), p. 12. Paul Methuen (1723–1795), was a subscriber to Thomas Hearne's edition of *Leland's Itinerary* (Oxford, 1745).

An inquisition held on 11 September 1562 into the condition of the property reported 'the manor house of the Lady, the Queen [Elizabeth I] is much ruined.'[3] Sir Christopher Hatton had leased a derelict house, which he was probably unable to rebuild because of the heavy debts he had incurred entertaining Queen Elizabeth at Holdenby, his principal seat in Northamptonshire.[4] After holding Corsham for three years, Sir Christopher sold it in 1575 to Thomas Smythe (1522–91), a native of the town who had made a successful career in London, eventually becoming the Collector of Customs for that city. Like Sir Christopher Hatton, Smythe enjoyed the costly patronage of Queen Elizabeth. It was probably Smythe who began the erection of the Elizabethan house slightly north of the medieval house. The remaining stonework of the medieval building that John Leland saw in 1541 was perhaps incorporated into the new house. The date '1582' on the semi-circular pediment of the south porch may denote the date of completion of the house.

Two documents have survived which provide a description of the Elizabethan house.[5] The first is a 'Survey of Mr Henry Smythe's lands 1602 at Cossam,' the manor and grounds having passed from Thomas Smythe to his third son Henry in 1591. The survey gives a brief description of the house, showing that it contained a suite of state apartments of the period:

Imprimus, a faire stronge howse, newly built with freestone having a hall and ij parlers at each end theroff wainscotted, a great chamber, and longe gallery verrie faire, & dyverse other rooms parte wainscotted, a faire new built gatehowse, and stable with stone, glased & covered with slatt, with loftes over them, ij faire green courtes with a high wall about them coped with freestone, a fountaine in the middest of the garden, & a still howse & banketting howse with cesters & condgtes to convey the water to every office in ye howse . . . all which cost the buylding £4,000.

There is a marginal note in another hand, 'I will give noe thynge for ye howse.' The second document describing Corsham is Richard Greene's report to the first Viscount Weymouth of Longleat House, written from Corsham on 18 January 1706–7. It was sent to the trustees of Henry Frederick Thynne who

---

[3] Brakespear, p. 515.

[4] For an account of Sir Christopher Hatton and Holdenby, see Emily Sophia Hartshorne, *Memorials of Holdenby* (London & Newcastle-upon-Tyne, 1868).

[5] Both documents are in the Marquess of Bath's archives at Longleat House, Wiltshire. They are: No. 6711, 'The Survey of Mr Henry Smythe's Lands at Cossham,' and No. 6713, a letter written by the Reverend Francis Richard Greene, Vicar of Corsham to the first Viscount Weymouth, dated Corsham 18 January 1706–7, when the latter was contemplating the purchase of Corsham. Henry Smythe sold the estate to Sir Edward Hungerford of Rowden, Chippenham, on 21 June 1602.

subsequently purchased the Corsham estate in 1707 from Thomas Lewis for £11,607.[6] In his report, which is more evaluative than Henry Smythe's descriptive survey, Greene emphasised what he considered some admirable qualities in the house and its situation:

the firmnesse of the buylding and the pratiness of the situation . . . the fineness of the air not much exceeded as I have heard by that of Highgate near London, so that tis a very healthy place, and many persons of quality have declared that they thought it one of the compleatest compact seats in the West of England for a gentleman to live in. Wilton, indeed, Longleat and Badminton are very august seats, which, therefore, Corsham must not be mentioned in competition with, and yet the late Lord, Duke of Beauford [Beaufort] was pleased to say, of it, that it was, "Multum in parvo," very much admiring it for the stateliness of the great staircase together with the uniformity of the mansion howse and the correspondency of the other buyldings in subserviency to it.

We do not have any contemporary plans of the Elizabethan house, but the evidence that has survived, the surveys of 1602 and 1707, and drawings made before the alterations of 1749 and 1760 (see **2** and **27**), show that the original ground plan was E-shaped and symmetrical with the main block on an east-west axis 120 ft long by 30 ft wide. The two projecting wings on the south side were 25 ft wide and extended 45 ft from the main block, providing symmetrical east and west fronts of 75 ft. The present porch of the south front forms the centre of the E-shape.

A subsequent addition, designated as 'domestic premises,' was made to the west of the house nearest the town (see **2**). This extension had a thin irregular wall system; the window-frames possibly of wood. These features contrast sharply with the rigidly symmetrical plan of the original house, with its thicker wall system and the heavy stone mullion windows. Greene mentions in his report that Colonel Richard Lewis improved the house between 1694 and 1706, including the 'offices.'[7] Greene's report also suggests that the domestic premises in the ground floor of the west wing were being used as a parlour before 1707

---

[6] The original receipt is at Longleat, Document No. 6712. The sequence of owners after the Hungerfords sold Corsham in 1684 until it was purchased by the Longleat Estate were: Richard Kent of London, MP for Chippenham; Richard Lewis of Edington, Wiltshire, who purchased Corsham through the Court of Chancery in 1694; Thomas Lewis, his son who sold Corsham to the Longleat Estate for Henry Frederick Thynne in 1707.

[7] The Reverend Greene's report states, 'The Colonel Lewis gave for all together £7,500 a cheap purchase. He hath laid out the House and offices above £1,000 put leaden pipes underground for conveying water to all places, and been at considerable charge in bringing flood waters out of the Town and main road which hath wonderfully improved the herbage . . .' Longleat House archives, document 6713.

(see **27**). The location of the original domestic quarters is similar to those at Barrington Court (*c.* 1530) whose plan closely resembles Corsham's (see **3**).

Summerson regards Barrington Court as an early isolated example of symmetrical planning.[8] The house evolved from a late medieval type of manor house. Corsham reflects the early Tudor planning of Barrington Court; both have advancing wings, a porch, and a hall. However, Barrington Court does not show the influence of the Renaissance in its architectural details, and at Corsham more attention has been given to the interior planning; the staircase is more elaborate, and the banqueting-hall is a single storey.

Some information on the interior planning of Corsham is provided in the report of Mr Henry Smythe's lands of 1602. This report is the only evidence we have that the house contained the suite of state reception rooms customary in an Elizabethan mansion. The state reception rooms of a mid-16th-century Elizabethan mansion consisted of a great chamber, a withdrawing chamber and a long gallery, usually situated on the first floor leading off the principal staircase adjacent to the banqueting-hall. The arrangement of the rooms at Corsham followed this plan, but their precise location has not been ascertained, as the surviving drawings only provide details of the ground-floor plan of the house. What remained of these reception rooms was destroyed by John Nash in 1800 when the centre section of the Elizabethan house was converted into a Grand Hall.

The ground-floor plan of the house shows the location of the hall and the arrangement of the principal rooms (see **2**). The banqueting-hall was one storey high with a screen at both ends, and was set with its long axis at right angles to the main entrance.[9] The earliest Tudor banqueting-halls were placed on axis with the main entrance to the house but, as they gradually lost their place as the focal point of entertainment in the house, the long axis of the hall was placed at right angles to the main entrance.[10] This orientation is found at Barrington Court (*c.* 1530), Longleat (1567–72), and Montacute (1587) as well as at Corsham. The height of the earlier banqueting-halls rose through two floors, as at Barrington Court and Longleat. Later, they were reduced to one floor as more importance was given to the great chamber (often situated on the first floor above the ban-

---

[8] Sir John Summerson, *Architecture in Britain* 1530 *to* 1830 5th ed. (Harmondsworth: Penguin Books, 1969), p. 13.

[9] A lithograph made from a drawing of the screen that led to the principal staircase has survived. It was executed by John Adey Repton before the alterations of John Nash transformed the Elizabethan centre section of the house into a Grand Hall rising through two floors (see **21**). The pedestals of the screen have survived and are now used as supports for pieces of sculpture.

[10] Summerson, *Architecture in Britain*, p. 40.

queting-hall) where the private family entertainment took place. If the normal arrangement of state rooms was used at Corsham, the great chamber would have led off the first-floor landing from the principal staircase.

The location of the long gallery is not known; it may have been placed at the attic level on the east-west axis of the house as at Montacute, Somerset. A large mullion window in the attic gable of the principal staircase situated in the north-east corner of the house suggests that the long gallery had been entered at this level (see **5**). But if the great chamber was placed in the projecting east wing of the first floor, as at Montacute, then the long gallery could have extended across the centre of the house at the first-floor level.

Of the surviving Elizabethan rooms only those in the projecting wings of the attic level overlooking the south front of the house retain their original oak wainscotting and the original stone mantlepieces. This wainscotting, which forms a cupboard space in both rooms, has also been retained at the original floor level.

The symmetrical plan of the house exerted a powerful influence upon the designs of successive Revival architects. Even though the principal Elizabethan rooms on the ground and first floors were eventually remodelled or altered beyond recognition, the outer walls of the Elizabethan house always remained the core around which the later alterations were made. The Elizabethan Revival theorists, James Hakewill and James Dallaway, returned to the principle of symmetrical planning in the 1830s. Thomas Bellamy adopted this principle when he remodelled the house for the last time between 1846 and 1849 in the Elizabethan Revival style.

Of the exterior part of the house the south front alone has survived very much in its original condition. The other three fronts have been covered by subsequent additions. The west wall was the first part of the house to be concealed when domestic premises were added, most likely as a part of Colonel Lewis' improvements (see **2**). The north and east fronts have been altered beyond recognition, but surviving drawings show the original gabled-roof system preserved on the south front (**5** and **6**). The walls were divided by stringcourses at the first- and second-floor levels, continuing the entablatures of the south front. There were mullion windows two and three sections wide respectively on the ground and first floors. The attic levels had single windows in groups of three, except the north attic of the east front that lighted the principal staircase, where a cross-shaped mullion window was inserted. Sash bar windows had replaced some of the mullion windows by 1749. External stone chimney-stacks with square stone chimney-pots, a prominent feature of all three fronts, were subsequently encased in the wall system when later extensions were added. It is not known whether the north and east fronts were also finished in cut Bath stone like the south front. But the remaining Elizabethan gables on the east and west sides of the house that have survived in the complex roof-system are finished in dressed stone, suggesting that the lower walls were faced as well.[11]

The south front originally consisted of the present centre section of the house and single projecting wings (4). The present outer wings were added in the same style by Lancelot Brown between 1760 and 1766. From the south side of the house we can see the podium or high basement into which windows were inserted in the 18th century. This feature was probably derived from Longleat, where it was used to elevate the ground floor and thus provide a better view across the park. It was probably derived in turn from French sources such as the Château de Madrid, a building Sir John Thynne of Longleat could have known when he was in France.[12] The two principal floors of the south front are clearly distinguished by the entablatures dividing them, while the attic level is built into the gabled roof system of the house. The porch, consisting of a pair of triple-clustered columns that support the upper structure, occupies the central position of the south front. Like the pair of adjoining bay windows, the porch is two-storeyed, as are also the bay windows on the end of each wing. The front is executed in ochre-coloured cut Bath stone that blends harmoniously with the brown Cotswold stone tiles of the roof. The marks still exist where a stone balustrade with a centre gateway originally linked the east and west wings at the podium (7). A similar balustrade was used at Heanton House, Devon, but this house did not have a podium (8).[13]

Corsham follows the external planning of contemporary Elizabethan houses such as The Hall, Bradford-on-Avon, and Montacute, where many external architectural elements which have disappeared at Corsham can be seen. Many of these elements may have originated in the recommendations of Andrew Boorde in

---

[11] The north front was refaced with a Palladian facade in 1749 by Nathaniel Ireson. Lancelot Brown added his cabinet room and picture gallery to the east front between 1761 and 1766.

[12] Somerset House (1547–1552) had a basement, but it is not known with certainty whether it was introduced by the Duke of Somerset, or in the later remodelling for Anne of Denmark between 1609 and 1611. Mark Girouard, *Robert Smythson and the Architecture of the Elizabethan Era* (London: Country Life, 1966), p. 65. This study has provided much new material upon one of the principal Elizabethan architects. Another influential source for podiums is the illustrations in the treatises of du Cerceau and Serlio. Barrington Court, which shows no Renaissance influences, does not have a podium.

[13] This drawing was made by Edmund Prideaux in the 18th century. For a scholarly article on Edmund Prideaux, see John Cornforth, 'An Early Country House Enthusiast,' *Country Life*, 8 Mar. 1962, 526–528.

his *Dyetary of Helth* (1542).[14] They were part of the common practice of the builder when siting Elizabethan houses in the second half of the century. The survey of 1602 and Greene's report of 1707 confirms that these elements were used in the external planning of Corsham. Corsham House stands on slightly rising ground on the western edge of a 350-acre park. It has a fine view across the parkland on its eastern side into the distant countryside beyond. On the north side the ground continues to rise to the skyline. Boorde recommended a similar situation with woodland, water, fields, vales and hills and level ground. The Elizabethans gave particular attention to the purity of the air and healthiness of the site. Boorde recommended that the house should not be located near stagnant water, and Greene commented upon 'the fineness of the air not much exceeded as I have heard by that of Highgate near London, so that tis a very Healthy place. . .'

The layout of the grounds immediately before the south front follows Boorde's recommendation to have the gate-house located opposite the hall door and enclosed by a courtyard. The south front is described in the 1602 survey as having 'a faire new built gatehowse, and stable with stone, glazed and covered with slatt, with loftes over them,' opposite the south porch. The original Elizabethan stable blocks still exist on either side of the main entrance (see **22** and **75**). The 1602 survey also refers to 'ij faire green courtes with a high wall about them coped with free stone, a fountaine in the middest of the garden, and a still howse and banketting howse . . .' 'Ij faire green courts' may refer to the present south front, which is still bounded in part on its east and west sides by high stone walls with freestone coping that could easily be Elizabethan (see **1** and **59**). 'Courtes' may mean that other gardens were laid out on the east and north sides of the house such as still exist today at The Hall, Bradford-on-Avon, and Montacute. The locations of the fountain, the 'still' and the banqueting houses have not been ascertained. The latter could have been placed on an axis with the house, possibly on the north front near the boundary-wall with the park where extensive views would be enjoyed across the countryside. The banqueting houses at Montacute and The Hall, Bradford-on-Avon, erected contemporaneously with Corsham, are placed on the boundary-walls of the gardens. The overall picture is that of a typical Elizabethan house, essentially inward looking, bounded by high walls dividing enclosed courtyards and gardens from the park which lay beyond.

The construction of Corsham can be associated stylistically with the second building campaign (1553–67) of Sir John Thynne at Longleat House, Wiltshire, situated about 20 miles from Corsham. Sir John Thynne had been directing the

---

[14] Andrew Boorde, *A Dyetary of Helth*, ed. F. J. Furnivall (London: Early English Text Society, 1870), pp. 234 and 238.

construction of Longleat continuously since 1552, and he was then engaged on the fourth and penultimate building campaign (1572–75) when Corsham was begun in 1572.[15] Sir John succeeded in completing the house during his fifth and last campaign (1575–79) shortly before his death in April 1580. Sir John Thynne had been the steward of Edward Seymour, Duke of Somerset and Lord Protector of England from *c.* 1547 to 1552—while holding office under Somerset he superintended the construction of Somerset House, in the Strand, London.[16] After Somerset's fall from power and execution in 1552, Sir John retired to his estate at Longleat and began the construction of his own house. He incorporated into his building at Longleat many of the innovations of Somerset House, later used in modified form at Corsham.

The Strand front of Somerset House is important for Renaissance architecture in England because, in Summerson's opinion, it was 'probably the first deliberate attempt to build in England a front altogether composed in the classical taste.'[17] This design assimilated the latest developments of contemporary French architecture as found in parts of the Château de Ecouen, near Paris, remodelled in the 1550s for Anne de Montmorency, Constable of France. It can be argued that the stylistic influence at Corsham is derived from Longleat through Somerset House, which in turn reflects French Renaissance influences.

It seems unlikely that Corsham is directly dependent upon Somerset House. The excellent local tradition of working in Bath stone, of which Corsham is constructed, would hardly justify employing a mason from London where this stone was not commonly used. It is more likely that the mason employed at Corsham had been previously working at Longleat, and was familiar with the new Renaissance influences to be found there. The south front at Corsham, which has survived very much in its original form, is the most important evidence for this derivation.

The most significant link between the south front at Corsham and those of Longleat and Somerset House are the square bay windows (**9 and 10**). The bay windows are probably very similar in design to the windows which existed before the fire at Longleat on 21 April 1567. The original bay windows at Longleat were two storeys high, pedimented and with the gabled-roof system exposed to view as we see them at Corsham today. The gabled-roof system at Longleat was not

---

[15] Girouard, *Robert Smythson*, pp. 58–61.

[16] The Duke of Somerset, in addition to the new palace on the Strand, also owned the great house at Syon, Middlesex, and began a third house in Wiltshire at Bedwyn Broil. See John Edward Jackson, 'Wulfhall and the Seymours,' *Wiltshire Archaeological and Natural History Magazine* 15 (1875), 140–207.

[17] Summerson, *Architecture in Britain*, pp. 16–17.

concealed behind the third 'Corintian' level of bay windows until the fourth
building campaign (1572–75). After the fire of 1567 the design of the windows
was altered from two to three rows of windows in height because the new rooms
were larger and higher.

An analysis of the structural and decorative details of the bay-windows
confirms a strong stylistic relationship between those of the Strand front of
Somerset House, Longleat, and Corsham. An influence of Somerset House on
Longleat is established by documentary evidence. A contract has survived at
Longleat dated 1559, during the second campaign (1553–67), specifying the
erection of pedimented windows decorated with columns similar in scale to those
of the Strand front.[18] Thus the bay windows of all three buildings were pedimented. Structurally, the bay-windows at Corsham are similar to those of the Strand
front where the centre mullion subdivides the bay into a pair of cross-shaped
mullion windows, although the Corsham windows are completely plain, without
the decorative detail of those at Longleat and the Strand front. The projection of
the Strand front bay windows was too shallow to insert side windows. This may
well have been the case at Longleat in the windows erected in 1559, for the
Elizabethan bay windows at Corsham had no side windows. This fact is revealed
in the plans of Henry Keene in 1759 (**28**), more accurate than the earlier plan of
around 1749 (**2**), and the drawing of the Elizabethan south front (**4**).[19] Another
important similarity between the windows at Corsham and most of the windows

---

[18] The mason, Spicer covenanted to build 'a wyndowe of fytene foote wyde in the
gallery of freestone with colompnes.' Girouard, *Robert Smythson*, p. 55.

[19] Side windows are shown in the watercolour of the south front by John Buckler,
c. 1809. Sir Richard Colt Hoare commissioned from Buckler a set of watercolours
of the important buildings of Wiltshire. They are bound in two portfolio volumes
now in the Devizes Museum, Wiltshire. The north and south fronts of Corsham
House are in the museum collection, Volume 10, folios 26 and 27. This appears to be
the first exact illustration of the south front showing side windows. It is not known
whether side windows were inserted by Brown or Nash. It was most probably Brown
who had inserted the side-windows when he duplicated the existing Elizabethan
bay-window system for his additions to the South Front between 1759 and 1762.
An opportunity may have been taken to remodel all of the bay windows by Brown,
as they would have appeared old fashioned in the 1750s. Nash's remodelling did
not call for structural alterations to the South Front at this time (Corsham Archives
6011). John Britton's plan of Corsham, 1806 (**41**), which shows the bay windows
without side windows, is clearly at variance with the evidence to be seen in John
Buckler's watercolour of the South Front, *c.* 1809. Bellamy's plan of 1846 (**76**), and
his watercolour of the South Front (R.I.B.A. collection), show the window system
as it is today. Bellamy had inserted additional windows into the main walls on
either side of the bay windows flanking the porch that do not appear in Buckler's
watercolour. The solution to the bay-window designs will remain a problem until
further evidence is found.

at Longleat is the profile of the mullions (see **11** and **12**). Each window of the bay has its own stone enframement. The Longleat windows have a similar profile to those at Corsham, but they are slightly smaller and have a different moulding. In both houses the same profiles are used for the exterior and the interior of the windows. The same profiles could have been used before the fire of 1567, derived from those of the Strand front, but the drawings of the front do not clearly indicate the mullion profiles.[20] This analysis would seem to indicate that the stone-mason employed at Corsham was probably familiar with the window profiles at Longleat, and copied the bay-window system existing before the fire of 1567, modelled on the bay windows of the Strand front. Structurally, the stylistic link between Corsham and Longleat can be traced to the symmetrical planning, the use of a podium, and the similarity of the earlier bay-window system, which in turn is dependent upon the Strand front of Somerset House.

In addition to the planning and structural similarities between Corsham and Longleat, decorative elements used by the craftsmen at Longleat are repeated at Corsham. The influence can be traced to two principal craftsmen, Robert Smythson the master mason, and a French sculptor, Allen Maynard (Maenard). Girouard attributes the splendour of Longleat to the association of master and craftsmen, combining the energy and enthusiasm of Sir John Thynne, the skill and organisation of Smythson, and the carving ability and knowledge of French Renaissance architectural practices of Maynard.[21] Indeed, it may well be that Smythson or Maynard supervised the work at Corsham.

The major decorative element of the south front is the porch, the focal point upon which the ornamental decoration has been lavished (see **13**). Four elements of its design can be found in the work of Maynard and Smythson. The massive porch is supported by Doric columns. A cluster of three columns support the front on either side, and almost free-standing paired columns support the rear of the porch. Smythson used the Doric order in the carved screen of Wollaton Hall designed between 1580 and 1588 (his drawings have survived).[22] An elaborate

---

[20] A survey made of the mullion profiles at The Hall, Bradford-on-Avon, Montacute House, and Wollaton Hall designed by Robert Smythson the master mason at Longleat, all erected contemporaneously with Corsham, reveal that different profiles were used, and they were not repeated on both sides of the window as at Longleat and Corsham. I am indebted to Mr Mathews, head carpenter to the Marquess of Bath, for supplying measured drawings of the cross-section of the mullion windows at Longleat House used for (**12**).

[21] Girouard, *Robert Smythson*, p. 61.

[22] See Girouard, *Robert Smythson*, plates 33 and 34. Smythson took his source for the screen from Androuet Vedreman de Vries' *Variae Architecturae Formae* (Antwerp, 1563). He could have used and probably knew Sebastiano Serlio's *Regoli genrali di architetura spora le cinque maniere de gli edifice*, IV, ix, fig. 9, folio 63.

two-storey porch was erected at Longleat, probably dating from the third campaign (1567–72), or even later; it was taken down in the 17th century.[23] This porch was supported in front by three Doric columns, although not arranged in a cluster. Whether it was designed by Smythson is not known, but the appearance of clustered columns in his design for Wollaton suggests that he may have been responsible for the design at Corsham.

The bizarre treatment of the Doric entablature of the porch suggests that the Elizabethan masons relied upon illustrations rather than learning the rules. The metopes have bucrania and rosette designs like those found in Serlio.[24] But they are not arranged in the customary manner (see **14**); instead, a rosette is placed on either side of the centre triglyph, and the pair of bucrania on opposite ends of the frieze. Although half-bucrania are placed on the projecting ends of the entablature, they do not occupy the corner position as required by Vitruvius (see **89**).[25] On the side entablature two metopes (bucrania and rosette) are placed next to each other without the intervening triglyph. Another peculiar feature of the porch is the side lintel block which is cut in two instead of being a single block. The treatment of the porch shows that Elizabethan masons often did not understand the correct arrangement of the triglyphs and metopes and used them in a very free way.

The two decorative motifs forming the upper part of the porch can be traced to the architectural treatises of du Cerceau with which Maynard and Smythson were familiar; other motifs used at Longleat came from similar sources. The panel above the entablature contains a design similar to that found in what may be the earliest surviving drawing by Smythson, one which Girouard dates between Smythson's arrival at Longleat in 1568 and the commencement of the present windows in 1572.[26] This motif, frequently used for door panels and wainscotting,

---

[23] Girouard, *Robert Smythson*, p. 61.

[24] Serlio, *Regoli generali*, IV, Dell'Ordine Dorico, vi, and subsequent editions. Also earlier editions of Vitruvius such as the *De architectura* (Venice, 1511), IV, 37.

[25] Vitruvius points out that there should be half a metope at the corner of a temple or the outer column moved inwards by half a metope. Marcus Pollio Vitruvius, *Ten Books on Architecture*, trans. by Morris Hicky Morgan (1914; rpt. New York: Dover Publications, 1960), IV, iii, 2. The half metope is usually illustrated as having a rosette.

[26] Girouard, *Robert Smythson*, plate 21. In Smythson's drawing, this motif forms a part of the crowning decoration of the bay window, being capped with a curved pediment. At Corsham, there are two vertical sunken rectangular panels on either side of this motif.

is rarely found in ornamental stonework. A panel in a similar position and divided into three sections, but without the centre design, can be found in du Cerceau's *Le Premier Volume des plus excellants Bastiments de France* (Paris, 1576) on the plate entitled 'Front of the Fountain Court, Fontainebleau.' The three panels are situated in a position similar to those at Corsham above the Doric entablature of the main entrance and surmounted by a pediment.[27]

The most unusual motif found at Corsham is the fan-shaped pediment that surmounts the porch with similar semi-circular half-pediments abutting the main wall. This motif is derived from contemporary architectural decoration illustrated by du Cerceau with which the French sculptor Maynard might have been acquainted. This motif was not used at Longleat or Somerset House, and indeed seems to have no parallel in Elizabethan architecture at this date. Semi-circular pediments crowning gateways and towers had appeared in contemporary French architecture since 1565, examples of which were published in du Cerceau's *Bastiments de France* (1576) (see **15**).[28] This motif may well have been known to Maynard who was employed at Longleat from 1563 onwards where he introduced other French motifs such as the *oeil-de-boeuf* dormer window motif on the parapet.[29] Later Thomas Bellamy used this motif in prominent positions on the north front in his unexecuted design for remodelling the east front, and for the tympanums of the smaller doorways in the corridors, in order to create a more authentic appearance.

Maynard's probable influence may also be seen in the sculpture set in the pediments of the Elizabethan bay windows at Corsham. Occupying the centre of each pediment is the bust of a single person in contemporary Elizabethan costume,

---

[27] Thomas Bellamy in the nineteenth century used a similar motif to the design of the centre panel of the porch for the corridor ceilings of his extension, and for the projected decorations of the east front on a level with the coving of the picture gallery.

[28] Examples are found in plates of Jacques Androuet du Cerceau's *Le Premier volume des plus excellants Bastiments de France* (Paris, 1576) where semi-circular pediments are found in illustrations of the Chateau de Verneuil, begun in 1565. Many motifs used at Verneul occur there for the first time or nearly the first time. Verneuil is a variant of Monceaux-en-Brie, begun by Primaticcio in 1547 for Catherine dei Medici, and completed by Jacques du Cerceau the Elder. Cerceau in his *Livre d'Architecture* repeats similar motifs in two of his own designs on plates XI and XII. These designs were published too late to influence the pediment at Corsham, but had been frequently used in French architecture since the 1560s.

[29] A French joiner, Adrian Gaunt, was also engaged at the same time; they are the first French craftsmen working in England during the Elizabethan period whose names are known. Girouard, *Robert Smythson*, p. 54.

leaning slightly forward; the single busts of female figures adorn the inner pediments and male figures the pediments of the wings. It is uncertain whom they represent. Similarly, placed figures appear on the facade at Longleat and in the pediment of an interior doorway at Wolfeton House, Dorset, which is occupied by the bust of a man holding what appears to be a laurel wreath. Both figures at Longleat and Wolfeton have been attributed to Allen Maynard.[30]

The walls of the south front have distinctive entablatures and mouldings. The entablatures tie in the bay-windows with the main wall of the house by introducing a decided horizontal emphasis to counteract the vertical emphasis of the square bay-windows. A prominent moulding is used between the podium and the main wall. The attic gables are edged with an elaborate moulded coping.

Some elements of medieval decoration have been used on what is essentially a Renaissance front. The gables are surmounted by heraldic bears holding shields, an emblem of the Hungerford family, one of the 17th-century owners of Corsham.[31] The pediments of the bay-windows are each surmounted by three eagles, except the centre pedestal of the porch, where there is a group depicting a pelican feeding her young.[32]

The remaining fragments of the Elizabethan chimney-pieces at Corsham also provide evidence for a strong stylistic connection with Longleat in the work of Smythson, and possibly Maynard. All the Elizabethan chimney-pieces at Corsham have been removed from their original positions, except those already mentioned in the attic storey and one in the Chinese Room on the first floor of the east wing. Only the lower part of this chimney-piece has survived, telling little of its original design. It consists of the purple and white marble bolection moulding of the chimney-opening. Partial remains of other chimney-pieces were stored in the cellars, possibly at the time of Lancelot Brown's additions in the 1760s or even earlier; they have now been placed in the estate yard. The pieces do not seem to constitute a complete chimney-piece, and they are probably from at least two chimneys.

---

[30] Girouard, *Robert Smythson*, pp. 67–68, and plate 17.

[31] Similar heraldic beasts can be found at Longleat on the gables of the inner courtyard. They form a part of the gabled-roof system that formerly surrounded the exterior of the house before it was enclosed by the 'Corintian' level of bay windows in the fourth campaign of 1572–75. For illustrations of the inner courtyard gables see, Girouard, *Robert Smythson*, plates 14 and 15.

[32] The symbol of the pelican vulning herself forms the finials of gate pillars at a house between Upwey and Nottington, Dorset. This motif, usually called the Pelican in her piety, was exclusively connected with the crucifixion in the medieval period. Sidney Heath, *The Romance of Symbolism* (London: Francis Griffiths, 1909), p. 129.

From the remaining blocks two significant motifs have survived. The first design has a boldly cut egg-and-dart design on the ovolo moulding of the block, and on its face there is a ribbon strap-work design edged on either side with a single guilloche motif (see **16**).[33] These designs are similar to the remains of an elaborate black marble chimney-piece which has been dug up from the well at Wardour Castle, Wiltshire, where Smythson worked around 1576. These pieces contain strapwork designs that Girouard considers more Flemish than French, which would indicate that Smythson was familiar with de Vries' illustrations as early as 1576, before he went to Wollaton Hall.[34] Pieces of black marble among the fragments at Corsham may originally have formed part of a chimney-piece similar in design to the one attributed to Robert Smythson at Wardour Castle, especially as other fragments at Corsham have Flemish strapwork designs also found on the Wardour chimney-piece. The second design (**19**) is another strap-work motif of the kind found in de Vries' *Variae architecturae*,[35] and is similar to the underside of the lintel of the stone screen at Wollaton Hall (see **20**).[36] The use of strapwork motifs suggests that Smythson at least may have provided the designs for the Corsham chimney-pieces. The Elizabethan Revivalists, including Bellamy, attached much importance to them for their interior decoration.

It has been shown that Corsham is stylistically dependent upon Longleat for its planning influence, structural elements such as the podium and bay windows, and architectural motifs. The arguments of the 18th- and 19th-century architectural theorists concerning the classification of the Elizabethan style, in which Longleat is cited as an important example, can apply to a lesser extent to Corsham. The definition of the style by each Revival movement affected the kind of design

---

[33] A similar design of a more complex ribbon strap-work can be found in Vredreman de Vries' *Pictores, statuarii architecti* (Antwerp, 1563), plates II and IX. The ribbon design occurs in the frieze of the Ionic order and pedestal. These designs are more elaborately drawn, but the looping and overlapping of the ribbon-work in a similar form appears on the Corsham design. Robert Symthson copied the Doric order for the hall screen at Wollaton from this publication between 1580 and 1588. He also used a double guilloche design for the arch rims of the screen (See **17** & **20**).

[34] Girouard, *Robert Smythson*, p. 27.

[35] Girouard, *Robert Smythson*, plate 38.

[36] Smythson seems to have been fond of using a motif of pairs of spirals turning away from each other, such as in his drawing from de Vries' *Variae* (see Girouard, *Robert Smythson*, plate 38). This motif occurs in the Corsham design (**19**), and on the fan-shaped pediment of the porch (**13**). The three surviving chimney-pieces at Longleat were probably carved by Maynard, but it is not possible to find convincing similarities with the Corsham designs.

submitted by the Palladian and Gothic Revival architects for remodelling Corsham. The Elizabethan south front provided data for succeeding architects— each emphasising certain elements in their designs elsewhere in the house. Thomas Bellamy made a careful study of these elements for his Elizabethan Revival addition and used motifs from the south front to give a more authentic flavour to his exterior and interior designs.

The only other significant additions to the property after the improvements of Colonel Lewis and before the Palladian additions, were the present main entrance to the south front of the house, and the piers of the park gates at the southern entrance to the park. The main entrance was a replacement of the Elizabethan gatehouse described as 'newly built' in the survey of 1602. The form of the entrance with its characteristic curved pediment, rusticated stonework and oval-shaped scrolls buttressing the piers is Baroque (see **22**). The entrance piers of the south avenue have channelled rusticated stonework, surmounted by an entablature with ball finials held in acanthus leaves on pedestals as on the main entrance. Pevsner dates the gateway to the late 17th or possibly early 18th century.[37] The two entrances could have been erected by Colonel Lewis as a part of his improvements to the house, except that Greene's survey would probably have mentioned such an important feature in his report.

The other occupants of Corsham after the Lewises and before the Methuens were Lord Thomas Thynne and his trustees, 1706–16, and Benjamin Haskins Styles, 1716–45. It is doubtful whether such large gates were erected under Lord Thynne's brief occupancy at the court, because he died in 1710 and his widow, Lady Mary Thynne, moved to Old Windsor shortly afterwards.[38] Benjamin Haskins Styles was a brother-in-law of one of the governors of the South Sea Company, who owned in addition to Corsham, Moor Park, Hertfordshire, and another principal seat at Bowden Park, Wiltshire, before his estates were forfeited. During this time he had Moor Park remodelled, and began building Bowden Park.[39]

---

[37] Nikolaus Pevsner, *Buildings of England—Wiltshire* (Harmondsworth: Penguin Books, 1963), p. 171.

[38] Correspondence at Longleat deals with the removal of her possessions to Old Windsor, the management of the estate and attempts to sell the house and grounds.

[39] An extract from a diary of an unknown visitor describes his visit to Bowden House, Wiltshire, on Thursday, 29 September 1743: 'Called and saw Bowden House, the seat of Haskins Styles Esqre., it stands near Laycock, at the top of that hill from whence there is a prodigious prospect, the house is but a shell it having nothing finished about it, the design of it is grand, but it is going to ruin, the park is small and but little land belongs to it.' *Diary of an unknown traveller to Bath and Bristol in 1743*, mss 222111, Bristol Municipal Library.

Styles' immense wealth at this time makes him seem the most likely person to have had these gates erected. He employed Sir James Thornhill to re-model Moor Park in the Palladian style soon after 1720.[40] Christopher Hussey describes the articulation of the ground floor of the facade of Moor Park as having tall arched windows set in 'channelled rustication like that used by Vanbrugh at Blenheim.'[41] Similar channelled rustication is used at Corsham, especially on the piers of the park gates. Also, the curved pedimented archway of the main entrance has a typical Vanbrugh quality that indicates Thornhill's Baroque influences.

A date around 1716 for the entrances is strengthened by scrollwork motifs of similar design to those used on the main entrance being used as brackets for the door canopies of numbers 4 and 5 Church Street, Corsham; number four has a date of 1714 carved on the stonework under the canopy. This property has always belonged to the Estate. It is thus possible that Styles had the entrances erected soon after he purchased Corsham in 1716, from a design that he could have obtained from Sir James Thornhill, who remodelled Moor Park for him.

With the exception of the domestic premises added to the west wing, most probably by Colonel Lewis, and the main south gateway and the piers of the park gates possibly added by Benjamin Haskins Styles, Corsham had the general appearance of an Elizabethan manor house when the Methuen family began negotiations to purchase the estate in 1745. The Renaissance decorative elements and bay-window system show the influence of Longleat, and two of the important craftsmen, Robert Smythson and Allen Maynard. We have seen that the house contained the usual suite of state reception rooms, although their precise location has not been ascertained. Analysis of the surviving fragments of chimney-pieces indicates that these rooms also owed some of their decorative influence to Robert Smythson. It was around this Elizabethan-Renaissance house that subsequent Revival style additions were made between 1749 and 1849.

---

[40] The designs of Moor Park appear in the *Vitruvius Britannicus* (London, 1771), V, plates 50–55. The attribution to Leoni that appears in many texts is incorrect. See also, Howard M. Colvin, *Biographical Dictionary of English Architects* 1660–1840 (London: John Murray, 1954), p. 611. Styles took possession of Moor Park on 27 August 1720. T. P. Hudson, 'Moor Park, Leoni and Sir James Thornhill.' *Burlington Magazine*, 113 (1971), 658.

[41] Christopher Hussey, *English Country Houses* (London: Country Life, 1955), I, 43.

SECTION TWO—THE METHUEN FAMILY

Corsham Court has been continuously occupied by the Methuen family since 1747; three generations of the family were responsible for the Revival style alterations carried out between 1749 and 1849. They were: Paul Methuen (1723–95), the first owner, who commissioned Lancelot Brown to add the Palladian extension to the east front and landscape the park between 1760 and 1766; his son, Paul Cobb Methuen (1752–1816), who employed John Nash and Humphry Repton to add the Picturesque Gothic north front and remodel the park from 1795 to 1803; and his grandson, Paul Methuen (1779–1849), who became the first Lord Methuen in 1838, and who had Nash's extension demolished and replaced by one in the Elizabethan Revival style by Thomas Bellamy between 1846 and 1849 (see their portraits facing p. XX).

When Paul Methuen's trustees purchased the Corsham Estate in his behalf on 25 February 1745, it was not only with the intention of providing a country seat suitable to his social position, but also of choosing one with a setting of sufficient dignity to house the important picture collection he was to inherit upon the death of his older cousin, Sir Paul Methuen.

The subsequent architectural alterations during the remainder of the century were made expressly to meet this special requirement.

Sir Paul Methuen, KB (1672–1757), had spent a lifetime gathering this collection, housed at the time of his death in his home at 4 Grosvenor Street, London. No doubt the Corsham Estate was purchased with Sir Paul's approval; indeed he may have been instrumental in having the purchase made from the forfeited estates of Benjamin Haskins Styles (then in the Court of Chancery that acted, among other things, as trustees for bankrupt estates). Sir Paul had speculated in South Sea Company stock, having prudently sold his holdings before the bubble burst. As Corsham, one of Benjamin Haskins Styles' residences in Wiltshire, was offered for sale, it was an opportune moment to purchase 'one of the compleatest compact seats in the West of England,' as Richard Greene had called it in 1707.

The Methuens belonged to the group of powerful Wiltshire clothiers whose families intermarried for several generations, augmenting the family assets through shrewd marriage contracts. The Methuens carried on their business at Bradford-on-Avon, about three miles from Corsham; it was then an active centre of the woollen industry in Wiltshire.[42] Wool was one of the important staple industries of England in the Elizabethan period and continued to flourish in the 17th and 18th centuries. Despite periods of acute depression, the decline in the West of England woollen industry did not occur until after 1800. In the 18th century, like the Venetian Merchants of the 16th century, some of the clothiers disengaged from trade and invested much of their wealth in landed estates, taking on the role of country gentlemen. Another clothier, whose family later became ennobled like the Methuens, was Robert Child of Heddington, who transferred his business interests to the City of London.[43] Paul Methuen (1723–95), whose trustees had negotiated the purchase of Corsham for him in 1745, became a member of the landed class, his father, Thomas Methuen, the last member of the family to engage in the trade of clothier, having died in 1733 (see Appendix A).

The diplomatic career of the Right Honourable John Methuen (1650–1706), the father of Sir Paul Methuen, helped to advance the family's social position beyond the status of clothier, a trade in which the family had been engaged since 1615 when Paul Methuen (?–1667), settled in Bradford-on-Avon. The antiquarian John Aubrey in 1667 described him as the greatest clothier of his time.[44] The Rt Hon. John Methuen matriculated in 1665 into St Edmund Hall, Oxford, and was called to the Bar of the Inner Temple, where in 1685 he was appointed a Master

---

[42] A distinctive feature of the Wiltshire clothiers' trade was to supply the weavers with the wool to be woven in their homes. The latter were paid for the actual weaving process. Some clothiers organised their businesses along factory lines, with one even using the nave of Malmesbury Abbey. The clothiers held the cloth for sale to visiting buyers, while most foreign exports were sold through Blackwell Hall, London. The practice varied in different parts of the country. For references to the woollen industry and Wiltshire Clothiers, see Peter J. Bowden, 'The Wool Supply and the Woollen Industry,' *Economic History Review*, 2nd Ser., 9, No. 1 (1956), 44–58; *The Wool Trade in Tudor and Stuart England* (London: Macmillan, 1962); Christopher Hussey, 'Wiltshire Clothiers' Houses,' *Country Life*, 19 Nov. 1943, pp. 904–907; K. G. Ponting, *History of West of England Cloth Industry* (London: Macdonald, 1957); George Daniel Ramsey, *The Wiltshire Woollen Industry in the Sixteenth and Seventeenth Centuries* (London: Oxford University Press, 1943); John Smith, *Chronicon Rusticum-Commerciale or Memoirs of Wool* (1747); Charles Wilson, 'Cloth Production and International Competition in the Seventeenth Century,' *Economic History Review*, 2nd Ser., 13, No. 2 (Dec. 1960), 209–221.

[43] Robert Child's younger son became Sir Francis Child, the wealthy banker and ancestor of the Earls of Jersey. Christopher Hussey, 'Wiltshire Clothiers' Houses,' p. 907.

[44] John Aubrey, *The Natural History of Wiltshire*, ed. John Britton (London, 1847), p. 113.

in Chancery; he later retired to Portugal in 1690, after separating from his wife. In 1691, he was appointed the envoy to the King of Portugal to bring the Portuguese to the side of the allies, out of the French sphere of influence.[45] His son (Sir) Paul joined him in 1692 in the capacity as personal secretary. Paul had been educated at a Jesuit school in Paris (1681–84), where he acquired the facility for languages that proved useful for his future career. Both father and son spoke French and Spanish. In the following year, 1693, the Methuen Treaty of Alliance was concluded with Portugal, giving England preferential wine imports in exchange for British goods. Later, John Methuen was recalled to England to become Lord Chancellor of Ireland (1694–1701), and in the following year, Speaker of the Irish House of Lords. He was re-appointed ambassador to Lisbon in May, 1702, where he died 11 July 1706.

Sir Paul Methuen received the appointment of ambassador in his father's place. At the time of his father's death he was engaged in the campaign of the Duke of Savoy that ended on 7 September 1706, with the capture of Turin. When the news reached him in Turin, Paul Methuen returned to Lisbon. He stayed on as ambassador until August, 1708, when he returned to England after a disastrous year in the management of the Peninsula War. He was replaced as ambassador by the Earl of Galway. Sir Paul served as Lord of the Admiralty from November, 1709 to December 1710, but declined, on grounds of ill-health, to accept a mission to Holland for Robert Harley's Tory administration, or to go on a special mission at the request of Queen Anne to Milan.

When the Whigs regained power in 1714, James Stanhope, Secretary of State, sent Sir Paul to Madrid as a temporary ambassador where he remained from August until December, 1715, when ill health caused him to resign. From July to December 1716, he served as acting Secretary of State in the southern department during Stanhope's absence abroad; upon Stanhope's return he continued to hold the post until April, 1717, when he was forced to resign by his health.

In 1720 Sir Robert Walpole appointed Paul Methuen Comptroller of the Royal Household. In 1725, he was created a Knight of the Bath, an order of chivalry revived by George I. After transferring to the Treasureship of the Royal Household in the same year, he resigned this position in April, 1729, because, according to Lord Hervey, he was not appointed Secretary of State.[46] His

---

[45] For a scholarly account of the diplomatic service rendered by John Methuen and his son, Sir Paul Methuen, in Portugal, see Allen David Francis, *The Methuens and Portugal* 1691–1708 (Cambridge: Cambridge University Press, 1966).

[46] Lord John Hervey, *Some Materials towards Memoirs of the Reign of King George II*, ed., Romney Sedgwick (London: Eyre and Spottiswoode, 1931), I, 101–102.

personality caused him to make enemies in his own political party, and to fall out with Sir Robert Walpole. Meanwhile, since his return from Portugal, he continued to hold a parliamentary seat. Sir Paul's first seat was as member for Devizes, the seat formerly held by his father, from 1708 until 1711, when he was disqualified in a re-election. In 1714, Sir Paul stood for Brackley in Northamptonshire, a seat he held for the rest of his parliamentary career until 1747, when he retired at the age of seventy five.

Sir Paul knew everyone of note in his day through his political, social, and court connections. Despite his complaints of ill health, he seems to have led a long, active, social life. Although a bachelor all his life, he was much sought after in feminine society (being mentioned in the correspondence of the Duchess of Marlborough, Lady Cowper, and Lady Mary Wortley Montague), and he frequently dined out with Queen Caroline.[47] He also received dedications and flattering references from the literary figures of the day.[48]

Sir Paul amassed a considerable fortune in his lifetime, and left over a quarter of a million pounds, including an account with the Bank of England of £65,000.[49]

---

[47] Lady Montague considered him a 'handsome and well man, with a wit enough, and a romantic turn in his conversation.' She also gives an account of his flirtations with Madame Kilmensegg, a favourite of George I. Lady Mary Wortley Montague, *Works*, ed., Lord Wharncliffe (London, 1866), I, p. 132. Lady Cowper describes him 'as making sweet eyes' at a party of Madame Montandre's in Dec. 1714. *Diary of Mary Countess Cowper*, ed. Hon. C. S. Cowper (London: John Murray, 1864), p. 29.

[48] Voltaire in his *Oeuvres completes* (Paris, 1785), XII, 13–14, wrote of him: 'Le chevalier Methuen, Ambassadeur d' Angleterre auprès du Duc de Savoie, le plus généreux, le plus franc, et le plus brave homme de son pays qu'on ait jamais employé dans les ambassades, avait toujours combattu à côté de ce souverain.' John Gay, *The Poetical Works*, ed., John Underhill, 2 vols. (London: Lawrence & Bullen, 1893), I, 201–204, 'Epistle to the Rt. Hon. Paul Methuen,' and also in 'Mr. Pope's welcome from Greece,' (I, 209), written in 1720 on Alexander Pope's completion of the translation of the *Iliad*. Gay's reference occurs in Verse VII, lines 53–56 (p. 209). Sir Richard Steele dedicated the 7th volume of *The Spectator* (1712–1713) to Sir Paul. Horace Walpole was antagonistic towards him, describing him as 'a dull, formal, romantic braggadochio' in notes on Dr Maty's Memoirs of Chesterfield, printed in the Philobilon Society's Journal, II, 7. Sir Paul's motion in Parliament in 1741 hastened the collapse of his father's administration, something for which Walpole never forgave him (Francis, *The Methuens*, p. 350).

[49] This amount is verified in a letter written shortly before his death to Throphilies Jones at the Bank of England, 9 February 1757. Sir Paul enclosed his account book and £270: 'the balance in my favour will be again reduced to sixty-six thousands pounds and if you find it so, I beg you would be so kind as to have my account balanced.' Sir Paul Methuen died on 11 April 1757 (Corsham archives).

The source of his fortune has caused speculation. The nucleus must have come from his father's legacy and his own ambassador's salary, which included a final discharge of £1,272-15-0d for the ambassadorial gold and silver plate he was allowed to retain, and £5,583-5-0d for expenses. In 1709, Parliament approved his accounts as paymaster for the Gibraltar Campaign totalling £202,071-1-0d.[50] But perhaps it was through his business connections, such as those with the Childs, Benjamin Haskins Styles, and the Hoares, which allowed him to take advantage of speculation in the South Sea, East India, and other companies, that he became so wealthy.

Sir Paul Methuen, with his command of European languages, was a knowledgeable connoisseur of paintings who assembled one of the well known 18th-century collections. He was also a bibliophile; his cousin Paul Methuen inherited an impressive collection of architectural treatises from him. A visit to Rome in 1694–95 as a young man of twenty-two may well have formed his tastes, reflected in particular in the collection of architectural books (later in life he was especially interested in Italian treatises). Rome, then at the height of her Baroque splendour, was the home of many important picture collections (subsequently dispersed). This trip probably gave him the opportunity of visiting Florence and other cities en route to Rome. His participation in the Duke of Savoy's campaign to recapture Turin allowed little time for connoisseurship, but his diplomatic appointments in Spain and Portugal no doubt provided him with opportunity to see the royal collections and important private collections. Sir Paul seems to have begun his own collection after his return to England in 1715, according to the careful records he made of his personal expenses over the years, especially noting his purchases of china, books, and pictures, many of which he bought at auction sales.

Of the important collections assembled in the 18th century, Sir Paul's is one of the few to remain in the possession of the same family. Among the important collections of his contemporaries were those of Dr Richard Mead, MD, Sir Gregory Page of Blackheath, Sir Richard Child of Wanstead, Mr Henry Hoare of Stourhead, Field Marshall Wade, General Guise, the Duke of Chandos, and William, 4th Duke of Devonshire. Sir Paul Methuen was able to enrich his own collection when some of the collections of his contemporaries were dispersed. He made purchases amounting to £160 at the Duke of Chandos' sale at Cannons on 12 May 1747, and he recorded an entry for 20 March 1754, 'laid out at Dr Mead's auction, one hundred pounds.'

Some records have survived showing the range of his activities as a connoisseur. Among his important acquisitions still at Corsham and listed among his

---

50 Francis, *The Methuens*, p. 327.

records is one recorded in the entry: '22 May —— For a large Vandyck of Our Saviour betrayed by Judas to the Jews, one hundred pound.' This large painting (107¾ × 87¼ in. canvas size) was given a prominent position in Lancelot Brown's plans for the new picture gallery. Sir Paul also purchased pictures directly from dealers and agents abroad. An entry of 28 November 1727 records a list of expenses incurred in shipping pictures from Leghorn (9 cases), signed Captain Thomas Townsend ex 'Europe.'[51] A few letters have survived out of correspondence with an agent in Florence. On 7 February 1730, Francis Colman wrote from Florence to Sir Paul about Monsignor Sampien's pictures, followed by another letter from Colman on 18 February 1730, indicating 'that Monsignor Sampien does not wish to deplete his pictures.'[52] Sir Paul knew other connoisseurs, among them his friend at Court, Thomas Coke, a Vice-Chamberlain, who had been responsible for checking the inventory of Queen Anne's paintings between 1706 and 1710.[53] Alexander Pope mentioned Sir Paul's collection in correspondence with Ralph Allen of Bath.[54]

Sir Paul increased his knowledge of paintings by visiting other collections: in 1736, he made a journey to the Low Countries to visit important Dutch and Flemish collections, leaving London on 10 June and returning 1 August. His carefully written list of expenditures records the inns he stayed at with his friends, the connoisseurs he met, or to whom he had letters of introduction, and the various collections he visited. His itinerary took him to Rotterdam, Amsterdam, Antwerp, Ghent, and Brussels. This seems to have been his only recorded journey to the Continent after his return from Madrid in 1715. During the summer parliamentary recesses he made a habit of visiting various parts of England, and probably saw other important picture collections. His expenses for these journeys have survived, but give little indication where he stayed and what he saw, except that we know he was a frequent visitor to Bath and knew Ralph Allen.

---

[51] For expenses of shipping pictures from Leghorn, see Corsham documents, 4081A, 4082, and 4098.

[52] For the correspondence between Francis Colman and Sir Paul Methuen, see Corsham documents, 5029, and 5031.

[53] This reference was supplied by Miss Scott-Elliott, Royal Library, Windsor Castle. See, Denis Mahon, 'The Dutch Gift to Charles II,' *Burlington Magazine*, 91 (1949), 349, n. 10.

[54] Alexander Pope mentioned Sir Paul Methuen's collection to Ralph Allen when he was corresponding with him concerning the choice of subject matter for hall pictures at Prior Park, Bath. Benjamin Boyce, *The Benevolent Man: A Life of Ralph Allen of Bath* (Cambridge, Mass.: Harvard University Press, 1967), p. 105.

Sir Paul Methuen's picture collection had become known nationally in his own lifetime. After his death in 1757, Horace Walpole considered it sufficiently important to include in a catalogue published by the Strawberry Hill Press in 1760.[55] The collection was then housed at Sir Paul's home in Grosvenor Street, London. Walpole's catalogue was the earliest to be printed of the collection; two other contemporary descriptions also appeared in the 1760s.[56]

The first part of Sir Paul's collection of pictures was brought to Corsham between 1768 and 1772 after the completion of Lancelot Brown's picture gallery. When John Nash's north front was completed (*c.* 1800), the second part of the collection was transferred from London, to be hung in the salon and music room where Nash had designed a special gallery to house it.

Although today the original collection is depleted, it was enlarged when a second collection, that of the Reverend John Sanford of Nynhead Court, Somerset, came to the family by marriage in 1844. It included, in addition to fashionable Italian Renaissance and Baroque painters, Italian primitives that Sanford had purchased in Italy during the chaos that followed the aftermath of the Napoleonic Wars.[57]

In addition to the picture collection, Sir Paul Methuen assembled a comprehensive collection of architectural books which remains almost intact at Corsham today. In many respects, Sir Paul's purchases of books are recorded in even more detail than his picture collection, because some of the auction-sale catalogues have survived with his annotations in them (see Appendix B for a list of Sir Paul Methuen's architectural treatises).

The architectural taste of Sir Paul and of his cousin Paul Methuen was formed by the prevailing style of the first half of the 18th century, the Palladian. Through his Wiltshire connections Sir Paul probably knew William Benson, one of the

---

[55] *Catalogue of the Collections of Pictures of the Duke of Devonshire, General Guise and the late Sir Paul Methuen.* Sir Paul's collection is subtitled on page 26 as 'Catalogues of Pictures etc., on the two first floors of the house of Paul Methuen, Esq., Grosvenor Street.' The collection of the 4th Duke of Devonshire is still in the possession of the Chatsworth Estate, and General Guise bequeathed his collection to the Ashmolean Museum, Oxford.

[56] *London and its Environs Described* (London: R. & J. Dodsley, 1761), III, 83–100; Thomas Martyn, *The English Connoisseur containing an account of whatever is curious in painting, sculpture, etc., in the seats of the nobility and principal gentry of England, both in town and country* (London, 1766), II, 17–37.

[57] For information on the present collection see, Tancred Borenius, *Catalogue of the Methuen Collection*, private ed. (London 1939), and Benedict Nicolson, 'The Sanford Collection,' *Burlington Magazine*, 97 (1955), 207–214.

initiators of the 18th-century Palladian Revival; Benson is credited with erecting one of the earliest Palladian houses, Wilbury, Wiltshire (*c.* 1710). His brother-in-law was Henry Hoare the Elder, of Stourhead, Wiltshire, who was one of the Methuens' bankers. Benson was briefly associated with Colen Campbell (from around 1715 to 1719), who published the first volume of his influential *Vitruvius Britannicus* in the spring of 1715. Sir Paul was in England when the first volume was published, but his name does not appear on its list of subscribers. He was a subscriber to the second volume of the *Vitruvius Britannicus* (1718).[58] Campbell dedicated plates 89 and 90 in this volume to Sir Paul, as Principal Secretary of State. By the time of publication Sir Paul had relinquished this temporary government position.[59] Campbell probably had the plates engraved, and may have sent specimens of them to Sir Paul when he was still in office. This dedication was possibly a form of political lobbying by Campbell for an official position; he dedicated other plates to prominent members of the government. Campbell describes the design as being in the 'Theatrical Style,' which was influenced by the town house of Count Valerio Chiericato (Palazzo Chiericati), Vicenza, illustrated in Palladio's *Quattro Libri*, II, plate 2 (see **23**). Whatever Campbell's motives were in dedicating the plates to Sir Paul, he did not receive a commission. At the time Sir Paul may have contemplated building a country seat, for he owned an estate at Bishops Cannings, near Devizes, Wiltshire, purchased from the Bishop of Salisbury.

Other members of the Government to whom Campbell dedicated plates were Sir Robert Walpole and the Rt Hon. James Stanhope, one of the signatories to the approbation of the *Vitruvius Britannicus*.[60] The design Campbell dedicated to him was a slight variation of the Palazzo Valmarana-Braga, Vicenza, designed by Palladio. Walpole received a design influenced by Palladio's Villa Pisani at

---

[58] The three volumes of the *Vitruvius Britannicus* in the library at Corsham contain Sir Paul Methuen's bookplates. The second volume published in 1718, describes Sir Paul as principal Secretary of State and in the third volume published in 1725, he is described as Comptroller of the House. This edition was printed before Sir Paul received his knighthood in May of the same year.

[59] Campbell's dedication to Sir Paul Methuen states 'This new design of my invention in the Theatrical style, is humbly inscribed to the Rt Hon. Paul Methuen, Esqr., principal Secretary of State, etc.' Plate 90. On page 5, Campbell provides a description of the design, 'A New Design inscribed to Mr Secretary Methuen, plates 89 & 90.' See, Colen Campbell, *Vitruvius Britannicus* (London, 1718), II, 5, and plates 89 and 90.

[60] In July 1716, Sir Paul was made acting Secretary of State during Stanhope's absence abroad. Sir Robert Walpole appointed Sir Paul Comptroller of the Royal Household in 1720. Francis, *The Methuens*, p. 350.

Montagna. This resulted in a commission for Campbell to prepare designs for Houghton (*c.* 1721), which was eventually erected in a much modified form of the Pisani design. This commission was the only one Campbell received as a direct result of publishing his *Vitruvius Britannicus*. The design of Houghton influenced William Kent, and later Lancelot Brown, who erected the Palladian east front of Corsham Court between 1761 and 1767, where some of Campbell's Houghton motifs appeared on the east front.

Through Colen Campbell's subscription lists in the *Vitruvius Britannicus* we learn the names of persons associated with Sir Paul Methuen, politically and socially. They were the early patrons of the Palladian movement, even if Campbell did not receive many actual commissions from them. Campbell also mentioned other persons indirectly associated with the later alterations at Corsham, persons whose tastes were in part formed by Campbell's treatise.

Other subscribers to the *Vitruvius Britannicus* and patrons of the Palladian Revival were neighbours of the Methuens in Wiltshire. Their names will be mentioned indirectly in connection with the subsequent alterations at Corsham. They include Lord Shelburne, who later purchased Bowood near Corsham and employed Henry Keene to extend it from 1755 to 1760; Viscount Weymouth of Longleat, who gave Lancelot Brown his first commission in Wiltshire to remodel the park at Longleat, and Henry Hoare the Elder, who commissioned Campbell to design Stourhead House.[61] The contractor for Stourhead, Nathaniel Ireson, was employed later at Corsham between 1747 and 1749 to design and erect the north front.

Personal friends and acquaintances of the Methuen family who also subscribed to the *Vitruvius Britannicus* included the Duchess of Buccleugh, the Duke of Argyll, Lord Dalkeith and the Duke of Bridgwater. The Duchess of Buccleuch was the mother-in-law of Lady Caroline Dalkeith, who was a friend of Mrs Paul Methuen. From Lady Dalkeith's correspondence we learn of references made to Sir Paul's picture collection, and a visit of Lancelot Brown to Corsham. Brown was paid for plans submitted to remodel the park at Adderbury, Oxfordshire, for the Duke of Buccleugh. John Campbell, second Duke of Argyll, Lord-Steward of the Household and father of Lady Dalkeith, purchased two copies of each volume.[62] Lord Dalkeith, Lady Caroline's husband and heir of the Dukedom of

---

[61] Henry Hoare's wife was Jane Benson, a sister of William Benson who designed Wilbury House, Wiltshire, *c.* 1710.

[62] Colen Campbell dedicated the first unsolicited design to the Duke who was the hereditary chief of the clan Campbell.

Buccleuch, subscribed for a copy. The Duke of Bridgwater had two copies of each volume; at one time he was Sir Paul's landlord in London, and later Sir Paul acted as trustee for his estate. Lancelot Brown remodelled the house and park at Ashridge, Hertfordshire, the Bridgwater country seat, between 1759 and 1768; Sir Paul had stayed there in the summer of 1742.

The death of Thomas Coke, a subscriber to the *Vitruvius Britannicus* and colleague of Sir Paul's at court, contributed indirectly to the growth of Sir Paul's collection of books. Coke, Vice-Chamberlain to the Royal Household, also a connoisseur and book collector, died in office in May, 1727.[63] At the sale of his possessions in February, 1728, Sir Paul purchased a collection of Coke's architectural books.[64] These, together with Sir Paul's own subscription copies of the *Vitruvius Britannicus* were the foundation of his architectural collection. Sir Paul purchased a further collection of books at the auction sale on 18 November 1754, following the death of Dr Richard Mead.[65] A well-known connoisseur, Mead had assembled an important picture collection and library. He also subscribed to the *Vitruvius Britannicus*, although Campbell did not dedicate a plate to him.

Besides the *Vitruvius Britannicus*, Sir Paul acquired two other important English Palladian publications which mentioned the names of associates, and craftsmen later employed at Corsham. The first was Thomas Coke's subscription copy of Giacomo Leoni's *The Architecture of Andrea Palladio . . . Revised* (London, 1715), which included among the subscribers Lord Shelburne of Bowood and James Stanhope. The second was a copy of William Kent's *Designs of Inigo Jones with some additional Designs* (London, 1727), whose subscribers included Henry Keene, a carpenter and father of Henry Keene, who provided designs for Corsham in 1759, and Peter Scheemaker, a sculptor who supplied the marble chimney-piece for the picture gallery.

The books from Sir Paul Methuen's architectural collection, which in those days were printed in very limited editions, were at Paul Methuen's disposal to study when he was in London. His subsequent choice of the Palladian style for the extensions that were added to Corsham House—the north front of 1749, and

---

[63] For Thomas Coke's obituary notice see *The Political State of Great Britain*, A. Boyer, ed., 23 (1727), 528.

[64] The sale was held at Mr Cooper's auction rooms in the Great Piazza, Covent Garden. The annotated catalogue of Coke's sale is preserved at Corsham, in which is recorded Sir Paul's purchases totalling £208-13-0d.

[65] The sale catalogue consisting of 242 pages with annotations by Sir Paul Methuen is preserved at Corsham.

Lancelot Brown's east wing of 1761–67—reflects in part the continuing influence of Colen Campbell's *Vitruvius Britannicus*, in which a plate had been dedicated to his cousin.

Thus through the political careers of the Rt Hon. John Methuen and Sir Paul Methuen, and the wealth accumulated by the latter, the Methuen family established themselves as members of the Whig landowning class in Wiltshire. Sir Paul's connoisseurship and literary tastes added further lustre to the family's reputation through the splendid art collection with which Corsham was eventually endowed following his death in 1757. The collection remains a great cultural and social attraction of the property to this day.

CHAPTER TWO

The Alterations of Lancelot Brown

The architectural alterations of Lancelot Brown demonstrated a sympathy for the Elizabethan style unusual for the period. This sympathetic treatment extended to both the plan and elevations. The symmetry, flat wall-surfaces, regular window-openings and simple cubic spaces of the Elizabethan–Renaissance style enabled the Palladian architects to integrate their designs into the house with a minimum of alterations. The Elizabethan–Renaissance proportions suited Palladian forms. Similarly, the Renaissance elements of the south front—the entablatures, the pediments and the porch—helped to preserve the Elizabethan form and character of the front in the face of remodelling. When Brown doubled the bay windows of the wings to preserve the symmetry of the south front it constituted an early archaeological treatment of the facade. In this way the architects emphasised the classical forms to be found in the Elizabethan–Renaissance style, and ignored the Gothic elements in their designs for the north and east fronts.

Although Paul Methuen's trustees had purchased the Corsham estate in 1745, legal delays prevented him from taking possession of the property until 25 March 1747, at the age of twenty-three. This was a significant year in English architectural history, and for the Gothic Revival in particular. The young Horace Walpole, who was twenty-nine, and the fourth son of Sir Robert Walpole, purchased a small estate at Strawberry Hill, Twickenham, in the same year. Horace Walpole began as a creator of taste, whereas Paul Methuen was a follower of the latest fashion.

In 1747 the Palladian Revival was still the prevailing architectural style, but was losing the authority it had enjoyed in the two previous decades. Although it continued to be used extensively on facades, the interior style of decoration was changing. Within a Palladian exterior were rooms decorated in distinctive

Revival styles. The use of classical as well as Rococo and Gothic decoration was a reaction to the heavy Palladian interior decoration associated with the Burlington School, whose principal decorator was William Kent. The interior decoration at Corsham reflects this departure from the prevailing Palladian style.

The Palladian movement became fashionable in part through the patronage of Richard Boyle, 3rd Earl of Burlington, and 4th Earl of Cork. After an early association with Colen Campbell and his own studies of Palladio, Lord Burlington was able to turn the taste of the English nobility and landowners towards the Palladian style. His status as an amateur architect gave him a place of authority within the Palladian Revival. William Kent, who was Lord Burlington's principal protégé in developing the movement, died in 1748. Kent's work furthered the development of English landscape gardening that became almost inseparable from the Palladian Revival country houses; Kent also helped to spread the Rococo–'Gothick' Revival beginning *c.* 1730. Burlington's widespread influence also extended to architects like Henry Flitcroft, Isaac Ware, Roger Morris and the aristocratic amateur Henry Herbert, 9th Earl of Pembroke. When Burlington died in 1753, the movement was an established style; of the movement's early initiators only he lived into the 1750s.

The two architects associated with the remodelling of Corsham House between 1759 and 1766, Lancelot Brown and Henry Keene, were in 1747 young men at the beginning of their careers. Brown was born in Kirkharle, Northumberland, in 1716, the year following the publication of Campbell's first volume of *Vitruvius Britannicus*. In 1739, Brown moved southwards and obtained a commission from Sir Charles Browne, 2nd Bart., of Kiddington Hall, Oxfordshire, where Brown created a lake mentioned by John Penn in his *History & Descriptive Account of Stoke Park*, 1813. Shortly afterwards, according to Penn, Brown came to the notice of Lord Cobham at Stowe where he took up his appointment in 1740.[1] Brown was 24 when he moved to Lord Cobham's mansion at Stowe where he stayed until the owner's death in September 1749. Brown's close association with Kent at Stowe had an important formative influence upon his landscape planning and architectural design. Kent had been re-designing Stowe from the 1730s until his death in April 1748. In 1747 Brown was probably engaged upon laying out the Grecian valley in conjunction with Kent. This was Brown's first opportunity to lay out a landscape from uncultivated land, rather than merely

---

[1] Dorothy Stroud, *Capability Brown* (new ed. 1975), pp. 47–9.

altering the more formal layout of Charles Bridgeman who had worked at Stowe before Kent.[2]

Henry Keene was also at the beginning of his career as an architect in 1747. Ten years younger than Brown, he was born on 15 November 1726.[3] His father was a builder who was able to provide his son with an architectural training; in 1746, when Henry Keene was barely twenty, he succeeded Thomas Hinton as Surveyor of Westminster Abbey. Later in 1752 he was appointed to the second Surveyorship offered by the Abbey authorities, and was responsible for the fabric of the abbey itself. This association with one of the most venerable examples of Gothic architecture in England enabled him to become familiar with the Gothic style, of which he was one of the earliest practitioners in the 18th century. The Gothic style had continued to be used in the 17th century by Sir Christopher Wren, Hawksmoor, and Vanbrugh. The influence of these essentially Baroque architects declined with the rise of the Palladian School; even with the revival of an interest in the Gothic, their own Gothic buildings were not very influential.[4] Keene's early Gothic work included the restoration of the chapel at Hartlebury Castle, Worcestershire (1750) for Bishop Maddox, and a design for the gate of Worcester Cathedral also in 1750. Thus Keene's experience of designing and building Gothic structures from the beginning of his documented career, enabled him to provide both Classical and Gothic designs for his proposed work at Corsham.

Paul Methuen belonged to the same generation as Henry Keene; he was seven years younger than Lancelot Brown. In the tradition of his family Paul Methuen was educated at Winchester College; he then entered Oriel College, Oxford, matriculated on 4 April 1741, and obtained his MA from Oriel on 23 August 1744. He endeavoured to follow a parliamentary career upon leaving Oxford, and was returned as member for Westbury in 1747; because of some irregularity at the polls he was subsequently unseated after a petition for a recount. After this setback he abandoned his political career until he became a member of Parliament for Warwick from 1762 to 1764, and for Great Bedwyn

---

[2] Christopher Hussey considers that much of Brown's repertory originated in William Kent, especially in their joint work in the Grecian Valley at this time. Christopher Hussey, *English Gardens and Landscapes 1700–1750* (New York: Funk and Wagnall, 1967), p. 47.

[3] Howard M. Colvin, *Biographical Dictionary of English Architects 1660–1840* (London: John Murray, 1954), pp. 333–337.

[4] Kenneth Clark, *The Gothic Revival*, 3rd ed. (1928; rpt. London: John Murray, 1962), pp. 15–18. In writing about the Gothic Revival, Clark makes the distinction between survival and revival; he considers that the Revival began in the 18th century with William Kent.

from 1774 to 1781. On 25 June 1749, Paul Methuen married Christian Cobb, the daughter of Sir George Cobb, Bart, of Adderbury, Oxfordshire and his wife Anne Langton of Newton Park, Bath.[5]

In June 1747, a journey to Edinburgh to trace his Scottish ancestry at the Scottish Office of Heraldry gave Methuen the opportunity to see some important examples of architecture; some notes of this journey have survived.[6] They constitute the only architectural writings of Paul Methuen that have survived. They indicate a familiarity with architectural terms and styles of the day. On Monday, 20 June, he visited Chatsworth House, Derbyshire, and recorded the following impressions of its facades and gardens:

It has four handsome Fronts of great elegancy and neatness of Building, the most ornament'd one is 180 feet long, it forms a quadrangle in the middle of wch has a bason of water in the middle of it. The beautiful colour of the house is a great addition to the appearance of it. One front has 12 windows, nine in another. . . . The gardens are finely disposed in Lawns and Plantations. . . .

Passing the great Elizabethan mansion, Wollaton Hall, Nottingham, erected between 1580 and 1588 by Robert Smythson, Methuen commented that it was, 'situated in a well planted park and is a fine old seat belonging to Lord Middleton.' He was apparently equally interested in the Gothic style, which he introduced in later architectural and decorative alterations at Corsham. He mentions several Gothic structures, including Lichfield Cathedral:

Tis a small cathedrall of Gothick Architecture, the west front like Wells was full of statues most of wch were demolished in the Rebellion, and indeed those that remain are much disfigured and all the ornamentary part of the outside much injured in those times.

These notes indicate Paul Methuen's appreciation of architecture and landscape gardening. His comment upon Wollaton Hall shows that Methuen regarded the Elizabethan style as old-fashioned and must indirectly reflect his opinion of Corsham at this time. He was far more impressed with the classical fronts of Chatsworth House, with the beautiful effect of its Derbyshire stone, and with its ornamental gardens. Chatsworth provided an excellent example to which a country landowner could aspire. Although Corsham could not be remodelled on the scale of Chatsworth, it was possible to add a modest classical front to the old house and carefully planned pleasure-gardens to provide a suitable setting.

---

[5] Lord Methuen, *Corsham Court* (Bristol: Holloway & Son, 1965), p. 6. It was through her residence at Adderbury, Oxfordshire, that Mrs Paul Methuen knew Lady Caroline Dalkeith (Campbell), whose father-in-law, the Duke of Buccleuch had a country seat at Adderbury.

[6] The notebook, marked number three, dates from 8 June, to Monday 27 1747; it covers a section of the route southwards from Carlisle to Lichfield. There is also a partially burnt page remaining from book number two. (Corsham archives.)

THE PALLADIAN FACADE OF THE NORTH FRONT

Perhaps the most important result of Paul Methuen's journey was his decision to have a Palladian facade, no doubt inspired by those he had seen at Chatsworth, added to the Elizabethan north front of Corsham. Two designs for the north facade are preserved at Corsham. (The Palladian facade was subsequently refaced and incorporated into the extension built beyond the Elizabethan north wall of the house by John Nash.) A drawing has survived (see **27**), made by Henry Keene in 1759, that shows his proposed modifications to the then existing Palladian facade. Another engraving (published in William Watt's *Seats of the Nobility and Gentry* London, 1779), depicts the north front after Brown's extension on the east side was added (see **24**).

Who was the architect and builder of this facade is not known with certainty, but it has been attributed to Nathaniel Ireson of Wincanton on the basis of strong stylistic evidence and a note of his name on the unexecuted design.[7] Ireson was born in 1686 probably at Nuneaton; his early training is unknown. His first documented work was the construction of Stourhead House, Wiltshire, for Henry Hoare the Elder from 1720 to 1723, in accordance with Colen Campbell's design (*Vitruvius Britannicus*, III, plates 41 and 42). That Ireson worked at Stourhead again in the early 1740s for Henry Hoare the Younger is confirmed in two letters from Henry Flitcroft (1697–1769) to Hoare dated 18 August and 25 August 1744.[8] It was probably through Paul Methuen's connections with Henry Hoare the Younger, who was his banker, that Ireson came to Corsham.[9]

---

[7] For the identification of Ireson's name on this design see, H. St George Gray, 'Nathaniel Ireson of Wincanton: Master Builder,' *Somerset Archaeological & Natural History Society Proceedings*, 87 (1941), 81–84; ———, 'Nathaniel Ireson: Master Builder and Potter,' *Country Life*, 22 April 1939, 423–425. Also, George Sweetman gives a biographical account of Ireson in his *History of Wincanton* (London: Henry Williams, Wincanton: George Sweetman, 1903), 209–211. In addition to other activities Ireson was a sculptor.

[8] I am indebted to Kenneth Woodbridge, author of *Landscape and Antiquity* (London: Oxford University Press, 1970), and 'Henry Hoare's Paradise, Stourhead, Wiltshire,' *Art Bulletin*, 47 (1965), 83–116, for this information. The letters cited are in the Stourhead House archives correspondence I (1736/37–1835).

[9] Other houses erected by Ireson include: Ven House, *c.* 1730; Crowcombe Court, 1734. Ireson was also associated with John and William Bastard at Blandford Forum, Dorset. For references to Ven House, see *Country Life*, 24 June 1911, pp. 924–934; Christopher Hussey, 'Crowcombe,' *Country Life*, 22 April 1933, pp. 414–419; Geoffry Webb, 'John and William Bastard.' *Burlington Magazine*, 47 (1925), 144–150, and Arthur Oswald, *Country Houses of Dorset*, 2nd ed. (London: Country Life, 1959), p. 32.

Ireson's first design for a north front is dated 1747 (see **25**). This design for a two-storey elevation with a hipped roof was somewhat old-fashioned at the time, characteristic of Carolean country houses such a Hugh May's Eltham Lodge (1663–4), and Roger Pratt's Coleshill House, Berkshire (*c.* 1650), although William Benson's Wilbury (*c.* 1710) and Colen Campbell's earliest house, Shawfield, Glasgow (1712) both had hipped roofs. Pilasters divide the facade into three bays of which the centre one is pedimented. He intended to use 'composed capitals,' of Baroque form originally introduced into England by Thomas Archer, who had studied Borromini's architecture while in Italy.[10]

Other elements of the facade show Ireson's indebtedness to Colen Campbell. The venetian window motif used for the entrance is almost identical to that used for the garden front at Stourhead. The eared window-mouldings also came from there. The curved pediments and pulvinated friezes of the centre windows of the ground-floor side bays could have come from Campbell's Roll's House 1718, (*Vitruvius Britannicus*, III, plates 44 and 45). The chimney stacks were to be disguised as piers with urns standing in front of them. The urns are characteristic features of Ireson's work and appear elsewhere.[11] But the difficulty and the cost of demolishing the Elizabethan gables on the outer sides of the two chimney stacks (see **25**) made Ireson's first design unsatisfactory.

The second design, dated 1749, overcame the problem of the gabled roof by adding an attic storey with a crowning cornice (see **26**). The tripartite division of the front was maintained, the projecting pedimented centre being formed by the projection of the chimney stacks from the main wall of the house. He substituted quoins for pilasters to define the pedimented centre bay, echoing Campbells' use of quoins on the Roll's House, a source also for the string-courses dividing the ground and first floors of the north front. The entrance to the north front was now formed by an aedicule motif consisting of a pair of attached Ionic columns supporting a pulvinated pediment derived from Campbell's Hedworth House (1716). The aedicule motif enclosed a round-arched entrance with a prominent keystone, a motif characteristic of Campbell's work at Wanstead.

---

[10] Thomas Archer (?1668–1743) had travelled in Italy between 1689–1693, and had closely studied Borromini's architecture. Ireson is thought to have derived his use of these capitals from the Bastards of Blandford. See Oswald, *Dorset Country Houses*, p. 33, and Marcus Whiffen, *Thomas Archer* (London, 1950).

[11] The urns on the gate piers of Couper House, Blandford, show a strong resemblance to those used for the designs at Corsham. This house has been attributed to Ireson by Arthur Oswald, see *Country Houses of Dorset*, p. 33. For an illustration of the gate piers see, Geoffrey Webb, 'John and William Bastard,' *Burlington Magazine*, 47 (1925), 144–145, plate iif.

The arrangement of the windows in the second design is basically the same: nine windows grouped into three bays, and an additional attic level. Because of their regular placement most of the window-openings of the Elizabethan north front could be used without cutting fresh apertures for the new facade. The pediment has an elaborately carved, foliated design carrying the Methuen coat-of-arms. It was upon detail such as this that Ireson was able to display his skill as a sculptor.

Ireson's designs for the north front show his fundamental reliance upon Campbell's architecture, and his indebtedness to Stourhead in particular. By concealing the Elizabethan gables rather than using a hipped roof, Ireson was also following Sir John Thynne; Thynne had already done this at Longleat in his last building campaign (1575–79) when he added the 'Corintian order' of bay windows and a balustrade to the house. Henry Keene later proposed the same method of remodelling the south front in 1759. The symmetrical plan of the house, its division into three bays with regular window openings, and its floor-levels of a suitable height made it easy for Ireson to adapt the Palladian front to the existing north front. The entrance was in the same position as that of the Elizabethan north door, directly opposite the south door of the house (see **27**).

Thus Ireson introduced a Palladian design drawn largely from his knowledge of Campbell's work that evinced a correct sense of proportion and provided a set of architectural elements that Brown was able to harmonise with his east front.

THE GOTHIC INFLUENCE AT CORSHAM

It has been generally assumed that the Rococo–Gothic influence at Corsham was introduced during Lancelot Brown's alterations, when the library was decorated in this style.[12] However, Paul Methuen had developed a taste for the Gothic before it had become generally fashionable in country-house decoration. The only evidence for this survives in several brief entries in three accounts.[13] The location of the rooms which he had redecorated in this style are not known, because of Brown's and Nash's later remodelling of the interior.

References to Gothic decoration occur in two items on an account rendered by John Dlimmers, paid on 15 June 1753 (Corsham document 5040). The first item is a fretwork ceiling priced at £15, and the second a Gothick cornice 75 ft 8 in. long at two shillings per foot, priced at seven pounds ten shillings. This

---

[12] Stroud, *Capability Brown* (new ed. 1975), p. 88.

[13] Corsham documents: 5040, John Dlimmers £89-19-0d; 5042, John Hutchins £30-8-0d; and 5044, John Hicks £61-15-0d.

suggests that a fairly large room, possibly one of the principal living rooms, was being remodelled with Gothic decoration. The measurements are approximately those of the Green Drawing-room in the plan of 1759 (see **27**). Another item on the same account is for a marble chimney-piece, but it is probably only a replacement of an older Elizabethan chimney-piece. The important thing is that the decoration of the cornice is specifically called 'Gothick' in the account.

The source of the Gothic influence could have been Lacock Abbey only three miles away from Corsham. Here Methuen's neighbour, John Ivory Talbot (1687?–1772), was employing Sanderson Miller to build a new hall. Miller was one of the leading authorities upon the Gothic style, and Lacock was one of his earliest important commissions. The old hall at Lacock was demolished in 1753; work began on the new one in the following year and it was completed in 1755.

Paul Methuen must have been aware of these alterations and may have met Sanderson Miller. In the following year, 1756, Talbot had the arms of his friends emblazoned in the fretwork design of the ceiling of the new hall; Paul Methuen's are included. Talbot wrote to Sanderson Miller about a ceremonial opening of the hall: 'when all my friends who are in the country and whose arms are emblazoned on the ceiling will do me the honour of their company and a grand sacrifice to Bacchus will be the consequence.'[14] This confirms our supposition that Paul Methuen knew of the work being done on Lacock Abbey in the Gothic style, contemporary with Walpole's innovations at Strawberry Hill. It may have been Paul Methuen's growing interest in the Gothic style and his desire that the decoration should not be exclusively Palladian, that led him to invite Henry Keene to submit designs for remodelling Corsham in 1759.

HENRY KEENE'S DESIGNS OF 1759

On the death of Sir Paul Methuen in 1757, Paul Methuen of Corsham was able to put in hand the long-cherished scheme of adding an extension to the house, ostensibly to house the picture collection. Henry Keene (1726–76) was the first architect engaged to submit plans for the proposed alterations. Before coming to Corsham, Keene had acted as architect from 1755 to 1760 for Methuen's neighbour John, Earl of Shelburne, at Bowood House, about four miles from Corsham.[15] Eleven of Keene's drawings are preserved at Corsham. In 1760,

---

[14] Janet Burnett-Brown, *Lacock Abbey, Wiltshire* (Bolton: Tillotsons, 1969), p. 8.

[15] Keene was employed upon remodelling the office block and portico in the Palladian style. He also erected for Lord Shelburne a classical Guildhall at High Wycombe, Bucks, in 1757, and carried out Gothic alterations to the church at High Wycombe in 1754.

there is a record of a payment of 30 guineas for the designs submitted.[16] They did not meet with Paul Methuen's approval; meanwhile Lancelot Brown had been asked to remodel the house and landscape the park.

The ideas suggested in Keene's designs, which formed the basis for Lancelot Brown's own designs, were his principal contribution to the remodelling of Corsham. Two important needs had to be taken into account in the planning; first, the provision of a suitable picture gallery, and second, of a library for Sir Paul's collection of books, also at Grosvenor Street. The only place available for the picture gallery was the Elizabethan east front still in its original state (see **5**). Although the north front would have provided a more even light, it had only been refaced in 1749. To destroy this relatively new facade would have been unduly expensive. As for the library, Keene decided to house it in the west wing, the only suitable place available, although it was then occupied by domestic offices. The area chosen was being used as the butler's pantry and the housekeeper's room, behind the proposed new bay window of the west wing at ground-floor level (see **2** and **27**).[17]

In adding a Palladian extension to the east side of the house Keene showed a sensitivity—unusual for the period—toward the existing style of the Elizabethan south front. He solved the problem of the projection of the east wing on its south side by doubling the bay-windows of both wings of the south front. Keene also proposed to classicise the existing south front, integrating its Renaissance elements into his design without entirely destroying its Elizabethan character. In providing for the addition of the picture gallery, Keene maintained the principal amenities of the house, such as the hall and staircase, thus preserving the Elizabethan plan of the house and the symmetry of the south front.

The evolution of Keene's ideas for remodelling the house at Corsham is preserved in three plans (see **27, 28,** and **30**). The earliest (**27**) appears to be the plan of the house after 1749, showing the proposed design for remodelling the west wing to include the library and relocated domestic premises. Here for the first time the principle of doubling the bay windows of the south front has been sketched in.

The second plan (**28**) is Keene's first complete drawing for the contemplated alterations. It shows the proposed east wing with the picture gallery on the

---

[16] This entry is recorded in Paul Methuen's Day Book on 12 January 1760, 'Pd Mr. Keene the Architect for plans of Alterations at Corsham, £31-10-0d.' (30 gns)

[17] The library was converted into the present breakfast room during the alterations of John Nash.

ground floor, and bedroom-space on the first floor. The east wing does not extend to the north front; Keene evidently wished to preserve the two windows at the north end of the existing east wing that lighted the main staircase (see **5**). This idea was retained in his third plan (**30**). The floor plan of the Elizabethan east wing remained unchanged (see **27**). The picture gallery is the same length as the adjoining wing, approximately nine feet wider, and the same height as the Elizabethan rooms. The bay-window at the south end of the gallery was to be concealed behind a false wall, as in the cabinet-room today. Although the gallery is wide, its low ceiling would have made it dark; apparently little consideration was given to the arrangement of the pictures at this stage of the design.

Keene provided a side elevation for this extension (see **29**). Of Palladian design, it consists of seven bays, with two principal floors and an attic level. The attached temple front of three bays in the Ionic order, raised upon a rusticated ground floor with balustrades linking the plinths of the columns, would have been the principal feature. Keene's second design would have given a dignified, monumental appearance to the east front in its arrangement of an attached Ionic order, and would have been a more sculptural compliment to the shallow temple front of the north facade.

In Keene's third plan the interior arrangement of the rooms in the east wing (see **28** and **30**) has been carefully integrated, and the shape of the Elizabethan rooms altered into Palladian forms. He reduced the length of the former yellow drawing-room, turning it into an octagon, one of the favourite Palladian forms used in suites of rooms. He also provided new entrances. The main purpose of the third design was to create a suite of inter-communicating state rooms.

Keene also paid attention to the design of the picture gallery in this plan, which centres the gallery in the middle of the Elizabethan east wall. The fireplaces would be on the north and south walls of the picture gallery because a doorway now occupied the position of the fireplace in the second plan. This plan had an advantage over the second in the communicating-doors between the rooms.

Keene provided two elevations for the Palladian east front with his third plan (see **31** and **32**). The first elevation has a front of five bays, and an attached temple front of three bays, consisting of the ground floor and mezzanine level of windows. This may possibly indicate that the height of the picture gallery had been raised to include a coved ceiling. The second elevation incorporates an attic storey at the pediment level, the same height as the north front.[18] Neither of these elevations

---

[18] Keene also provided an elevation of the north end of the east wing with the second elevation (see **33**).

is as monumental as that of the elevation to go with the second plan (**29**); instead, they appear to be mere wings jutting out from the main block of the house.

The size of the proposed library also changed in the third plan. In Keene's second plan (**28**), the library was to be the same width as the picture gallery, whereas in the third plan (**30**), the library was left the original width of the existing rooms (see **27**). Instead a muniment room was planned at the angle of the two walls, with steps leading into it from the library (see **43** for an exterior view of the muniment room).

Keene's designs contained several defects that must have caused Paul Methuen to reject them. Keene did not provide an acceptable solution for a picture gallery, which was, after all, an important addition to the house, designed specifically to display the principal pieces from Sir Paul Methuen's collection. His second design for the gallery gave too much space to openings for doorways and fireplaces, although the gallery was better integrated into the house through a system of communicating rooms imaginatively remodelled into different shapes within the limitations of the existing space. The second problem Keene failed to solve was how to light the main staircase if the proposed east wing were to be brought up to the level of the north front, necessary if the external symmetry of the house was not to be spoiled.

Although Keene doubled the bay-windows of the south-front wings, he intended to classicise the front in keeping with the conception of Palladian design. The designs he submitted all used the same principle adopted by Ireson for the north front—masking the attic gables with a parapet wall, although the cornice is not heavy enough in relation to the height of the front. The most interesting design is shown on **34**; it was intended as the elevation to correspond with the second plan (see **28**). Here Keene has removed the pediments from the bay windows, and the fan-shaped pediment from over the porch, and placed balustrades in front of the attic windows. The attic windows have been given triangular pediments with scroll-like motifs on either side. The bay-windows of the wings are linked by short superimposed colonnades in the Doric and Ionic orders, which appear to be attached to the main wall. The Ionic order carries a balustrade between those of the attic windows. Although Keene provides interesting designs for the attic windows, the thinness of the cornice is a real weakness of the front.

The second design of the south front (**35**) retained the original pediments above the bay windows, except for the porch where a triangular pediment has been substituted for the fan-shaped one. The attic windows have straight entablatures, with low parapet walls forming a small balcony over each bay-window. This design seems to have been scaled down in the interest of economy.

The third design of the south front follows the wall articulation of the second design (see **36**). But here, rather than adding a second bay-window to the wings, Keene proposed to add a single storey with a hipped roof. The projected gallery has been pencilled into scale on the east wing. In his design for the new windows Keene followed the original Elizabethan form; this is evidenced by a separate drawing (preserved at Corsham) that Keene supplied. This third design may chronologically be a part of the initial idea of providing a suitably balanced South front for the 'intended library' marked on **27**, before he doubled the bay-windows to incorporate the picture gallery on the East side in the second and third plans (**28** and **30**).

Keene planned to enliven the surface of Ireson's relatively plain north front by adding an Ionic porch to the centre section at the ground-floor level (see **37** and **38**), and balconies to two of the first-floor windows.[18a] These decorative elements would have made it more in keeping with his own designs for the east front.

Keene's designs formed the basis for Brown's subsequent work at Corsham. Keene was able to integrate his Palladian designs around the Elizabethan–Renaissance characteristics of the house, such as the symmetrical plan. This principle was followed by all the later architects. His proposal to duplicate the existing wings of the south front which he regarded as Gothic, shows a sensitive solution to the problem of preserving the character of the south front.

CAPABILITY BROWN'S EXTENSIONS

Exactly why Keene's plans were rejected is not known, but the employment of Brown offered the advantage that he could provide a unified scheme for remodelling the house and laying out the park. Paul Methuen had been considering designs for remodelling the pleasure gardens and park; but plans for these schemes submitted by Greening and Oram had not been carried out. Brown had gained a considerable reputation for treating both the house and grounds of estates; thus his employment offered to a prospective client the advantage of avoiding any possible conflict between architect and landscape gardener. Humphry Repton discussed combination of function in his *Observations on the Theory and Practice of Landscape Gardening*.[19] He quotes from a letter by the poet William Mason, written on 24 April 1792: 'Brown, I know, was ridiculed for turning architect, but I always thought he did it from a kind of necessity, having found the great difficulty which must frequently have occurred to him in forming a picturesque

---

[18a] An unidentified design for a Doric porch by Henry Keene (**39**) in the V & A Museum (E898–1921) may also refer to remodelling the North Front porch.

[19] Humphry Repton, *Observations on the Theory and Practice of Landscape Gardening: including some remarks on Grecian and Gothic Architecture* (London: J. Taylor, 1803), p. 71.

whole, where the previous building had been ill placed, or of improper dimensions.'[20]

When Brown was invited to Corsham late in 1759 or early 1760, his professional reputation was well-established and he was nearing the summit of his career. In 1758, an unsuccessful petition was made to the dilatory Duke of Newcastle, First Lord of the Treasury and dispenser of Royal patronages, to appoint Brown to the post of Royal Gardener. In the following March a reminder was sent, signed by 14 peers and one commoner; this also failed.[21] Brown's appointment was delayed until 1764, early in the reign of George III. He had worked for many of the signatories of the petition, among them George William, the 6th Earl of Coventry for whom Brown designed the house and laid out the grounds at Croome Court in 1751; this, his first combined treatment of a property, helped to establish his reputation in this dual role.

Another noble client who had signed the petition was the Earl of Exeter, owner of Burghley, the great Elizabethan–Renaissance mansion where Brown worked for 27 years, beginning in 1756. Here Brown was careful to design buildings to harmonise with the architectural style of the mansion. Lord Dacre commented upon this in a letter to Sanderson Miller in 1756: 'He [Brown] tells me that he has the alterations of Burleigh, and that not only of the park but of the house which whatever it is Gothick he intends to preserve it in that stile: and whatever new ornaments he adds are to be so.'[22] Brown's bath house or banqueting-house, near the lake at Burghley, has strap-work finials decorating the roof, copied from an Elizabethan banqueting house at Chipping Camden, Gloucestershire.[23] In choosing this style for a summer-house, Brown was careful to distinguish at Burghley between the Elizabethan–Renaissance style appropriate to the architecture of the house, and the Rococo–Gothic style then in vogue, thus demonstrating his archaeological attitude towards the various styles that he encountered when remodelling country houses before he came to Corsham.

Who introduced Brown to Corsham is not known. Paul Methuen's neighbour, John, Earl of Shelburne, had asked Brown's advice about planning the park at Bowood around 1758, but the actual work was not begun until April 1761,

---

[20] William Mason was the author of the 'Heroic Epistle to Sir William Chambers,' 1772, concerning the work of Brown and Chambers at Richmond and Kew Gardens; he was also the author of *The English Garden, A Poem* (London, 1772).

[21] Stroud, *Capability Brown* (new ed. 1975), p. 121.

[22] Stroud, *Capability Brown* (new ed. 1975), p. 77.

[23] For an illustration of the garden house at Burghley, see Stroud, *Capability Brown* (new ed. 1975), plate 14a.

after the Earl's death. Brown's first commission in Wiltshire was at Longleat House for the first Marquess of Bath, according to an agreement of 10 October 1757 (Longleat archives, 281–282). The Methuen family may also have been aware of Brown's work through their acquaintances. Brown visited the Duke of Bridgwater at Ashridge, Hertfordshire, several times in 1759, supplying sets of plans in 1760; the late Sir Paul Methuen had been a trustee of the Bridgwater estate and stayed at Ashridge in 1742. The Duke of Buccleuch of Adderbury House, Oxfordshire, had his park remodelled by Brown. Thus the Methuens must have been attracted by the improvements Lancelot Brown was making to the properties of their friends and neighbours.

Only one of Lancelot Brown's drawings and plans for Corsham has survived, a large map of the house and grounds marked, '. . . at Corsham Wilts, The Seat of Paul Methuen Esqr., by L.B 1761.'[24] This map has been damaged by water and folding; certain areas along the folds are now lost (see **40**). There is also a list of 'Mr. Brown's plans,' probably in Paul Methuen's handwriting (see Appendix C), but the drawings mentioned have not survived. However, the estate records showing the expenditure have been preserved at Corsham. They were kept at this time by the steward, Richard Boucher, who wrote in a neat and legible hand. Many of the supporting accounts and their receipts have also survived. Although the Corsham archives do not include the drawings, the costs of Brown's alterations are well documented. Five letters have survived between Brown and Paul Methuen, most of which refer to payments or acknowledge amounts received on account for work done. Other letters survive between Brown and the stuccoture, Thomas Stocking of Bristol.

When Lancelot Brown was consulted to remodel the house at Corsham in 1760 he had Keene's designs as a basis upon which to begin. Brown's problem, like Keene's, was to integrate the proposed picture gallery with the Elizabethan ground plan, and preserve the character of the Elizabethan south front. Lord Dacre's letter to Sanderson Miller in 1756 confirms Brown's sympathetic attitude towards the Elizabethan style at Burghley House. But even more than his reputation for dependable building, it was Brown's ability to remodel the grounds that formed the principal attraction for engaging him.

Brown accepted the alterations which Keene had proposed in his third plan for the new library in the west wing (see **30**), but rejected Keene's design for attaching the picture gallery to the Elizabethan east front. Keene had failed to resolve two weaknesses in his designs: the problem was firstly to provide a

---

[24] The first part of the title has been lost.

maximum amount of wall-space in the picture gallery to house the collection; and secondly to fill the whole extent of the Elizabethan east front with the gallery. Keene failed to use the entire length of the east wall, because it meant lighting the principal staircase from the north windows only, and making it much darker. Brown decided to expand his gallery beyond the north front, ignoring the staircase lighting. These ideas were sketched in pencil on Keene's third plan, possibly by Brown or Paul Methuen (see **30**), indicating that Keene's plans had been discussed. Brown's solution was an improvement over Keene's since it emphasised the principal object of providing an adequate gallery, whereas Keene had been more interested in the external appearance of his extensions and the hall lighting.

Using the third plan submitted by Keene (see **30** and **41**) Brown made the following alterations to the extension of the east wing. He created a cabinet-room 28 ft × 24 ft at the south end of his extension in place of the small room Keene proposed, of which the new south-east bay-window formed a part. The picture gallery which adjoins the cabinet room on its north side (see **42**) is a triple cube 72 ft × 24 ft covered by a high coved ceiling. A door in the centre of the north wall of the cabinet room links it with the gallery, which also opens on to the octagon room (see **41**). The gallery is lighted by five windows on the east side overlooking the park. Brown's aim in landscaping the park was to obtain the principal view from the gallery-windows, thus creating a harmonious relationship between the gallery and landscape. In enlarging the gallery, Brown had to extend it 27 ft beyond the existing north front erected by Ireson in 1749, thus blocking the east windows of the main staircase so dear to Keene (see **28** and **31**).

The large picture collection made it necessary to design a gallery on a greater scale than the surrounding state rooms. The windows are on the east wall, which is the dark side of the gallery; between them pier-glasses and console tables help to lighten the wall.[25] The pictures occupy the other three walls. Considerable attention must have been devoted at this time to their placement, to obtain at once maximum coverage and a symmetrical arrangement. Since it was customary to arrange them over the entire wall-surface, as one might arrange postage-stamps in an album, the shape of the picture was as important as its subject matter. Keene could not have paid enough attention to this aspect of the planning; he broke up the wall-space in his gallery with three doorways and two chimney-pieces, compared with two doorways and one chimney-piece in Brown's plan. Many of the paintings had been recently cleaned and re-framed in the most

---

[25] Designs for the pier glasses were supplied by Robert Adam. There is an entry in Paul Methuen's day book, '20th Feb., 1770, pd Mr. Adam for designs at the Great Room, Corsham, 19 guineas.'

ornate gilt frames of the period to match the new decorations and furnishings.[26] The rich gilding of the frames, hanging before a background of crimson silk damask, gives the whole the air of a sumptuous Italian palace.

Four large paintings from Sir Paul's collection occupy the principal positions in the picture gallery. The largest is Van Dyck's equestrian portrait of Charles I accompanied by M. St Antoine, considered to be the Whitehall Palace version listed in the catalogue of Charles I's pictures sold after his execution; it was placed in the centre of the north wall (see **42**).[27] Over the mantle-piece is a version of the Wolf Hunt by Rubens. In the centre of the walls on either side of the Rubens are two slightly larger canvases, a Betrayal of Christ by Van Dyck on the north side, and the Baptism of Christ by Guido Reni on the south. Around these four large paintings smaller ones are arranged symmetrically, including pendants by Salvator Rosa, Bernardo Strozzi, and Luca Giordano. The four principal paintings have occupied the same positions in the gallery since the late 1760s.

Because of the size of Sir Paul Methuen's collection the other state rooms were also used to display his pictures. The cabinet-room at the southern end of the picture gallery has a slightly higher ceiling than the Elizabethan rooms in order to raise it to the height of the gallery cornice. Two windows adjoin those of the gallery that overlook the park; between them is placed another mirror designed for the room by Robert Adam. In accepting Keene's general design for the state dressing-room, Brown substituted a regular octagonal form for the four alcoves of Keene (see **30** and **41**). The octagonal form was probably chosen because its walls would be more suitable for hanging pictures than the alcoves. The design of the state bedchamber remained the same as Keene's third plan, except that the door on the north side of the fireplace was no longer required.

Brown's treatment of the south front followed Keene's principle of doubling the bay-windows of the projecting wings. However, he left the Elizabethan front intact, without adding any further classical decoration as Henry Keene proposed (see **1**). Brown's sensitive handling of the original Elizabethan style in his addition to the south front was an unusual example of remodelling for this period. While there is no evidence that Brown made a theoretical distinction between the Elizabethan and Gothic styles, his handling of the bay-windows suggests that he

---

[26] The Adam Brothers designed the frame for Rubens' Wolf Hunt over the chimney-piece.

[27] The measurements (canvas size) of the four paintings are: Charles I on Horseback $135\frac{1}{2} \times 99$ in.; The Betrayal of Christ $107\frac{3}{4} \times 87\frac{1}{4}$ in.; The Baptism of Christ $107\frac{3}{4} \times 87\frac{1}{4}$ in.; A Wolf Hunt $79 \times 109\frac{3}{4}$ in.

was aware of it. In doubling the windows he also preserved the symmetry of the Elizabethan ground plan. The only irregularity that he created was the projection of his picture gallery beyond the east side of Ireson's north front. This posed a major problem for later architects who were called in to add a new extension to the north front.

Brown's extension was erected by the estate craftsmen under the direction of the steward, Richard Boucher. Only in the final stages of the decoration were specialised craftsmen brought from London and elsewhere. This seems to have been the normal practice at the period, when a force of labourers and craftsmen was kept on landed estates to keep up the mansion, its out-buildings, and tenanted property. Boucher's accounts disclose the same craftsmen working elsewhere on the estate as well as on the new extensions. Much of the timber was supplied from the estate,[28] and the stone was quarried locally. The additions were well built and have stood the test of time, compared with Nash's extension in 1797 built by the contract method.

THE WEST WING

Work began on the first part of Brown's architectural alterations on the west wing of the house. A new kitchen-block was built west of the 'chapel' to provide space for the housekeeper's room and the butler's pantry in the former kitchen. To enlarge the former kitchen-area Brown had to demolish the west wall of the kitchen and set it forward approximately six feet, the width of the new muniment-room to be erected in the corner between the west wall of the library and the south wall of the new extension (see **2** and **30**).

The interior of the original Elizabethan west wing was remodelled by re-arranging the staircase (see **27**). The staircase next to the common parlour was to be moved to the small room next to the dining-parlour, thus permitting access to the new library, and enlarging the common parlour in the west wing somewhat. The new staircase also gave access to a landing on the first floor and new bedroom-space above the new extension of the old kitchen. The old kitchen must have been one storey high, possibly with a pitched roof abutting the exterior Elizabethan west wall.[29]

---

[28] An entry in Paul Methuen's Day Book, 24 July 1760, records a payment to Robert Hulbert (the carpenter) for cutting down 207 oaks at Wraxall, Biddestone, and Warley, £11-1-0d.

[29] Entries in the accounts indicate that new bedrooms were erected over the new rooms provided for the butler and housekeeper.

Work on the new west-wing extension began in late 1759 or early 1760. The outside walls of the extension that was to house the new library were re-faced with Bath stone to match the Elizabethan wings, and a new bay-window added, matching the one already there, during 1760–61. The west wall was also re-faced; the windows at the library level were blocked up and two quatrefoil windows inserted; finally, the entablature was continued around the west side at both levels (see **43**). The Venetian-style window on the first floor may also have been inserted at this time, for Brown used a similar motif on the false wall at the north end of the picture gallery (see **24**).[30]

Methuen had a muniment-room built into the corner of the library wall and the butler's pantry. The room has a curved hip roof which was probably added at this time. The stone-facing of the library wall also continues around the exterior of the room. Incorporated into the substructure of the muniment-room is a Gothic vault with ribbed vaulting having a centre boss and liernes.[31] The vault supports the floor of the room above it. Thought to have come from another building whose name has now been forgotten, its incorporation into the building is a further indication of Paul Methuen's interest in the Gothic style.[32] The stone-facing of the adjoining new extension is much plainer, and has string-courses connecting the window sills, a device Brown used on the east front (see **43**).

The most important addition in the remodelled extension was the new library to contain Sir Paul Methuen's books. In an unidentified design the library is decorated with bookcases and a chimney-piece in the Rococo–Gothic style (see **44**); bookcases, laid out as shown in this design, have been neatly outlined in pencil on Keene's third plan, the one subsequently used (see **30**). The design probably already existed before Lancelot Brown was called to take over the alterations, for it was not included in the list of 'Mr. Brown's plans' (see Appendix C). It may well have been the one Brown used. The draughtsmanship is very similar to that of an unidentified design by Keene for an octagonal Gothic

---

[30] The octagonal turret, now partially dismantled, was added by John Nash in 1797, to balance one used on the south corner of the east wing. The crenellation on the kitchen wing was also added by Nash.

[31] In January, 1762, a payment of 12/3d was made to Robert Hulbert (carpenter) for making a centring for the arch of the muniment room.

[32] Lord Paul Methuen (4th Baron) suggested that this vault may have been brought from an old house at Bradford-on-Avon. It may also have come from the demolished Elizabethan gatehouse; they were often vaulted. The lower archway under the muniment room has a doorway on the south side that gives access to the west wing; this is a recent addition.

pavilion or chapel (see **46**).[33] In both designs there are similar ogee arches with prominent finials, drawn with dots by the draughtsman. The plan and elevation of the library walls are more carefully drawn, but both have the same characteristics. An attribution to Keene seems reasonable.

The basic idea for the library may have come from Horace Walpole's library at Strawberry Hill, which Paul Methuen might have known at first hand (see **47**). In 1760, Walpole included Sir Paul Methuen's collection of paintings in his catalogue published by the Strawberry Hill Press. Paul Methuen may have seen the library at Strawberry Hill in 1759 or even earlier.

Strawberry Hill may also have inspired the theme for Paul Methuen's library ceiling at Corsham, which displays the Methuen family genealogy (see **48**). Walpole himself designed the ceiling decorated with the coats-of-arms of his ancestors.[34] John Ivory Talbot had Sanderson Miller design a similar ceiling in the hall at Lacock Abbey (1753–55), though strictly speaking it is not a family geneology, because some of the shields contain the coats-of-arms of Talbot's friends and neighbours. Tracing the family pedigree was in vogue among the new landed gentry, especially among the Whig members of this social class. Paul Methuen now had the opportunity of having his ancestors' coats-of-arms emblazoned on his own library ceiling. That Methuen chose to place the genealogy on the library ceiling as at Strawberry Hill, rather than on the hall ceiling as at Lacock, seems to indicate that he modelled it on the former.

Although the general arrangement of the library at Corsham, with its Gothic bookcases, quatrefoil windows, and family pedigree displayed on the ceiling, has its genesis in Horace Walpole's ideas at Strawberry Hill, stylistically a more decided influence came from a school of Rococo stuccotures in Bristol. The surviving design for the library bookcases and chimney-piece may lead us to presume that Keene knew of the Gothic library at Strawberry Hill. But Keene was quite capable of designing such a library, even without the example of Strawberry Hill.

The Gothic design of the library shows a considerable Rococo influence. The ceiling is essentially Rococo in style in spite of its coats-of-arms, and stylistically does not depend upon Strawberry Hill. The design consists of roundels of

---

[33] The unidentified design by Henry Keene is preserved in the Victoria and Albert Museum, drawing no. E901–1921.

[34] For references to the library at Strawberry Hill, see Paget Toynbee, *Strawberry Hill Accounts* (Oxford, 1927), pp. 75–77, and W. S. Lewis, 'The Genesis of Strawberry Hill,' *Metropolitan Museum Studies*, 5 (1934–36), 57–92.

different sizes, in which the coats-of-arms are painted, linked together by elaborate ribbon-work on a plain white ground (see **48**). The bookcases and the chimney-piece also show a Rococo influence, especially the scroll designs of the mirror on the mantle-piece, and the brackets on the north-wall elevation (see **44** and **45**). Unlike Walpole's bookcases which have shelves behind the Gothic ogee arches that open like doors, Paul Methuen's bookcases have the ogee decoration above the shelf-level, which is, incidently, a more convenient design (see **47**). A notice-able Strawberry Hill influence was the pair of quatrefoil windows formerly on the outside of the west wall of the library at Corsham, but now sealed up. A pair of similar windows is found above the bookcases on either side of the large window at Strawberry Hill (see **43** and **47**).

The stucco work was carried out by Thomas Stocking of Bristol, who was responsible for all the ceilings of Brown's alterations at Corsham. Only the ceiling and the Gothic cornice of the library have survived.[35] The arcaded cornice is made up of a mixture of classical and Gothic elements. Exquisitely modelled heads act as corbels to support the tiny Gothic arches of the cornice, in the centres of which are acanthus leaves (see **49**). Stocking's cornice is quite unique in the Bristol area.[36] The over-mantel of the library chimney-piece, shown in the drawing on **45,** is similar to the chimney-piece still in the dining-room of the Royal Fort House, Bristol, erected in 1760, where Stocking is known to have worked. The Fort House overmantel is carved in wood and painted, having a mixture of Gothic and Rococo scrollwork and stalactite designs as in the Corsham design.[37] Thomas Stocking was one of a group of stuccotures working in Bristol in the second half of the 18th century who used a distinct Rococo style characterised by the use of garlands, ribbon work, leafy-scroll work and flower motifs. Their work represents a late provincial florescence of the Rococo style at a time before

---

[35] The bookcases and the fireplace overmantel Stocking carved were removed by Nash when the library was converted into a breakfast room in 1797.

[36] Stocking executed a less elaborate cornice in the Bath House, Arno's Court, Brislington for William Reeve, with acanthus leaves and a series of medallic heads modelled after Reeve and his daughter. Stanley Hutton, *Guide to Arno's Castle, Brislington, Bristol* (Bristol, no date), p. 9. What remained of the Bath House facade as a result of air-raid damage between 1939 and 1944 has been re-erected by Sir Clough Williams-Ellis at Portmeirion, N. Wales. Lord Paul Ayshford Methuen, *Corsham Court*, 2nd rev. ed. (Bristol: Holloway & Son, 1971), p. 24, n. 3.

[37] For illustrations of the dining room see, H. Avary Tipping, *English Homes, Early Georgian Period 1714–1760* (London: Country Life, 1921), plates 400–402.

the more restrained classical influence of the Adam School became widespread in the 1770s.[38]

Considerable attention was given to the chimney-pieces at Corsham, one of the principal ornaments of the 18th-century room. They were often panelled with expensive rare marbles imported from Italy and elsewhere; different marbles of brilliant colours were often combined in one chimney-piece. Writing on the use of marbles for chimney-pieces, Isaac Ware recommends the following for the guidance of workmen: 'instead of bestowing the richest coloured marbles upon these chimney-pieces where he intends the greatest expense of ornament, he will reserve these painted kinds for such as he intends should be wrought with less assistance of the chisel; and he will adopt for these high sculpture pieces always a plain marble of one uninterrupted colour.'[39] The more sculptural chimney-pieces installed in the state rooms at Corsham are of plain white marble, whereas coloured marbles were used to ornament the chimney-pieces in the library and other rooms.

Prince Hoare of Bath supplied the coloured marble chimney-piece for the Gothic library (see **48**). Designed by Brown, it was quite an expensive item, costing 72 guineas according to Hoare's account (Corsham document 5046). Hoare also supplied chimney-pieces for the enlarged common parlour next to the library, the dressing-room in the west wing, and the bedchamber, and dismantled and re-polished other chimney-pieces then in the house.[40]

Work continued on the library until August 1763, when the last payments were entered in Boucher's accounts.[41] Brown's library, which was probably based on Keene's design, represented a combination of Gothic and Rococo decorative motifs. The provincial Rococo influence apparent at Corsham was current in Bristol, then the second city of England in size and importance.

---

[38] Other works attributed to Stocking in the Bristol area are the nave ceiling of St Nicholas Church, Bristol (now destroyed), the Bath House, Arno's Castle, Brislington (recently removed), and possibly Ston Easton Park, Somerset, where Stocking may have worked with the three Paty Brothers, who were also responsible for the stucco work at the Royal Fort House and Kings Weston House.

[39] This quotation is taken from Isaac Ware, 'Of the appropriation of the materials to chimney-pieces,' *A Complete Body of Architecture* (London, 1768), VI, iv, p. 558.

[40] A sketch for this chimney-piece was made on the reverse side of Hoare's account £116-12-0d paid on 8 November 1763 (Corsham document 5046). When Nash converted the common parlour into his new library the chimney-piece was moved to a new position. His specification includes an item for 'cleaning and repairing old chimney piece and slab and refixed, five guineas' (Corsham document 6011). This chimney-piece contains a beautiful panel of Siena marble, and was transferred to the breakfast room in 1964 (see **68**).

[41] The entry reads 'Aug 27, To ditto [To Cash] pd Robt. Hulbert for acco[un]t of ye Floors £53-12-0d.'

THE EAST FRONT

Lancelot Brown had two existing fronts to consider when integrating his design for the east front of his new extension: the Elizabethan south front and the Palladian north. He chose the Palladian style. On the southern end of his new wing Brown added an Elizabethan bay-window and gabled roof to correspond with the adjoining Elizabethan wing. This new bay-window also balanced the one added to the west wing that contained the new library. He thus preserved the symmetry and character of the Elizabethan south front, and emphasised the Palladian principle of symmetrical ground-planning. On the north front, Brown had to integrate his design with the relatively plain Palladian front erected by Ireson in 1749.

The genesis of Brown's design for the east front in the Palladian style was influenced primarily by William Kent. He also drew upon Colen Campbell's *Vitruvius Britannicus* for illustrations of country-house designs, and upon his own wide knowledge of English architecture gathered while travelling around the countryside in the course of his work. Most of the architectural elements Brown used occur at Croome Court, which he erected for George William, 6th Earl of Coventry, in 1751. His first major architectural commission, Croome Court shows the stylistic influence of Holkam Hall, Norfolk, erected by William Kent for the Earl of Leicester (1734 ff.); Holkam Hall in turn was influenced by Campbell's Houghton facade erected for Sir Robert Walpole (1722 ff.).

Brown's extension to the east wing was designed principally to house a cabinet-room and picture gallery on the ground floor, with a basement below and a mezzanine floor above. The mezzanine floor provided for the high coved ceiling of the picture gallery, over which is a suite of rooms. Another room over the cabinet-room, nearly as high as the adjoining room in the Elizabethan wing, led on to the first-floor corridor of the Elizabethan wing. The mezzanine floor over the gallery was reached from the attic level. Architectural drawings of the east front have not survived; two surviving illustrations of the front, and comparison with other examples of Brown's architecture help us to reconstruct its design.[42] An analysis of these illustrations, and the surviving documentary

---

[42] The first illustration is an aquatint by an unknown artist (7 × 4¼ in.), published 1 October 1792, by A. Robertson and R. Faulder (50). It is a distant view of the house which cannot be relied upon for accuracy. The second illustration was published by Humphry Repton in his *Observations on the Theory and Practice of Landscape Gardening*, opposite p. 188. 'Corsham House—East Front added by Brown.' Repton's illustration does not show the quoins or the entablature between the gallery and attic level windows to be seen in 50. The quoins on Brown's North extension are clearly visible in 24. They also harmonise with the quoins edging the centre section of Ireson's pre-existing North front, see 26.

evidence, help us to reconstruct the North and East fronts that were completely refaced by John Nash in 1797.

Brown's Palladian design for the north and east fronts of Corsham reveal a limited architectural vocabulary, largely worked out in his first major commission at Croome Court in 1751. His careful handling of the motifs at Corsham produced a well-designed front but one which does not show much originality. String-courses divide the front horizontally between the basement and ground floor, and the ground-floor window sills; an entablature between the ground-floor windows and the mezzanine level divides the facade again. A cornice and balustrade mark the roof-line. The only new element in the design is the use of a string-course at sill level which appears here for the first time in his work.[43] Kent used this motif at Holkham Hall, on the north and south fronts.[44] The entablature that separates the gallery and mezzanine-level of windows was probably inserted to decorate the wide gap between the gallery and mezzanine-levels created by the high ceiling of the picture gallery.[45] The entablature would have also linked with that on the same level of the south front.

Brown divided the front vertically into three bays with quoins, creating an effect of angle towers at each end of the front. This motif is taken from Croome Court where he used it at the four corners of the building. One of the most characteristic features of English Palladian country-house design, angle towers were introduced by Inigo Jones and Isaac de Caus for the south front of Wilton House (*c.* 1648), where they are similarly edged with quoins.[46] Colen Campbell

---

[43] The string-courses used by Brown at sill level for the windows in the domestic premises of the west wing still survive (see **43**). Brown used them later at Broadlands, Hampshire, in 1767, when he remodelled an Elizabethan house for the 2nd Viscount Palmerston. For an illustration see, H. Avary Tipping, *English Homes, Late Georgian Period* 1760–1820 (London: Country Life, 1921), plate 382.

[44] This motif is found in Palladio's architecture at the Villa Cerato, *c.* 1540; the Villa Pisani, Montagnano, 1553; the Villa Pojana, 1545–50, and the Villa Caldagno, *c.* 1560–65.

[45] In 1797 Nash replaced the entablature with the Gothic moulding that we see today. A cornice was used in a similar position by Kent at Wakefield Lodge, Northants, completed in 1751 after his death. For an illustration see, Margaret Jourdain, *The Work of William Kent* (London: Country Life, 1948), fig. 38.

[46] The corner or angle towers are derived from the Villa Trissino at Cricoli, near Vicenza, erected between 1530 and 1538. The design of the villa has been attributed to Palladio's patron, Count Trissino. Palladio used angle towers for the Villa Thiene, Cicogna, built during the 1550s, now destroyed and illustrated in the *Quattro Libri*, II, plate xlv.

used them at Houghton, and so did Kent for the central block at Holkham Hall, although he did not edge them with quoins as Brown did later at Croome and Corsham. Brown's partition of the east front with quoins creates a vertical emphasis to counter-balance the horizontal string-courses and entablatures.

The architectural details for the windows, mouldings, cornices and balustrades that Brown used at Corsham occur in his other buildings. Of the seven windows on the ground floor the end windows and the middle window of the centre bay had curved pediments, while the others had triangular pediments. Their form must have closely followed those used at Croome Court, and later at Broadlands. The mouldings of the mezzanine windows, poorly indicated in the illustration, probably followed those used at Croome Court. In his estimate for later alterations Nash mentions that the front was crowned with a cornice surmounted by a balustrade much like those used at Croome Court (1751), Broadlands (1767), and Claremont (1769).[47] An unidentified account (Corsham document 5048) refers to the 'provision of four large stone carved ornaments' for the parapet balustrade. Such ornaments were used to silhouette the skyline of the balustrade and provide a classical emphasis to the front (see **24**).

Brown carefully integrated the north and west ends of his extension with Ireson's facade of 1749. Brown's north-front extension is illustrated in an engraving made by Thomas Hearne (see **24**).[48] It projected approximately 27 ft beyond Ireson's front. It was to partially conceal this effect that Brown edged the north front with quoins to create the appearance of an angle-tower similar to those on the east front. The north end of the extension has a Venetian-window motif on the ground floor, a pedimented window on the first floor corresponding in size to those of Ireson, and an eared window at the attic-level. The two lower windows are blank to mask the north end of the picture gallery; a pair of stone vases were set in the Venetian window.[49] Brown used the Venetian-window motif on his south front angle-towers at Croome Court, and it was used by Kent at Holkham Hall in the angle-towers of the north and south fronts.[50] The cornice

---

[47] Nash's instructions were '. . . take down the present parapet wall and cornice, cut away all roman moulding' (Corsham document 6011).

[48] The printer's proof states that the view was engraved by Thomas Hearne from a sketch by the Reverend Mr Gooch. It was subsequently published by W. Watts, 1 May 1784, Kemp's Row, Chelsea. The measurements are $7\frac{1}{4} \times 5$ in.

[49] These items are charged on the mason's account at three pounds each (Corsham document 5048).

[50] Colen Campbell used the Venetian window motif at Houghton. This motif was used by Palladio in his Villa Pojana, Maggiore, c. 1545–50.

and parapet wall surmounted by stone vases joined Ireson's north front at the parapet-level. At Croome the Venetian windows are supported by Ionic columns, which Brown may also have used at Corsham.

The architectural details that Brown used for his north and east fronts reveal him as an architect thoroughly conversant with the Palladian style. Brown's approach was essentially conservative; he handled his design sensitively, always conscious of its relation to Ireson's north front. The east front at Corsham is a modification of the wall-treatment in his earlier work at Croome Court (1751), with the exception of the window-sill string-course and the entablature between the ground and mezzanine floor. Brown took his details from the work of Kent, particularly from Holkham Hall, whose architecture Brown must have studied when he began to lay out the grounds in 1759. The surviving front perhaps nearest to Brown's east front at Corsham is at Broadlands, Hampshire, which Brown erected in 1767. Humphry Repton testified to the quality and dependability of his architectural work: '. . . if he was superior to all in what related to his own peculiar profession, he was inferior to none in what related to comfort, convenience, taste and propriety of design, in the several mansions and other buildings which he planned.'[51]

THE DECORATIONS OF THE STATE ROOMS

Brown was responsible for the decoration of the state rooms; according to 'Mr. Brown's list' he supplied 11 designs (see Appendix C). The names given to the rooms on 'Mr. Brown's list' are not those in current use: the octagon room (ante-room), the state bedroom (alcove or state bedchamber), the cabinet-room (dressing or vestibule room), and the picture gallery, sometimes described elsewhere as the Great Room (see **41**).

Although the evidence is slight, it appears that the Elizabethan hall may have been remodelled at this time (see Appendix D). In a memorandum made by Paul Methuen of 'Stocking's estimates delivered,' he noted that the cornice of the cabinet-room and state bedroom was the same as that of the hall (see **21** and **51**). Also, certain items on the unidentified mason's account indicate that other changes were being made to the hall.[52]

---

[51] J. C. Loudon, ed., *Landscape Gardening and Landscape Architecture of the Late Humphry Repton, Esq.* (London: Longman and Co., 1840), p. 266.

[52] This account must be contemporary with Brown's alterations, because it refers to the stone vases supplied for the east wing of the house. Items possibly connected with the hall include, 44 feet of straight architrave on the screen, 93 feet of architrave in the panels, 65 yards (?) of plain stucco on the walls, and the ceiling to the design at thirty pounds (Corsham document 5048).

These items suggest that the Elizabethan hall may have been redecorated in the classical style to harmonise with the decorations of the new suite of rooms in the east wing that led off the hall at ground-floor level. The only surviving illustration of the Elizabethan hall is a part of the staircase-screen drawn by John Adey Repton (see **21**). A comparison shows that the cornices are indeed similar. We have no means of telling whether Brown copied the original Elizabethan cornice for the state rooms, or if Repton was unaware that he was drawing the cornice added by Brown to the Elizabethan screen.

Identical decoration on the doors and walls of the state rooms give a sense of unity to the suite. Each room has a skirting with an elaborate moulding, a plain dado, and a matching dado (chair) rail (see **52**). Crimson silk damask covers the wall-surface above the rail and the plaster cornice consists of an egg-and-dart ovolo moulding, a carved modillion, and a bead and reel cyma.[53] The skirting, dado and cornice of the picture gallery are more elaborately carved.

The design of the doorways is also the same throughout the suite, except in the picture gallery where it is more decorative. The doors were made by John Hobcraft of mahogany with elaborate paterae and fluted mouldings.[54] The white-painted doorcases match the dado. The heavy enrichments of the earlier Palladian designs associated with Kent have given way to a lighter form of entablature for the doorcase. It has a straight Ionic cornice and a concave frieze decorated with wheat-ear garlands, an Adamesque motif.

Although Brown provided designs for the ceilings, the personal style of handling the Rococo motifs is that of Thomas Stocking, the Bristol plasterer responsible for all of Brown's ceilings at Corsham. The ceiling of the octagon room has a circular centre panel with octagonal panels surrounding it. These are filled with lively Rococo scrollwork of the kind filling the cove of the picture

---

[53] The walls of the state rooms are still hung with the original crimson silk damask. In 1769 Morris and Young supplied 700 yards at 13/6d per yard. The walls were originally lined with crimson flock paper which is still in place, either to show the final effect or pending the purchase of the silk. The paper was supplied by Bromwich and Leigh, the Golden Lyon, Ludgate Hill. This firm supplied papier maché work for the Guildhall, London, for the Coronation Banquet of George III, 1761. They supplied paper to Horace Walpole; and Mrs Lybbe Powys also mentions their paper in her visit to Fawley Court.

[54] John Hobcraft carried out the joinery at Croome Court where some of the rooms were decorated by Robert Adam. This may explain the Adamesque decoration of the doors and door cases at Corsham. Hobcraft was also a subscriber to Adam's *Spalatro*, 1764. Lancelot Brown employed Hobcraft later at Broadlands (1767), and Claremont (1771).

gallery.[55] Around the outside of the state bedchamber ceiling is a raised reeded border wrapped with acanthus leaves. In the corners are quarter circles filled with a palm-leaf design. In the middle of the ceiling, set in a plain ground, is a large circular medallion edged with a fluted design and a centre rosette (see **51**). The restrained design of the state bedroom is in contrast to the gay Rococo decoration of the octagon.

The ceiling of the cabinet-room is second only to the picture gallery in the richness of its effect (see **53**). It has raised segmented panels edged with a double guilloche design. A chandelier hangs from a large rosette in the centre circular panel. Two diagonals divide the ceiling into four: in the centre of each segment, surrounded by an elaborate palm-leaf scroll design is a female head with a classical profile. Each one has a different hair-style, and a portion of her garment shows at the base of the neck. The use of an octagonal centre panel edged with a guilloche design seems to be a Kentian influence, as in the hall ceiling of Raynham Hall, Norfolk.[56] The design of the cabinet-room ceiling mixes the more formal Palladian elements probably derived from Kent, like the sub-division of the ceiling, with Stocking's Rococo elements such as the palm-leaf scroll and classical heads, also found at the Royal Fort House, Bristol.[57]

Of all the rooms in the suite the picture-gallery ceiling has the most imposing decoration. Dorothy Stroud found a design similar to the ceiling at Burton Constable, Yorkshire, in 1939 (see **90**).[58] Brown had offered the design for the hall to Mr Constable of Burton Constable in 1758, who found it unsatisfactory and accepted instead one submitted by Thomas Lightoler. Brown may have retained a copy of this design and re-submitted it to Paul Methuen for the picture gallery at Corsham.[59]

There are minor variations between the Burton Constable design and the work executed by Stocking. The cornice frieze for example is more richly decorated. The scroll-like motifs forming the coved area, which occur in Stocking's

---

[55] Similar scrollwork can be seen in Stocking's work on the hall ceiling of the Royal Fort House, Bristol. For an illustration see, Avary Tipping, *English Homes, Early Georgian*, plate 398.

[56] For an illustration see, Jourdain, *William Kent*, Figure 65.

[57] A similar treatment of the female heads in profile, but partially veiled, can be found on a stucco keystone facing the main staircase of the Royal Fort House.

[58] Dorothy Stroud, 'The Architectural Works of Lancelot Brown,' *Country Life* (6 Jan. 1940), 14–18.

[59] Brown later used a similar design in the gallery at Claremont (1771–74); the design of the coved area is the same as Corsham, but the ceiling design shows the influence of Adam. Brown also used coffered ceilings at Croome Court.

work at the Royal Fort House, Bristol, add a certain lightness to the deep coffering above them. The latter shows the influence of Kent, especially when compared with the large octagonal panels he used for the hall ceiling at Raynham Hall, Norfolk (*c.* 1730). The precast ceiling rosettes resemble the centre rosettes used in the other state rooms at Corsham Court. Four medallions, each containing two putti, decorate the centre of each side of the coved area. Their iconographical meaning has not been solved. In the corners are elaborate baskets of fruit and flowers; each one is different. Both the medallions with the putti and the baskets of fruit are hand-modelled.[60] The coffered ceiling adds a touch of splendour to the gallery, necessary in a lofty room where the finer decoration of the Adams would tend to become lost in the half-shadows.

Brown's ceiling designs at Corsham show the waning influence of the heavier Palladian decoration of William Kent's work. While Brown's exterior architectural treatment at Corsham is strictly Palladian, his interior decoration reflects changes in contemporary taste towards the lighter, more elegant Rococo forms. The ceilings at Corsham represent an intermediate stage when the strict Palladian designs mingled with Gothic and Rococo forms, and had not been subject to the purifying influence of the Adamesque style.

Brown devoted the same careful attention to the selection of the chimney-pieces for the state rooms as the library and the west wing. The all-white marble chimney-pieces ordered for the state rooms follow the advice given by Isaac Ware: 'instead of bestowing the richest coloured marbles upon these chimney pieces where he intends the greatest expense of ornament . . . he will adopt for these high sculptured pieces always a plain marble of one uninterrupted colour.'[61] The white marble blends with the decoration of the state rooms, where coloured marbles would distract the eye. The white marble contrasts with the crimson silk damask and matches the white-painted dado. The most expensive item, the sculptured chimney-piece installed in the picture gallery, serves as the focal point of the room (see **54**). It was supplied by Peter Scheemakers for £325, according to the terms of an agreement with Paul Methuen dated 22 April 1763 (see Appendix E), after Methuen had approved a model of the proposed chimney-piece. It has a garland design in the frieze below the mantel-shelf, which is supported by a caryatid at each corner. Their outside arms are raised to hold tasselled cushions on their heads that support the cornice, while each figure's other arm holds the

---

[60] Similar baskets of fruit and flowers are met with in Stocking's work at the Royal Fort House, Bristol, and at Ston Easton Park, Somerset.

[61] Isaac Ware, *A Complete Body of Architecture*, p. 558.

hem of her himation. They both stand in a graceful *contrapposto* pose, turning slightly at an angle from the mantle-shelf.

The chimney-piece that Peter Scheemakers supplied for the cabinet room has a classical subject matter for its frieze which extends across the top of the chimney architrave.[62] It was probably chosen to match the classical heads of the ceiling-design modelled by Thomas Stocking. The mantle-shelf has an Ionic entablature, and is supported by a pair of consoles that also encase the frieze. The choice of a classical frieze for the chimney-piece may reflect Paul Methuen's interest in the antique at this time: his name appears on the list of subscribers to Robert Adam's *Ruins of the Palace of Diocletian* (London, 1764), (see **55**).

The last important chimney-piece, the white marble one in the state bed-chamber, which has a garland design on its frieze, was supplied by William Atkinson of Bath in June 1765. Atkinson lists a charge on the account for sending his men over from Newton Park, Bath, to install the chimney-piece at Corsham (Corsham document 5053).[63] Peter Scheemaker's workshop provided chimney-pieces requiring relief carving; the provincial examples were relatively plain, except for the occasional coloured-marble inlays.

While Brown conceived the decorative scheme of the state rooms mainly in terms of Kent's style, more contemporary influences permeated his designs. With crimson silk damask, richly gilded frames, the sculptured chimney-piece, and white stucco decoration he created a setting for Sir Paul Methuen's collection of an Italianate splendour. The arrangement of the pictures is as important to the effect as the decorations themselves. The unity of design achieved throughout the suite of rooms justifies Repton's assessment of Brown's architectural and decorative abilities, especially when we remember that for Brown the profession was secondary to his landscape activities.[64]

The construction of Brown's east wing at Corsham can be followed in considerable detail, because of carefully documented accounts kept by the steward, Richard Boucher, which provide a unique chronology of the building-operations. While Corsham's location between Bristol and London made it comparatively easy for skilled craftsmen and sub-contractors to come from either

---

[62] The subject has been taken from James Stuart's engraving of the Choragic Monument of Lysicrates in Athens. Pevsner, *Buildings of England—Wiltshire*, p. 173.

[63] Newton Park was the home of Mrs Paul Methuen's mother, Lady Anne Cobb, where Repton later remodelled the grounds. The cost of this chimney-piece was eighty guineas, plus a fitting charge.

[64] J. C. Loudon, ed., *Landscape Gardening of Humphry Repton*, p. 266.

city, most of the labouring work was carried out by the state employees, whose names appear in the accounts. It was they who carried out the routine work. Over 78 names of craftsmen, suppliers, tradesmen, and even labourers appear in the accounts, as well as an unspecified number of joiners, quarrymen, labourers, and haulage-contractors. The most important craftsmen involved in the work on the new wings were James Rawlings, the stonemason, and Robert Hulbert, the carpenter. As far as one can tell from the records, the work was supervised by the steward, Boucher. Brown made regular visits to Corsham, sometimes for three or four days, to inspect the sub-contractors' work.[65] Although he did not employ a resident clerk of works to supervise the house-contruction, Brown employed a Mr Smith to supervise laying out the park at Corsham.[66] The new extensions at Corsham seem to have been erected at a leisurely pace, the family being adequately housed in the rest of the mansion. Even such a comparatively modest extension was quite a complex undertaking, one which required that the labour-force and building supplies be well organised.

Work began on the extension of the east wing in January 1762, when weekly charges appear in the accounts for men working at the quarry and for hauling stone, timber and other building-materials to the site. The scaffolding was erected at this time. The work of excavating the foundations continued until May when the carpenters' and blacksmiths' charges appear. In August three sets of blocks and tackle were paid for: the outer walls had risen high enough to require lifting-materials. In September the mason, James Rawlings, was paid £100 for freestone to face the outer walls. John Lewis, the tiler, was employed between September and October upon the roofing operations. In November and December bricks arrived for the interior partition walls, chimneys and doorways. By the end of the year the outside walls, floor-joists, and the main roof were complete.

---

[65] Lady Caroline Dalkeith, writing to Mrs Paul Methuen on 16 September 1762, comments, 'I think you was lucky to keep Mr Brown four days, I thought that place in Wiltshire had been Lady Shelburne's for her life' (Corsham archives). Lady Dalkeith was referring to Bowood where Brown was also remodelling the grounds at this time. Lady Mary Fitzmaurice, Countess of Shelburne, was the widow of John, Earl of Shelburne, who employed Henry Keene at Bowood between 1755–1760, and who consulted Brown about the grounds in 1758, before his death in 1761.

[66] Brown's building contractor, Henry Holland the Elder, who was working nearby at Bowood in the 1760's under Robert Adam, may have kept an eye upon the operations at Corsham for Brown. At this time, Brown was laying out the grounds of Bowood. Later in 1767, Holland was employed by Brown as the contractor to remodel Broadlands, Hampshire.

During 1763, work began on plastering the interior walls and ceilings, laying floor-boards and internal joinery. During April lathes were ordered for plaster-work. In July and August quantities of oak-boarding and beams were ordered for the flooring of the cabinet-room and picture gallery. In October, new cellars under the east wing were excavated and paved. Also in October, James Ludgate, the carver, began work on the wood mouldings for the state rooms, where he was employed until September 1769. In December, joists were put over the new cellar. By the end of 1763 the fittings of the new extension were beginning to be installed.

In 1764 skilled craftsmen began to work upon the fittings for the state rooms. In May, John Hobcraft was employed to install the 'great sashes' of the cabinet-room and picture gallery, and to furnish the mahogany doors. In June, freightage of £3-18-6d was paid on deals (timber) and glass. The windows were probably glazed soon after the arrival of the glass, permitting Stocking to begin work on the picture-gallery ceiling in the autumn when he received two large payments on account of £190. Scheemaker's splendid chimney-piece for the picture gallery arrived from London in December in accordance with the agreement of 22 April 1763, and was installed by his workmen.

The work of decorating the state rooms continued through 1765 until the spring of 1767. In June 1765, William Atkinson had installed the marble chimney-piece in the state bedroom. On 30 March four labourers were paid for clearing 'ye gallery.' Apparently the rough work was substantially finished before the finer decoration was added. On 20 April, the joiners were at work, probably on the mezzanine level; they continued to work on and off in the east wing until April 1768. Meanwhile, the painters and carvers were employed to complete the final decorations. At last a gilder, at work in the state rooms from September 1766 until March 1767, finished enriching the mouldings, putting the final touches to the long work.

THE SEQUENCE OF STOCKING'S WORK IN THE STATE ROOMS

The ceilings at Corsham represent the most complete cycle of Thomas Stocking's work still surviving. The payments for his work are well documented and the surviving correspondence refers to some of the difficulties encountered during the course of the work. Although Brown was responsible for the designs of the ceilings, his plans have been lost, except for a design similar to the picture-gallery ceiling now at Burton Constable, and so it is difficult to judge to what extent Stocking was free to introduce his own innovations.

Thomas Stocking resumed working at Corsham in the early summer of 1763, this time in the east wing, having completed the stucco and carving in the library in the summer of 1762.[67] By 1763, the interior construction of the east wing had advanced sufficiently to permit Stocking to decorate the ceilings of the smaller state rooms. On 17 May 1763, Paul Methuen wrote to Brown, 'I hope to have the pleasure of seeing you at Corsham some time next month and imagine by that time there will be sufficient specimen of stuko work finished to judge of its effect' (Corsham archives). Unfortunately, Methuen did not give the location of the new stucco-work, but he may have been referring to test-pieces of moulding being placed in position on the gallery ceiling to judge their effect before the main work began.

Some of the surviving documents tell us about the work carried out in 1763. One is a memorandum in Paul Methuen's handwriting dated 11 November 1763, giving details of estimates for the ceilings that Stocking had sent; no date is given of their actual delivery (see Appendix D). During December 1763 Stocking was forced to delay his work, he wrote to Brown on 27 December that he had completed the cornices of the cabinet-room and the state bedchamber, but had not received the designs for the ceilings. He complained, 'I have been obliged to keep my ornament hands on mouldings for sum time past which is hurtful to me' (Corsham archives). Stocking was referring to the ornamental plasterers who received a higher rate of pay, because they modelled directly onto the ceiling, than the plasterer who made plaster-of-Paris castings into moulds that were stuck on to the ceiling when dry. Stocking also complained that the ceiling of the state bedchamber would be too dry to apply the ornamentation unless the designs were sent quickly.

Stocking had been working at Corsham since May 1763, and must have done more than decorate the octagon room, and fix the cornices in the cabinet-room and state bedchamber. Paul Methuen notes that the cornice of the cabinet-room and state bedchamber were the same as the hall; so Stocking may have been working in the hall during the early part of the summer.

When work began upon the picture-gallery ceiling is uncertain, but most likely it was decorated in the autumn of 1764, after the windows were glazed. Two payments made to Stocking amounting to £190-0-0d in the autumn of 1764 suggest that the ceiling may have been decorated at this time. Since much of the ceiling, such as the cornice, coffering, rosettes, and possibly the scrollwork, consisted of precast stucco ornament, it was less expensive than the smaller,

---

[67] Paul Methuen made an entry in his daybook on 7 June, 'Pd Mr. Stocking the stukoman in full for stuko work and carving done in the library £52-19-0,' making a total of 130 guineas.

hand-modelled ceilings that Stocking had done elsewhere. Only the four medallions and the corner baskets of fruit were modelled by the ornamental plasterers.[68]

Stocking's account includes an unspecified amount for work done on the greenhouse. The only reference to this building occurs in a letter from Brown to Paul Methuen on 16 March 1764. Stocking received an advance of £50 in April that may have been for the greenhouse. It has completely disappeared, leaving no indication of Stocking's work. This structure may have been executed in an ornamental style in keeping with his work elsewhere in the house.[69]

Although Stocking's correspondence indicates that he employed two kinds of plasterers, those who carried out a routine operation of making castings, and those who worked directly on to the ceiling, how many there were is not known. As he was entrusted with all the stucco-work at Corsham, he must have had an experienced workshop capable of carrying out a variety of stucco decorations on a large scale. Although his role was that of skilled craftsman and foreman rather than that of originator of the designs, his personal style is apparent in the handling of the Classical, Gothic and Rococo motifs.

BROWN'S OUTSIDE ARCHITECTURAL WORKS AT CORSHAM

Lancelot Brown was commissioned to design three structures in the park. The Bath House has survived in a slightly modified form. The greenhouse, or orangery, was subsequently demolished and its foundations removed. A projected pair of lodges were not erected.[70] The Bath House demonstrates Brown's ability to design a small garden-pavilion in a Rococo–Gothic style.

The Bath House is situated on the west side of the North Avenue near the sunken fence that divides the pleasure-garden from the park. Originally it overlooked the west end of a small lake that appears in the engraving of Corsham House (see **24**).[71] The Bath House is listed as No. 15 on the list of 'Mr. Brown's

---

[68] The accounts disclose that Stocking received £573-12-11½d for work on the east wing, making a total payment of £710-11-11½d for his work at Corsham, including the library.

[69] Two further balancing payments were made to Stocking in April and July 1766, amounting to £33-12-11½d.

[70] The lodges were to have been erected on either side of the North Avenue on the London Road and marked as item XII, 'Pair of intended lodges,' on the list of 'References' of Brown's 1761 plan for the house and grounds (see **40**). Their designs have not survived; they are not even mentioned on the list of 'Mr. Brown's plans.'

[71] The lake was filled in with the rubble from Nash's north front of the house in 1846.

plans' (Appendix C, where it is described as 'Mr. Brown—Cold Bath, Room over and drawings of dito'). It is not listed on Brown's map of 1761, although a rectangular building has been drawn on the map on the approximate site of the present Bath House.[72]

The pavilion consists of two floors (see **56**). The cold bath is sunk into the arcaded ground floor, and a flight of steps at the rear leads to a dressing-room above. Another doorway at the rear leads through a short tunnel to a walled garden at the back of the pavilion.[73] A triple-arched opening with a single arch on either side presently decorates the front of the building at the ground-floor level. On the first floor there is a Gothic window with a niche on either side (see **56**). Single windows appear on the sides of the pavilion at the same level. The roof is pointed with an entablature, crenellation, and pinnacles.[74]

The ogee-shaped side archways, the windows, the Gothic niches, and the pinnacles of the roof remain from Brown's pavilion. Nash removed three archways which were probably incorporated into a sham ruin on the west side of the house, next to the boundary-wall of the stable block. Intended to screen a view of the house from Church Street, next to the court, the ruin forms a high wall made of discarded pieces of masonry including some architectural elements such as windows and archways. The archways Nash removed have a more depressed ogee-shape than the side archways of the Bath House, also inserted by Brown. They are characteristic of the arches preferred by Rococo–Gothic architects found, for example, in Kent's design for the Courts of Chancery (*c.* 1735), and Batty Langley's design for an 'Octangular umbrello to terminate a view' (*c.*

---

[72] This building is located on Brown's map at the west end of item XI described as a 'piece of Water altered,' a small lake formed from a series of stew ponds that lay inside the boundary of the old pleasure garden on the north side of the house. Stew ponds are ponds or tanks where the stews (fish) are kept until needed for the table. They are usually arranged at different levels in order to be drained for cleaning, and for catching the fish.

[73] It was fashionable to take a cold plunge, which had been recommended some fifty years earlier by Dr William Oliver of Bath in his *A Practical Dissertation on Bath Waters* (London, 1707). Lord Methuen has collected a list of similar baths to be found in the neighbourhood: The Georgian House, Great George Street, Bristol, where it is located in the basement; in the basement of a Georgian House, Bradford-on-Avon, belonging to Mr Underwood; the ground floor of Ston Easton Park, Somerset, and St Catherine's Court, near Bath.

[74] An account has survived from James Rawlings the Mason, giving details of the work carried out on the Bath House under John Nash. This work was measured for payment on 10 June 1799 (Corsham archives). See **57** for the side archways of Brown's Bath House.

1747).[75] Pinnacles similar to those used on the Bath House appear in both illustrations.[76] During his formative years at Stowe Brown was fortunate to work with Burlington's favourite disciple, Kent, who was one of the most influential architects, interior decorators, and landscape-gardeners in the second quarter of the 18th century. The ideas of both Kent and Langley are reflected in Brown's use of Rococo–Gothic motifs. For example, Brown employed shallow ogee-shaped arches in the design for the Park Farm granary, Blenheim (1765), and in alterations at Tong Castle, Shropshire (1765). At Tong Castle, the main entrance has a triple archway with a centre ogee-shaped arch; the first-floor windows above are treated in like manner.[77] Similarly placed arches may have been used for the pavilion at Corsham before Nash remodelled the entrance. A form of broken pediment is used for the entablature of the Bath House, but its ogee-shaped arch in place of the normal classical pediment surmounted by a pinnacle reflects Batty Langley's 'Gothic' order of architecture.

Even beyond the specific influence of Kent and Langley, the ogee-shaped roof is traditional for Elizabethan summer houses. They appear in the design of John or Robert Smythson (RIBA Collection 1.9) for a summer-house at Chelsea (see **58**), and were used for the two corner pavilions of the garden-front at Montacute House (1587). Triple entrances are also found in the Elizabethan banqueting house or pavilion at Montacute, and at The Hall, Bradford-on-Avon (1597). Brown's design at Corsham followed a well-established form for the Elizabethan pavilion, which he embellished with Rococo–Gothic decoration.[78]

We may never know to what extent the orangery or greenhouse that Brown

---

[75] For an illustration of Kent's design see, Jourdain, *William Kent*, Fig. 28; and Batty and Thomas Langley, *Gothic Architecture Improved by Rules and Proportions* (London, 1747), plate LII.

[76] The surviving pinnacles designed by Nash on the stable block and the cloister adjoining the Gothic dairy are plainer in form, without any crocket decoration (see **75**).

[77] For an illustration of the Blenheim design, and Tong Castle, see Stroud, *Capability Brown* (new ed. 1975), plate 30b, and Stroud, 1950 ed., p. 111, respectively. The triple arch motif could have been taken by Brown from Kent's design for Esher Lodge, Surrey, restored for Henry Pelham, 1729–39. For an illustration see, Jourdain, *William Kent*, fig. 121.

[78] Paul Methuen must have been interested in garden pavilions at this time, because he subscribed to Thomas Collins Overton's *The Temple Builder's Most Useful Companion* (London, 1766). For details of Overton see the brief entry in Colvin, *Dictionary of English Architects*, p. 426.

erected near the mansion was influenced by Kent's Gothic style.[79] It is not listed on 'Mr. Brown's plans' (Appendix C), nor does it appear on the remains of the 'References' of the 1761 map, but it may well have been one of the missing items XIV to XVI. The employment of Stocking suggests that the structure had ornamental stucco decoration but there is no indication of the architectural style of the structure.[80]

LANCELOT BROWN'S ALTERATIONS TO THE GROUNDS AT CORSHAM

Brown transformed the park at Corsham into a landscape-setting for the house whose principal view was to be from the windows of the picture gallery and cabinet-room. When Brown surveyed Corsham in 1759, the gardens on the north and east sides of the house were most probably surrounded by stone walls, and beyond them lay the field-system of the estate. Three avenues of trees radiated from the vicinity of the house; much of the east avenue was removed during Brown's improvements. He had the advantage of laying out a park without too many existing obstacles: the only limitation to his freedom in creating a design was the fixed position of the house.

Other minor features that Brown had to consider were a series of pools or stew-ponds located on the north side of the house, and two small pools in fields on the north side of the east avenue. Several public footpaths and lanes criss-crossed the area of the present park, and the Bath turnpike-road to Chippenham passed along the northern boundary of the park. The vicarage on the south side of the churchyard was later demolished and a new vicarage built on the Lacock Road that forms the boundary on the south side of the park.

Paul Methuen had consulted two other landscape-designers before Brown. The first was Greening, who submitted a design to alter the pleasure gardens (see

---

[79] Lord Paul Methuen (4th Baron) considered that the greenhouse lay on the same side of the gardens as the Bath House but further south towards the house. The remains of foundations were removed when the pleasure gardens were extended in the 19th century.

[80] Brown erected a Gothic greenhouse at Burghley after 1756, and later he built an orangery with a classical portico at Broadlands, after 1767. For illustrations of the 'Gothick' greenhouse at Burghley, and the Orangery at Broadlands, see Stroud, *Capability Brown* (new ed. 1975), plate 13a, and Stroud, 1950 ed., p. 208. There is a record of a payment dated 6 Sept. 1760, to Sir George Cobb's gardener, for carriage and expenses for bringing orange trees from Adderbury, Mrs Paul Methuen's former home (Corsham archives).

60).[81] The exact date of Greening's plan is not known, but it is probably on or before 1749, because it does not show the steps leading from Ireson's facade. Greening's plan with its use of serpentine lines and walks through wooded areas reflects the earlier school of William Kent at Stowe. At the northern end of the garden is an oval-shaped pool to be converted from the existing stew-ponds shown in the 1745 map (see 59). A circular colonnaded temple stands on the far side of the pool from the house. Serpentine paths thread through a small plantation on the east side of the garden joining the existing eastern avenue of trees near the house. On the south side of the house is a large rectangular lawn with a carriageway around it.

Paul Methuen also obtained a design from a landscape-gardener called Oram, whose work is unknown. In extending the boundaries beyond the immediate pleasure-gardens to create a parkland, Oram's design reflects the development of landscape design of the 1750s. His plan must date after 1749 for it shows the steps of Ireson's north front (see 61). The plan shows a broader treatment of landscape design than Greening's plan, which is limited to the pleasure-gardens. Oram's scheme covers the area lying to the north and east of the house and extending into the surrounding field-system, but paid no attention to the southern part of the present park. Oram wanted to introduce a belt of trees along the west side of the north avenue, now called the Mynte Wood, one of Brown's plantations. He proposed screens of trees for the west side of the pleasure-gardens north of the house, and around the churchyard and vicarage. A large wood was to be planted on the eastern boundary of the property. The ponds on the north side of the east avenue were to be enlarged into a pear-shaped lake, continuing almost to the boundary of the northern pleasure-garden. The stew-ponds on the north side of the house would be filled in.

In some respects Oram's plan foreshadows the alterations that Brown eventually carried out, especially in planting belts of trees in different parts of the grounds and in creating a large lake from the existing ponds on the eastern side of the park. Oram's plan lacked the pictorial effect of Brown's plan, because he

---

[81] Two versions of this design exist; a large drawing and a smaller one, on the reverse side of the latter is a note 'Mr. Greening's plan for Corsham House, not executed,' probably in Paul Methuen's writing. The identity of Greening has not been established beyond doubt. Dorothy Stroud considers that it is most probably the Thomas Greening who died in 1757, 'a late Gardener to his Majesty'.' Thomas Greening also submitted plans for the grounds at Kirlington Park, Oxfordshire, *c.* 1746–51. Two other less likely candidates are, Robert Greening, a brother (?), and James Greening, Master Gardener, who was succeeded in this appointment by Brown in 1764. Stroud, *Capability Brown* (new ed. 1975), pp. 69, 83n. 7 and 122.

intended to retain the eastern avenue of trees which would have blocked the view of his proposed landscape in the north-east corner of the park. He showed little sensitivity to the contours of the ground for his plantations, or for the serpentine line essential to Brown's design.

Brown's plan of 1761 for remodelling the pleasure gardens and laying out a park was more comprehensive than Oram's (see **40**). Richard Boucher, the steward, kept careful records of the alterations, as he did of those carried out in the house. An account has survived for Brown's fees and services that lists the major work he carried out in the grounds, beginning 6 December 1760:

To wit the making the great walks and sunke fence between the house and the Chippenham Road. The draining the ground between the sunke fence and the line of garden. To making the Water in the Parks, as also the leveling round it. The leveling round the House, as also on front the New Building. The sunke fence on the front of the churchyard. All the planting included Mr. Methuen to find trees and alterations which have been made in the Garden. The above articles comes to one thousand and twenty pounds.[82]

Around the perimeter of the park Brown planted screens of trees. The 'great walk' along the west side of the north avenue was also proposed by Oram. A serpentine pathway leads through the 'great walk' (Mynte Wood) from the house to the top of the north avenue, where Brown proposed to erect the pair of lodges. In the north-east corner of the park Brown proposed a small lake, item XVIII, 'the intended piece of water' on the map. An avenue of trees beginning near the lake was to pass along the eastern and southern perimeters of the park, ending at the park gates of the south avenue; the avenue, wide enough for a horse and carriage so that visitors could be driven around the grounds to admire the view, was never built. One alternative route was to pass immediately behind another new lake in the south-east corner of the park, item XVII, while another was to continue around the perimeter of the park.[83] Brown followed Oram's plan in planting a screen of trees around the churchyard. The east avenue was drastically thinned, and small clumps of trees were planted on the east side of the house and in the park.

The proposed lake in the south-east section of the park was eventually constructed when Humphry Repton improved the grounds. In the meantime Brown seems to have enlarged the existing ponds on the east side of the park. Repton, in

---

[82] Corsham archives.

[83] Brown has a note at the bottom of his list of references 'The ride would be much better as at A, if Mr. Methuen does not chasse to . . .' possibly the hounds. The ink has faded here making the writing too faint to read.

his *Sketches and Hints on Landscape Gardening* (1794), paid tribute to Brown's skill in situating the lake in his landscapes, and stressed the importance of having a body of water. Viewed from the house the reflection of light off its surface creates the illusion that the lake is larger than it is, thus maximising the available resources. He also stressed the need for naturalness. Brown was always careful to observe this when forming a lake 'so that it would not fail to be agreeable.'[84] The Reverend Richard Warner, who visited Corsham 14 September 1800, soon after Repton had finished the lake that Brown had planned, said the park reminded him of a landscape by Poussin.[85] Poussin often placed bodies of water in the middle distance reflecting in their waters the dark masses of trees that surround them, as for example in his 'Landscape with a man killed by a snake,' 1648, the National Gallery, London.

Brown sank all the boundary hedges within the perimeter of the park to create a view from the house of gently undulating ground falling away towards the distant lake. The sunken fences were hidden on the far side of the rolling ground out of view from the house. Brown mentions levelling the ground before the east front of the house. A lawn was planted here to create a transition into the parkland beyond, with an uninterrupted view eastwards to the lake.

The combination of the pastoral setting of the park at Corsham and Brown's Classical east front resembles the classical landscapes of Claude and Poussin. In both the trees seem to have sprung up in a natural, artless arrangement in contrast to the formal and ordered elegance of the architecture. Thomas Whately stressed this association of art and nature in his *Observations on Modern Gardening* (1770) while arguing that gardening is 'as superior to landscape painting as a reality to a representation.' Brown's conception of landscape design developed from his work with William Kent at Stowe, especially in laying out the Grecian Valley. Kent's theories were based upon the idealised landscapes of Claude and Poussin that he had studied in Rome, his familiarity with the Roman Campagna and, upon his return to England, the influence of Pope. Pevsner considers Brown's elaborate formal asymmetry in landscape planning an aspect of Rococo that reflects a synthesis of a feeling for nature with classical order.[86]

The relationship of the villa and landscape had been stressed earlier by Palladio in the *Quattro Libri* (1570), where he states the villa should be sited upon hills or

---

[84] Loudon, ed., *Landscape Gardening of Humphry Repton*, p. 76.

[85] Richard Warner, *Excursions from Bath* (Bath and London, 1801), p. 195.

[86] Nikolaus Pevsner, 'The Genesis of the Picturesque,' *Architectural Review*, 96 (1944), 140.

rising ground and near water.[87] Palladian architects had the authority of Palladio for the design and setting of their villas, but the influence of the idealised landscapes of Claude and Poussin on the development of the English landscape garden should not be underestimated. As Brown had control of both the architecture and landscape design at Corsham he was able to stress this relationship. His object in providing the principal view of the park from the gallery windows was to create an association between the picture collection and the landcape in the minds of the visitors.

CONCLUSION

The alterations of Ireson and Brown at Corsham occurred in the period when strong classical influences were still to be found in the Palladian Revival. The Palladian and Elizabethan architects both derived their principles from the same theoretical source, whose ultimate origin was the treatises of Vitruvius, Alberti, and Serlio. Hence, it was possible to adapt the Elizabethan house to the Palladian style using, for example, the principle of symmetrical planning which they shared. The principle of doubling the wings on the east and west sides of the Elizabethan south front was established by Keene and followed by Brown, although Brown spoiled the symmetry of the north front by the extension of the picture gallery.

Because of the transitional nature of the style of the Elizabethan south front, it did not have to be completely remodelled in a classical form. Both architects must have recognised that the Elizabethan Renaissance elements in the south front could contribute to their own designs in such features as the entablatures, columns and pediments. Even Keene's designs to classicise the south front preserved its Renaissance characteristics, and concealed such Gothic features as the gabled roof-system.

Keene and Brown, who were sympathetic to the Gothic, decided to preserve the integrity of the Elizabethan south front by adding bay-windows to the existing style. Brown's comments about Burghley House testify to his archaeological attitude. His concern to add an extension in an existing style was unusual for the time, although an earlier example can be found in the work of Brown's master, Kent, in the Tudor addition to the Clock Court, Hampton Court Palace (1732). Hawksmoor was also adding the west towers to Westminster Abbey (1734) in a neo-Gothic style.

The picture gallery was the important architectural feature of Brown's

---

[87] Palladio is describing the villa of Count Marc'Antonio Sarego, Santa Sofia, near Verona. Andrea Palladio, *The Four Books of Architecture*, trans. by Isaac Ware (1738; rtp. New York: Dover Publications, 1965), II, xv.

extension. Brown's solutions to the problems of planning a gallery large enough to house the major items of Sir Paul Methuen's collection proved more satisfactory than those proposed by Henry Keene, an architect with more experience. Inside the gallery the placement of the pictures formed an important part of the overall decorative effect, for in the 18th century the layout of the pictures in a collection was of as much interest as the aesthetic value of the pictures themselves. Also important was the relationship of the pictures in the gallery and the view of the landscape from the windows, which was an integral part of the appreciation of nature and painting. At the end of the century, when Nash erected his gallery with top-lighting, this relationship between the collection and the view was sacrificed to provide better lighting conditions.

Although the exterior of Corsham reflected a strong Palladian influence at this time, the interior decoration of rooms in the Rococo–Gothic style reveals a decline in the authority of the Palladian style. Paul Methuen's interest in Sanderson Miller's work at Lacock Abbey, and his response to Horace Walpole's Gothic library at Strawberry Hill, brought the Gothic influence to Corsham as early as 1754. Rococo and Adamesque influences also permeated both the Gothic and Classical decorative schemes. These can be attributed in part to craftsmen employed at Corsham who had assimilated these influences elsewhere. The interior decoration of Corsham represents the end of the Palladian influence, typified by Kent's style at Holkam, and reflected in Brown's first major work at Croome Court (1751). The Rococo style was infectious: a decade later Brown had changed his decorative style under its influence. But Brown was too conservative to succumb completely to the Rococo style; he still retained the essential Palladian characteristics of Kent. While certain Adamesque influences are discernible at Corsham, mainly through the agency of Hobcraft, Brown was not influenced by Adam's style at this time.

Brown emerges as a competent architect and interior decorator at home in both Gothic and Palladian styles. His rather limited architectural vocabulary is drawn chiefly from his work at Croome, and the influence of Kent. We should view Brown's architectural work as secondary to his main interest in landscape gardening. At Corsham, although Brown had no opportunity to re-site the house, he provided a perfect harmony between his concept of a classical facade and a pastoral landscape setting whose principal view was from the gallery windows. The unity he created between the setting of the picture collection and the landscape view was something that 18th-century connoisseurs who related landscape gardening to the landscape paintings of Claude and Poussin were quick to notice. What looks today like a natural setting was an entirely artificial creation based upon this relationship of nature and art.

CHAPTER THREE

The Alterations of John Nash and Humphry Repton

When the second series of important alterations began at Corsham in 1797, the Gothic Revival and Neo-Classical Revivals had replaced the Palladian Revival as the prevailing fashionable styles. Two architects were consulted to submit plans; James Wyatt, whose designs were not accepted, and John Nash, who made more attractive proposals. Both sets of designs were in a Gothic Revival style. Paul Cobb Methuen decided to carry out further landscaping in the park, and commissioned Humphry Repton to do this work. He seems to have arrived at Corsham around the same time as Wyatt. Unlike Lancelot Brown's work in the 1760s, it was necessary for the architect and landscape gardener to cooperate in submitting plans that would not conflict.

Paul Methuen, the first member of the family to own Corsham, died in 1795. During his 48-year occupancy, he had transformed a relatively modest Elizabethan house into a distinguished Palladian country mansion overlooking a park converted from a field-system. Brown had enlarged the Elizabethan south front with the additional wings. Ireson and Brown respectively transformed the system of plain gables and mullion windows of the north and east fronts into distinctive Palladian facades. The interior of the house had undergone a partial remodelling, principally in the east and west wings. The east wing overlooking the park had been converted into a suite of state rooms and a magnificent picture gallery to hold some of the most distinguished pieces from Sir Paul Methuen's collection. In the west wing, a Rococo-Gothic library was added, and the adjoining Elizabethan room remodelled. In the main body of the house some of the Elizabethan rooms still existed, although they were probably decorated in Classical or Gothic styles. The great chamber on the first floor was still intact, but may also have been redecorated. The long gallery, whose location is uncertain, seems to have survived, although by now it may have been partitioned off. Practically all vestiges of the Elizabethan interior were destined to be swept away under Nash's alterations.

Both Wyatt and Nash had to consider three important problems in submitting their plans for Corsham. The first lay in the provision of an extension to the north side of the house, ostensibly to display the balance of Sir Paul Methuen's collection of pictures still in London. The second was the need to integrate the Elizabethan-Renaissance south front and the Palladian east front into their Gothic Revival designs. The third was to design their extension so as to preserve the symmetrical plan of the house. Brown had upset the symmetry to some extent by the projection of the north end of his picture gallery, although this was partially compensated by 'the chapel' on the opposite side of the north front (see **26**). The 'chapel,' which formed a part of the domestic premises containing the bakehouse and storeroom, was demolished by Nash.

According to Paul Methuen's will, his son and heir, Paul Cobb Methuen (1752–1816), was to bring all the pictures, plate, chinaware, and books then in London to Corsham within two years, and properly display them in the Tapestry Room (Corsham document 5046). This referred to the balance of Sir Paul Methuen's picture collection that had remained at Grosvenor Street since his death in 1757. The problems involved in carrying out the directions of his father's will were to occupy Paul Cobb Methuen for the rest of his life. Since the Tapestry Room was inadequate to house the collection, an extension to the house was necessary. James Wyatt was asked to submit plans, which, although subsequently rejected, influenced the alterations carried out at Corsham.

Paul Cobb Methuen decided to have the park enlarged and remodelled at the same time as the extensions to the house. Humphry Repton was consulted to submit designs for the park, and for the lake that Brown had proposed to build in the southeast corner of the park. Also some of the deficiencies of Brown's tree-planting were probably apparent after 40 years as the park began to assume a more mature appearance. In addition to landscaping the park, Repton was responsible for the architectural theory behind the new extension. His influence, as we shall see, seems to have led to Paul Cobb Methuen's rejection of Wyatt's designs, and to the employment of John Nash.

The rejection of Wyatt's designs was summary treatment for the most fashionable architect of the Gothic Revival movement. He was equally distinguished as a Classical Revival architect who had begun the Pantheon, Oxford Street, London (1770–72) at the age of 24. On the death of Henry Keene in 1776, Wyatt was appointed Surveyor of the Fabric of Westminster Abbey, the Palace of Westminster and Houses of Parliament, a position he held until his death in 1813.

He also succeeded Keene in directing the completion of the classically-designed Radcliffe Observatory, Oxford. Among Wyatt's earliest domestic Gothic works was the remodelling of Sandleford Priory (1780–86) for Mrs Elizabeth Montague, 'Queen of the Blue Stockings.' His work for Thomas Barret at Lee Priory (1782–90) earned the approbation of Horace Walpole. Writing to Thomas Barrett on 5 June 1788, Walpole said, 'My House [Strawberry Hill] is, therefore, but a sketch by beginners, yours is finished by a great master.'[1] Walpole employed him at Strawberry Hill in 1789 to design and construct an office block.

Wyatt became associated with the court and seems to have been on friendly terms with George III, who was interested in architecture. As a special mark of favour he was privileged to dine at the equerries' table.[2] He constructed a Gothic ruin for Queen Charlotte at Frogmore House in 1792, where George III used to have breakfast; in 1787 he began the restoration of St George's Chapel, Windsor Castle.[3]

Wyatt was commissioned to convert Windsor Castle into a Royal Residence in 1796, and in the same year, following the death of Sir William Chambers, appointed Surveyor General and Comptroller of His Majesty's Office of Works.[4] However, because of Wyatt's unpunctual and erratic manner, George III did not bestow a knighthood upon him. Among other distinguished honours, Wyatt was elected a Royal Academician in 1785 and, after a heated controversy over his restoration of cathedrals, elected a member of the Society of Antiquarians in December 1797.

It was most probably through the Methuens' indirect connection with the court that Wyatt was invited to Corsham. Paul Cobb Methuen's sister, Christian, had married Frederick Irby, second Lord Boston, who was a personal friend and

---

[1] Horace Walpole, *The Letters of Horace Walpole*, ed. Paget Toynbee (Oxford, 1903–1905), XIV, 47.

[2] James Greig, ed., *The Farington Diary by Joseph Farington R.A.* (New York: George H. Doran, 1923), I, 41.

[3] The Duke of Leeds wrote at Oxford on Thursday, 14 July 1791, 'Mr. Wyatt called upon me and shewed me the plan and elevation of the intended building in the Queen's Flower Garden at Frogmore.' British Museum MS. 28,570,50. Wyatt also constructed at Frogmore the stables, a hermit's cottage and a dovecote in the grounds. Anthony Dale, *James Wyatt* (Oxford: Basil Blackwell, 1956), p. 179.

[4] Farington entered in his Diary for 14 February 1794, 'Din'd at the club. Nineteen present. I sat by Wyatt, who told me that on 7th June last [1793] the King [George III] voluntarily promised him the place of Surveyor General of the Works in case he survived Sir William Chambers.' Greig, *Farington Diary*, I, 41.

Lord-in-waiting to George III. Lord Boston, who is mentioned by Joseph Farington in his diary, would have known of Wyatt's improvements at Frogmore House
for the Queen.[5] Wyatt had other commissions in Wiltshire at the time; he was
engaged upon improvements for Lady James at Hartham Hall, Pickwick (1790–
95), about a mile from Corsham. His most important commission was at Fonthill
Abbey for William Beckford. Wyatt had erected a ruin at Stop's Hill for Beckford
in 1790, but the planning of Fonthill Abbey did not begin until 1796.

We do not know precisely what James Wyatt's plan was for the alterations at
Corsham. In addition to gothicising Corsham House and possibly the out-
buildings, Wyatt probably intended to gothicise the main entrance and the forecourt leading into it.[6] We know that Wyatt's designs for the alteration of Corsham
House were exhibited at the Royal Academy in 1796. They must have been
completed towards the end of March at the latest, because the exhibition committee is recorded as 'examining' work on 2 April.[7] This suggests that Wyatt
surveyed Corsham in the previous summer or autumn of 1795. The only evidence
that survives of Wyatt's designs for the remodelling of Corsham is a watercolour
recently discovered by Lord Paul Methuen (4th Baron), (see **63**).[8] This watercolour
may have been executed by Dixon, Wyatt's draughtsman, who had been with him
since the construction of the Pantheon, Oxford Street (1770–72).[9] It shows the
proposed extension of the north front, and the east front remodelled to harmonise
with the new extension.

Wyatt had the problem of adding an extension to the north side of the house
that incorporated the end of Brown's picture gallery projecting 27 ft beyond
Ireson's facade. We can only judge Wyatt's design from the surviving watercolour;

---

[5] Greig, *Farington Diary*, III, 104.

[6] Some indication of them is given by Paul Methuen in a letter to his mother, Mrs
Paul Cobb Methuen, in 1809. See a further reference on p. 79.

[7] I am indebted to the Assistant Librarian of the Royal Academy of Arts,
Constance-Anne Parker for this information. For the 1796 Catalogue entry, see No.
831, 'Design for altering Corsham Hall, Wilts., the Seat of P. C. Methuen, Esq.'
Algernon Graves, *Royal Academy of Arts—A Complete Dictionary of Contributors
and Their Work from its Foundation in 1769–1904* (London: Henry Graves & Co.,
and George Bell & Sons, 1905–6), VIII, 372.

[8] When the watercolour was taken out of its frame to be cleaned a label was found
on the back marked, 'Design for Alterations Corsham Hall, Wilts, The Seat of
P.C. Methuen, Esq. James Wyatt, R.A.' This may have been the design exhibited
at the Royal Academy in 1796.

[9] Greig, *Farington Diary*, I, 35.

there is no indication of the interior arrangement of the rooms. In designing a symmetrical front and placing a tower of equal size at the western end of the north front Wyatt provided a 'classical' solution to the problem posed by Brown's extension. In the centre part of the north front Wyatt proposed to add a slightly larger tower projecting from the north wall of the house. In this design he has given the north and east fronts a sense of mass.

Wyatt clothed his boldly projecting symmetrical design with Gothic detail. The centre tower of the north front has two octagonal turrets at each corner; string-courses at the first and second levels extend across the east front to join the entablatures of the south front. There are three pointed-arched windows at each level. The sills of the upper windows form a part of the moulded string-course. At the lower level French doors lead on to a flight of steps. All the windows have prominent drip-moulds like those on the east front today. The projecting corner-towers have slightly higher staircase or buttress-towers rising above the surrounding crenellation. The crenellation gives the whole a castle-like air. In Clark's *Gothic Revival* he refers to two distinct classes of Gothic country houses built in the 18th century, the crenellated Windsor class, and the more adventurous Fonthill class.[10] Wyatt had often reserved the Windsor class with its battlements and massive towers for ducal clients with impressive pedigrees, while the Fonthill class, having a silhouette with ranges of cloistered galleries, lofty crossing-towers, and principal entrances like church portals, appealed to the more romantically disposed clients. Wyatt's design for Corsham follows the Windsor class, but it also prefigures characteristics of the slightly later Fonthill.

Wyatt intended to remodel Brown's classical east front in the Gothic style, using slightly projecting towers at each corner to mask the Palladian angle-towers. It is not known how drastically he intended to remodel the south front. In the watercolour the crenellation of a buttress-tower on the southeast corner suggests that Wyatt considered concealing the gabled roof-system behind the crenellated parapet wall, and heightening the bay-windows to transform them into towers. This means that he intended to transform the entire exterior of the house into a castle style.

Wyatt's scheme for Corsham is revealed in a letter written by Paul Methuen (1st Lord) in 1809, over a decade after Wyatt had been dismissed. On the subject of proposed improvements to the churchyard walls immediately outside the main entrance, he wrote, 'Mr Wyatt's suggestion is what I have repeatedly

---

[10] Kenneth Clark, *The Gothic Revival* (1928; rpt. London: John Murray, 1962), p. 82.

suggested my self, I am still of the opinion that the front gate should be gothicised and three other gates be gothic on a smaller scale.' Further on Methuen states,' . . . my larger plan for improvements means but in short to give the place an appearance of a college by Gothic walls round the churchyard in every direction . . . I have no fear of either Mr Nicholls or Mr Repton hearing these opinions of mine as I know they would agree with me, and I cannot leave Mr Wyatt in possession of all the merit of originality of this occasion'.[11]

The proposed new entrance to be aligned with the boundary walls before the stable-block was to replace 'the present nondescript' gateway (see 22). Wyatt created a Gothic forecourt with crenellated walls as a part of his improvements at Wilton House (*c.* 1801–14), and he may have submitted designs for a similar scheme at Corsham. The Collegiate Gothic, to which Methuen refers, was a domestic form derived from the Gothic associated with colleges and universities, such as Oxford and Cambridge. Repton refers to the suitability of college architecture for domestic use, but warns that if 'the building does not look like a house, and the residence of a nobleman, it will be out of character.'[12] Wyatt's proposals were taken over in a large measure by Nash, who did remodel the Elizabethan stable-block on the side facing the house, but no plans or estimates have survived to indicate that he intended to follow Wyatt's proposal to Gothicise the main entrance or its forecourt.

Wyatt's design for Corsham shows the development of his mature style. He had begun to develop the rectangular towers introduced in the design as early as 1783 at Lee Priory; they are to be found in a more fully developed form at Fonthill Abbey. According to Anthony Dale, Wyatt's experience in restoring cathedrals and colleges between 1787 and 1797 transformed his style from the more Rococo forms at Lee Priory into the monumental style of his later period beginning with Fonthill Abbey.[13] The Corsham design produced in the spring of 1796, immediately preceding the Fonthill designs, also possesses the monumental qualities of Wyatt's mature style, although upon a smaller scale than Fonthill.

Wyatt repeated the form of the centre tower of the north front at Corsham in the two massive crenellated towers set astride the southern end of St Michael's

---

[11] Corsham archives. Mr Nicholls is probably the Reverend Norton Nicholls, an expert in landscape gardening and a correspondent of Humphry Repton, see also p. 88, n. 32.

[12] Humphry Repton, *An Enquiry into the Changes in Taste in Landscape Gardening* (London, 1806), p. 113.

[13] At this time, the Corsham design had not been discovered. See Dale, *James Wyatt*, p. 143.

gallery at Fonthill. Later he added a similar tower to the north wing at Fonthill to form the vaulted corridor leading to the oratory. Wyatt also used massed tower-blocks at Windsor Castle (subsequently altered by his nephew, Sir Jeffry Wyattville), and at Ashridge (1808–13) for the 7th Earl of Bridgwater (this latter work has survived). The monumental castle-like appearance that Wyatt's proposed extension for Corsham would have presented when viewed from the park was fully in keeping with the picturesque concepts of Gothic Revival architecture, though still retaining the Renaissance symmetry of the Elizabethan ground-plan.

The circumstances leading to Wyatt's dismissal and the employment of John Nash are not absolutely clear. Wyatt's treatment of new clients may partly account for this. His nephew and pupil, Sir Jeffry Wyattville, mentioned that while it was his uncle's habit to be attentive to new clients, eagerly following their instructions to begin the work, he afterwards became indifferent and casual toward the commission.[14] This probably occurred at Corsham, because at this time Wyatt had become heavily involved with William Beckford's more lucrative commission at Fonthill, the plans to remodel Windsor Castle, and other public works for the Crown. Humphry Repton's presence at Corsham at the same time as Wyatt must also have influenced Paul Cobb Methuen to dispense with Wyatt's services. Repton had recently formed a business partnership with John Nash whereby Repton received a small commission on the contract price to introduce Nash to new clients. The advantages of such a partnership, that undertook both the architecture and landscape work at Corsham, may have been suggested to P. C. Methuen. Repton first visited Corsham on two occasions in November 1795 (3–5 and 23–24).[15] Wyatt had submitted his plans to Paul Cobb Methuen, probably in March 1796 before they were exhibited at the Royal Academy. On 19 May, Repton charged three guineas for meeting Wyatt at Corsham.

Surviving correspondence throws some light upon the circumstances of Wyatt's dismissal. A letter dated 16 August 1796 from Wyatt to Paul Cobb Methuen (Corsham document 6056) registered his indignant protest at the dismissal:

I never was more surprized in my Life than I am at every part of the Contents of your letter excepting one, which is, that a Plan has been submitted to you that you prefer to mine, I wish it may prove to have the merit which you have been given to understand it has; but if it is made upon the Principles which has occasioned your rejecting mine I am afraid you are most egregiously deceived; it is not an uncommon thing for some person's tongue to outrun their Reason, and I will venture to assert

---

[14] Dale, *James Wyatt*, p. 197.

[15] These dates are given on Repton's account submitted 23 January 1797 (Corsham document 6068).

that whoever has advised you to prefer any other light to a North light for Pictures had some other motive in preference to your interest and doing Justice to your Pictures for his suggestion . . . I find you are told that I have been deceiving you, for it is not to be supposed, nor will anybody suppose, that living amongst Artists which I have done all my life that I should not have heard (if it be true) that a North light is the worst light for Pictures. It must also have been suggested [to you] that I was too much employed to pay proper attention or to feel inclind to give you another Plan. . . . I hope Sir you will indulge my request that I may discuss the matter fairly and profit by the opinions of superior Talents.

Wyatt evidently did not know that meanwhile John Nash had been consulted (Nash had visited Corsham 3 August 1796, with Humphry Repton). Wyatt's remarks concerning the use of a north light suggest that Nash and Repton must have advised Paul Cobb Methuen at this time to place the picture gallery elsewhere in the house.

In a subsequent letter to Methuen of 20 April 1797 (Corsham document 6009), in which Wyatt enclosed his account, he refers directly to some kind of animosity which seems to have arisen between Humphry Repton and himself, probably during their meeting at Corsham on 19 May of the previous year. Wyatt requested an interview with P. C. Methuen on the following morning in the hope of retaining his commission. Methuen replied with a draft to settle the account and wrote, 'I am fully persuaded that an interview would be extremely unpleasant to us both' (Corsham document 6009, p. 3).

James Wyatt had a reputation as the leading Gothic Revival architect even if his treatment of cathedral restoration was controversial. Wyatt's design for Corsham, an early example of his mature style, reveals that he clearly understood the problem involved with Brown's picture gallery; Nash's Tudor-Gothic front was a thinly disguised copy. Bellamy also accepted the same principle in his design for the north front in 1846. Wyatt's disparaging remarks concerning Nash's original placement of the second picture gallery, which can only have been on the south side of the house, were sufficiently authoritative to make Nash change it to the north front. Nash was able to profit from Wyatt's longer and wider experience in his subsequent design for Corsham. Although Wyatt lost the commission at Corsham, his design was influential, and his suggestions were later respected by the family when Nash's work proved to be disappointing.

Humphry Repton (1752–1818), had experienced a disappointing career until his decision in 1788 to become a landscape gardener.[16] Repton was born in Bury St Edmunds, and received a grammar-school education there and in

---

[16] For an account of Humphry Repton's early career, see Dorothy Stroud, *Humphry Repton* (London: Country Life, 1962), pp. 15–26.

Norwich. His father sent him to Holland to be educated at the age of 12; he lived there for two years with Zachery Hope, one of the international merchant bankers of Rotterdam. Entering business at the age of 16, he met with little success, and gave it up after his father's death in 1778. He bought a small estate at Sustead, where he lived as a minor country gentleman, and formed important friendships, including one with William Wyndham, the politician. After the failure of a mail-coach venture he moved with his family to a cottage at Hare Street, near Romford, Essex. In 1788 he decided to become a landscape-gardener, taking over the mantle of leadership in the profession vacant since Lancelot Brown's death in 1783. Dorothy Stroud suggests that Repton may have met John Nash at Hafod, Wales, whose owner, Colonel Thomas Johnes, was a friend of William Wyndham. Nash and Repton were both acquainted with Richard Payne Knight and Uvedale Price, the leaders of the Picturesque movement in landscape appreciation.[17]

Repton himself became influential in the theory of landscape gardening. By 1794, when his *Sketches and Hints on Landscape Gardening* had reached the final proof stage, he became embroiled in a controversy with Richard Payne Knight and Uvedale Price over the qualities of the ideal landscape. Knight and Price favoured the wild and rugged scenery of nature so appealing to the artist. This conflicted with the cultivated, pastoral concepts of the Brown School.[18] The Reverend William Gilpin, another member of the group, defined the 'picturesque' in his *Observations Relative to Picturesque Beauty* (1789) as a landscape aesthetic denoting a specific visual quality of the more romantic and unkempt scenery. Later, in 1794, Gilpin attacked the formality and smoothness of Palladian architecture in his *Three Essays on Picturesque Beauty*, and pleaded for something more irregular, such as the Gothic style. In support of Gilpin's stand, Knight wrote a poem addressed to Uvedale Price, 'The Landscape,' that ridiculed the arcadian landscapes of Brown. Repton replied to these criticisms of Brown's landscape principles in a letter addressed to Uvedale Price published in Repton's *Sketches and Hints* (1795). The controversy caused much public comment. The aged Horace Walpole, then 79, wrote to William Mason, who had defended Brown against Sir William Chambers' criticisms, and asked him to write to Repton to express his support of his cause. Mrs Crewe of Crewe Hall recorded that when she entertained Burke, who wrote *A Philosophical enquiry into the origin of the*

---

[17] Stroud, *Humphry Repton*, p. 94.

[18] For a commentary on the Battle of the Picturesque, see Stroud, *Humphry Repton*, pp. 82–92; and Christopher Hussey, *The Picturesque Studies in a Point of View* (London: G. P. Putman's Sons, 1927).

Sublime and the Beautiful (1756), he had agreed with much Repton had written. By the time Repton was invited to Corsham he was one of the leading landscape gardeners in the country, who had established a reputation as a landscape theorist and leader of the Brown School.

Repton's introduction of his business partner Nash to Corsham gave him an opportunity to share a percentage of the architectural commission, which he would not have received from Wyatt. Joseph Farington recorded their arrangement in his diary—if Repton introduced Nash to an architectural commission where he was landscaping, Repton would receive $2\frac{1}{2}$ per cent. of the value of the architectural work, or vice versa.[19] Dorothy Stroud calculates that Nash would have had to charge 7 per cent., as his normal rate was $4\frac{1}{2}$ per cent.[20] At Corsham, Nash charged a commission of 5 per cent. for his professional services; thus it seems reasonable that Repton would have received about $\frac{1}{2}$ per cent.

Repton's architectural and landscape theories were certainly a factor in ensuring Methuen's commission. Repton had already scored a notable success in *Sketches and Hints on Landscape Gardening*, which he had published in 1795, the year before he came to Corsham. This book, which contained a reply to the attack made upon Lancelot Brown's methods, must have enhanced his prestige considerably in the eyes of his clients.

Repton, a serious student of Gothic Revival architectural theory, had incorporated the results of his research in his *Observations on the Theory and Practice of Landscape Gardening: including some Remarks on Grecian and Gothic Architecture* (London: J. Taylor, 1803). Some of his theorising upon the architecture of Corsham House was expressed in the Red Book, which he supplied to Paul Cobb Methuen in 1797.[21] This book has been lost, but extracts from it were quoted by Repton in his *Observations* of 1803, and also by John Britton, the antiquarian, in his *Historical Account of Corsham House* (Bath: Joseph Barrett,

---

[19] Greig, *Farington Diary*, I, 25.

[20] Stroud, *Humphry Repton*, p. 94.

[21] The Red Books, bound in red morocco approximately 6 × 8 in., set out a brief description of the property and the changes Repton proposed to make with the theoretical reasons for doing so. The text was accompanied by watercolours showing the present scene over which flaps could be placed to show the proposed improvements. Farington recorded that 'The King [George III] seen some of Repton's books on gardening [Red Books (?)], and seems to think them coxcomical works' (14 Feb. 1794); and on 29 April, Farington records, that Lord Orford 'thinks Repton a coxcomb,' that is, a pretender to learning and taste, Greig, *Farington Diary*, I, 42.

1806), and in *Beauties of Wiltshire* (London: 1801), II, 270–301.[22] The Red Book essentially provided a rationale for the architectural alterations at Corsham carried out by John Nash.

Apart from Repton's work few attempts were made in the 18th century to supply a theoretical foundation for Gothic Revival architecture. Batty and Thomas Langley published their *Ancient Architecture Restored* in 1741, followed by *Gothic Architecture Improved by Rules and Proportions* in 1742, which attempted to create orders of architecture for the Gothic.[23] They took Vignola's *Regole de' cinque ordini* (Venice, 1562), as the model for their treatises. James Essex was the first Gothic revivalist to complain in 1769 about a lack of theoretical foundation for the movement, but his manuscript on the 'History of Gothic Architecture in England' was to remain unpublished.[24] It is doubtful if Repton knew James Essex, who died in 1784, four years before Repton embarked on his landscape career, and equally unlikely that he knew of Essex's unpublished manuscript. But he probably had read Essex's articles in the *Archaeologia* and elsewhere.

In his unpublished notes Essex divided the evolution of the Gothic style into five periods. During the fourth period 'the modern Gothic was perfected from the time of Henry IV to Henry VII,' while the fifth period of 50 years is its 'decline under Henry VIII on the introduction of Greek and Roman in the following reigns.' Essex seems to have been influenced by contemporary French and Italian architectural treatises that discussed Gothic architecture, especially the Abbé M. A. Laugier's *Essai sur l'Architecture* (Paris, 1753), translated into German and English in 1755, and Conte Algarotti's *Saggi sopra l'architettura in opera* (Livorno,

---

[22] John Britton dedicated the third volume of his *Beauties of Wiltshire* to Paul Cobb Methuen. See the letter from Britton to Methuen, 27 October 1801, Devizes Museum. Subsequent references to Corsham in Britton's work occur in the *Beauties of England* (Wiltshire) (London: Vernor & Hood, 1814), XV, 510–520; *Auto-Biography of John Britton* (London, 1850), I, 344–347; II, 10.

[23] For a detailed discussion of Gothic Revival architectural theory, see S. Lang, 'The Principles of the Gothic Revival in England,' *Jour. Soc. Architectural Historians*, 25 (1966), 240–267.

[24] The notes for a 'History of Gothic Architecture in England,' are now in the British Museum, James Essex Add MS 6771 f.34v. See D. R. Stewart, 'James Essex,' *Architectural Review*, 108 (1950), 317–321. Papers on Medieval architecture by Essex were published in *Archaeologia*, the journal of the Society of Antiquarians of London, between 1776 and 1785. Other articles and plans of Gothic architecture were published elsewhere, see Howard M. Colvin, *Biographical Dictionary of English Architects 1660–1840* (London: John Murray, 1954), pp. 197–200.

1764), which expresses the earlier ideas of his master Carlo Lodoli (1690–1761).[25]

Like James Essex, Repton had studied the writings of the Abbé Laugier and Lodoli. Lang considers him to be the first to simplify Laugier's and Lodoli's theories and apply them to Gothic architecture.[26] Repton seems to have read most of the contemporary 18th-century Gothic architectural theory, which gave him a framework upon which to formulate his own theories. His writings were especially important for the Gothic Revival movement, since they influenced such later theorists as Augustus Welby Pugin and Edward James Willson. Some of Repton's theories were formulated by 1797 and included in the Red Book for Corsham as the principles upon which Nash and Repton remodelled the house.

In his *Observations* (1803) Repton set forth five principles applicable to all Gothic buildings. They were: (1) the use of a building should be considered before the ornament; (2) the ornaments should be placed where they are most conspicuous; (3) the principal parts of a building should have some conspicuous and distinguishing character; (4) some degree of symmetry should be preserved without insisting upon such regularity of design as to 'involve extra building'; (5) the degree of irregularity can add grandeur to the building. Repton's fourth and fifth principles are concerned with the problem of symmetry and the aesthetic effect of asymmetry. Rigid adherence to the principle of symmetry meant often unnecessary building as side wings and pavilions were duplicated. In his fifth principle, Repton has perceived that irregularity or asymmetry was one of the assumed qualities of Gothic structures, used by Walpole at Strawberry Hill and Knight at Downton Castle. Repton also grouped Gothic structures into three main categories: the Castle Gothic, the Church Gothic, and the House Gothic.[27] He discusses the relation of the architectural qualities of each to domestic architecture of the Gothic Revival. He considered Castle Gothic unsuitable for homes because the window apertures are too small; the Church Gothic would also be unsatisfactory because large areas of glass would create

---

[25] The first English translation of the Abbé Laugier's essay was *An Essay on Architecture in which its true Principles are explained and invariable Rules proposed* (London, 1755). Carlo Lodoli's theories were published by Andrea Memmo (1729–1793), *Elementi d'architettura Lodoliana, ossia l'arte del fabbricare con solidita e con eleganza non capprociosa* (Milano, 1834). See also Emil Kaufmann, 'At an 18th-Century Crossroads: Algarotti vs. Lodoli,' *Jour. Soc. Architectural Historians*, 4 (1944), 23–29.

[26] Lang, 'Principles of the Gothic Revival,' 258.

[27] Humphry Repton, *Observations on the Theory and Practice of Landscape Gardening; including some remarks on Grecian and Gothic Architecture* (London: J. Taylor, 1803), p. 190.

too much the appearance of a church. House Gothic remained the most suitable for domestic architecture.

Repton placed the Elizabethan style under his third category of 'House Gothic.' Few examples of earlier Gothic domestic architecture had survived suitable for designing country mansions. To overcome this problem, Repton defined Elizabethan architecture as Late Gothic, saying, 'the general character and effect of those houses [Elizabethan] is perfectly Gothic.' To justify this theory he accounted for the Renaissance elements to be found in the style thus: 'in the latter part of her reign [Elizabeth I's] bad taste corrupted it with the introduction of Grecian architecture in its ornament.' He cites Longleat and Wollaton as examples where the corrupting Renaissance influence is to be found. Repton's definition had an important influence on later Gothic Revival theorists who accepted his principle that the Elizabethan style was Gothic.

Repton included his architectural and landscape theories on Corsham Court in his *Observations* (1803),[28] having extracted them from the Red Book.[29] He claimed full credit for these theories in the *Observations*: 'Yet I claim to myself all that relates to the reasoning and principles on which the character of the house was adopted.[30] The *Observations* give us a good idea of the theoretical considerations behind the alterations carried out by Nash and Repton. When writing of his profession later in 1806, Repton defined precisely the role of the landscape gardener: 'To my profession peculiarly belongs the external part of architecture, or a knowledge of effects of buildings on the surrounding scenery.'[31] This statement helps us to understand how Repton visualised his role at Corsham.

Repton wanted the house kept in its present location and laid down principles for the preservation of its Gothic character. He contrasted the close proximity of Corsham House to the town with the modern practice of placing country mansions in the middle of parks, noting that it had been the custom of the English baron to live in or near the town or village whose name he took for his mansion or his title. Repton was especially thinking of the seignorial relationship that

---

[28] It forms a part of his discussion of 'the impropriety of improving the grounds without previous attention to the style, character, and situation of the house.' Repton, *Observations*, p. 190.

[29] Repton delivered his 'Red Book of Plans—Designs for the whole 40 guineas' during 1797. The item is charged on an account enclosed with a covering letter dated 23 January 1798 (Corsham archives, document 6068).

[30] Repton, *Observations*, p. 192, n. 1.

[31] Humphry Repton, *An Enquiry into the Changes in Taste in Landscape Gardening* (London, 1806), p. 71.

subsists in smaller country-towns and villages between the landowner and his tenantry. The nature of this relationship led Repton to propose to retain the high walls and massive gates surrounding Corsham as a symbol of the status of the Methuens. He discussed this point with an unknown correspondent as a post-criptum to a letter dated 13 February 1796: 'At Corsham I confirm your opinion that the stables should not be removed.'[32] The removal of the stables and walls in such circumstances, Repton believed, would imply the want of landed property, and hence a loss of social consciousness by the landowner, whose mansion had become a symbol of his wealth and social position.

In discussing the baronial status of Corsham, Repton referred to the kind of relationship that had existed between the landowner and tenantry before the Civil War when the manor house was the centre of all community activity.[33] Then the great hall formed the meeting place of the family, servants and tenants. This medieval relationship had long ceased to exist as the landowners preferred to have their business conducted by stewards and bailiffs. By the end of the 18th century the more intimate social contact between the landowners and tenants as in the Tudor period, when the tenants were invited into the great hall for enter-tainment, had been lost. Even in the later Elizabethan period, the great hall was reduced in size, as at Corsham, and the great chamber was used increasingly for private entertainment. Also, the introduction of the Palladian style in the 17th century, with its elegant marbled and columned halls, contributed to this separa-tion. These halls were unsuitable for the village-type of social gatherings, where the parish hall would be a more appropriate place. The landowner continued to discharge his social duties from a greater distance, perhaps representing a con-stituency in Parliament like the Methuens. A further factor was that an increasing number of county families, whose social outlook in the Tudor period was quite provincial, had succeeded in joining the ranks of the peerage, or held high offices of state.

As a genuine concern for beauty and elegance developed in the 18th century, country houses became show-places, and the traditional hospitality of the Eliza-bethan and Jacobean periods that centred around the country house gave way to

---

[32] The addressee of this letter is not indicated but it may have been the Reverend Norton Nicholls, a friend of Thomas Gray, and an authority on landscape garden-ing with whom Repton conducted a regular correspondence. Bristol University Library, MSS No. 180/4. For a reference to the Reverend Nicholls see, Stroud, *Humphry Repton*, p. 27.

[33] For a discussion on the changing social status of the English country house from the 16th to 18th centuries see, G. R. Hibbard, 'The Country House Poem of the Seventeenth Century,' *Jour. of Warburg and Courtauld Institute*, 19 (1956), 159–174.

stateliness. Suites of state rooms were shown to travelling gentry to impress upon them the taste and wealth of the owner. This occurred at Corsham with Brown's state rooms that housed Sir Paul Methuen's collection, and the later suite of rooms added by Nash for the second part of Sir Paul's collection. To allow for this show of magnificence the family was often relegated to the rest of the house, or had to retire to smaller rooms when the state rooms were on view. Nevertheless, landowners looked upon their country houses as retreats from the debilitating effects of high society life in London, like the Venetian merchants of the 16th century.[34] In the artificial atmosphere of the 18th century the nobility and gentry did not feel secure enough to risk lowering class barriers, or to return to the more informal social relationship with their tenants that existed in the Elizabethan period. The removal of the boundary walls at Corsham would have been a concession in that direction.

Repton took the Elizabethan south front as the style upon which the alterations should be based because it conformed to his definition of Gothic architecture. He stated that 'the original south front should become the object of proper imitation.' Although Repton accepted the south front as 'the standard of character' for the alterations, he sought to purge it of 'the Grecian [Renaissance] elements, which corrupt taste of King James' time had introduced', and substitute 'the true Gothic mouldings of Elizabeth's reign.'[35] Repton was referring to the early part of Elizabeth's reign when the Renaissance influence hardly existed. For Repton the south front was essentially 'House Gothic,' whose Renaissance elements merely showed the later degeneration of the style.

Repton advocated the remodelling of the north and east fronts of the house in an authentic Gothic style, rather than the duplication of the Elizabethan style; both of the existing fronts were quite unsuitable according to his theories. He described Ireson's north front as Grecian and Brown's east front as 'a correct but heavy style [Grecian] of regular architecture.'[36] They were inappropriate for the house owing to its close proximity to the town. From his aesthetic viewpoint, classical fronts should be set in more isolated surroundings. Moreover, he criticised the conjunction of different architectural styles on the fronts of the same house. The different styles did not seem quite so apparent until the walls and

---

[34] Palladio, *Quattro Libri*, II, xii.

[35] The term 'King James' architecture' also applied to the latter part of Elizabeth's reign including the Elizabethan–Renaissance style of Somerset House, Longleat, and Wollaton. Repton, *Observations*, p. 190.

[36] Repton, *Observations*, p. 188.

courtyards surrounding them were removed. One of Repton's reasons for re-modelling the Palladian east front in a Gothic style was to achieve a more harmonious union with the 'Gothic' south front.

Repton's primary concern with the picturesque silhouette of Gothic archi-tecture tells us that he approached architecture from the point of view of its purely visual effect upon the surrounding landscape. The silhouette of the Gothic style was more attractive than the gabled-roof systems and straight parapet walls of Elizabethan houses. He praised 'the stateliness and grandeur of lofty towers, the rich assemblage of turrets, battlements, and pinnacles, and the irregularity of outline in a large Gothic building unknown in the most perfect Grecian edifices.'[37] From this description we arrive at Repton's second principle of Gothic architec-ture, that 'the ornaments should be placed where they are most conspicuous.'[38] In using the Tudor-Gothic style to remodel the north and east fronts Nash and Repton created the kind of silhouette Repton had described; it was also one that suited his theories for remodelling the park.

Repton stressed the importance for the architect of imitating an existing Gothic building in an authentic style rather than to create his own design. Because an octagonal room was required on the north front, Henry VII's Chapel, West-minster Abbey, was chosen as an appropriate building to imitate. It is not known who suggested using this chapel but Repton claimed that the design was the joint work of Nash and himself.[39] Repton also gave another reason for this choice in the Red Book: 'Any building in such an aspect [northerly], however numerous the breaks, will always appear a flat facade, because there can be no sun to distinguish those breaks. But the tall and isolated turrets and flying but-tresses of Henry VII's Chapel, having the air playing round them and turning their octagonal sides and pinnacles to the sun, will produce a relief that no other means can afford in a north aspect, and exhibit catching light will dissipate in a great measure, its melancholy gloom.'[40] Their choice of 'Henry VII's Chapel' broke away from the flatness of Ireson's Palladian facade that cast the high north

---

[37] Repton, *Observations*, p. 189.

[38] Repton, *Observations*, p. 190.

[39] In a footnote to his *Observations* (1803) Repton states, 'In speaking of this house [Corsham], I use the plural number, because the plans were the joint effort a con-nexion and confidence which then so intimately existed between me and another professional person [John Nash], that it is hardly possible to ascertain to whom belongs the chief merit of the design.' Repton, *Observations*, p. 192. In 1803 Repton and Nash dissolved their partnership. Stroud, *Humphry Repton*, p. 112. Repton's claim to joint authorship was never acknowledged by Nash.

[40] Britton, *Beauties of England*, XV, 512.

front in deep shadow. The projection of the 'Chapel,' with the single storey-rooms on either side, created a variety of shapes, and gave some distinction to what was hitherto a dull and uninteresting front. As a landscape designer, Repton was preoccupied with the effect the picturesque silhouette of Henry VII's Chapel would create upon the surrounding scenery.

The design of Henry VII's Chapel complied with several of Repton's principles of Gothic architecture, for example, that 'the principal parts of a building should have some conspicuous and distinguishing character,' and 'the degree of irregularity can add grandeur to the building.'[41] These principles are embodied in the silhouette of the north front. While the symmetrical design of the north front could be said to involve unnecessary building, contradicting Repton's fourth principle, the west tower was necessary to balance the projection of Brown's picture gallery. To avoid a lopsided appearance was probably the reason Nash and Repton chose a symmetrical front as a suitable setting for Henry VII's Chapel, and ignored Repton's fourth principle. Corsham represents one of the last houses where Nash used a symmetrical design. Slightly later the influence of Richard Payne Knight's Downton Castle caused him to change his style to the castle-type house with an asymmetrical design.

Henry VII's Chapel, Westminster Abbey, so rich in English Flamboyant Gothic decorative carving, enjoyed a considerable vogue with the Rococo Gothic Revival. Horace Walpole had been among the first to show a preference for its motifs.[42] The chapel had attracted considerable public attention in the 1790s because of its delapidated condition. James Wyatt, surveyor for the Abbey, made a report upon the state of the chapel roof to the Dean and Chapter on 3 August 1793.[43] It may possibly have been through a chance remark of Wyatt's while visiting Corsham with Repton, 19 May 1796, that the idea developed of using the chapel as the prototype for the north front. This is suggested by a rough pencil sketch for the proposed north front showing a design based on Henry VII's Chapel that may date from the visit (see **64**). The sketch was made on the back of a letter addressed to Repton on which there is a postal mark, part of which reads

---

[41] Repton, *Observations*, 190.

[42] In a letter to Richard Bentley, September 1753, Walpole refers to 'the Westminster Abbey Style.' Horace Walpole, *The Letters of Horace Walpole*, Paget Toynbee, ed. (Oxford, 1903–05), III, 188. The gallery ceiling at Strawberry Hill (1763) is taken from one of the side aisles of the chapel which Walpole described as 'in Propria persona' (in appropriate character). Toynbee, *Strawberry Hill Accounts* (Oxford: Clarendon Press, 1927), p. 108.

[43] A letter has survived from the Chapter Clerk of Westminster to James Wyatt, touching the roof of the Chapel of Henry VII: dat Br(oa)d Sanc(turar)y, 3 August 1793. Copy 2 leaves. Westminster Abbey Muniments, document 24, 882.

'May,' but the year is not legible. Underneath the sketch is written 'Mr Methuen's House.' Although it may be a coincidence, it seems to indicate that Repton made a rough sketch of the proposed extension at this time, and handed it to Paul Cobb Methuen; it shows crudely the design that was adopted.

In his theory of landscape gardening Repton dealt with the different species of trees to be planted according to the style of architecture used.[44] He divided buildings into two principal categories of perpendicular and horizontal. The perpendicular included all buildings erected in England before and during the early part of Elizabeth's reign, even 'that peculiar kind called Queen Elizabeth's Gothic,' in which turrets prevailed, battlements were discarded and Grecian columns occasionally introduced. In the perpendicular class he cites Longleat and Wollaton as 'magnificent' specimens. The horizontal form applied to structures built since the introduction of classical architecture, when the remains of Grecian or Roman models were used.[45] Horizontal shadows are cast by the entablatures of classical buildings, and vertical shadows by Gothic buildings. From this he concluded that pointed and conic-shaped trees with a strong vertical emphasis were best suited to horizontal architecture of the Classical style, while the perpendicular lines of Gothic architecture were best contrasted with round-headed trees.

Repton developed his theory from an observation of the idealised landscapes of Claude and Poussin, where fir and cypress trees are usually grouped around classical temples. A similar relationship exists between the Roman ruins and isolated clumps of fir trees in the Roman Campagna. This type of tree would be unsuitable for Gothic architecture because both have a vertical emphasis. Linking the round-headed trees to Gothic architecture was particularly apt, for both are indigenous to England. Repton qualified the theory by stating that the Classical or 'the Grecian style will accord with either round or conic trees; but if the base is hidden, the contrast with the latter is most pleasing.'[46]

The 'Gothic' character of the Elizabethan south front at Corsham lent itself to Repton's tree-planting theory. The proposed Gothic extension to the north front and the re-facing of Brown's Classical front with Gothic elements would create Gothic silhouettes on the three principal fronts to use with round-headed

---

[44] Repton, *Landscape Gardening*, pp. 73–79.

[45] There was a third kind which was neither horizontal nor vertical, called 'Chinese', which was a confused mixture of both.

[46] Repton, *Landscape Gardening*, p. 76.

trees. In fact, Repton recommended the Gothic style in particular for additions or repairs to an old house. Henry VII's Chapel was especially appropriate for the application of this principle because of the decided vertical emphasis of its flying buttresses.

Repton's theories underlay the architectural and landscape work executed by Nash and himself at Corsham. His recommendation of the Gothic style for the north and east fronts, based upon his definition of the Elizabethan south front as Gothic, also fitted in conveniently with his tree-planting theory, for Brown had planted the grounds with mainly deciduous trees; the choice of a classical design would have meant extensive replanting with fir trees. Repton showed as great an interest in the picturesque silhouettes of the design for Corsham and his landscape theory as in the practical problem involved in constructing 'Henry VII's Chapel.' Unlike Thomas Bellamy he was not interested in repeating the Elizabethan style for the north and east fronts; his definition of the style precluded use of its Renaissance elements on these fronts. It was not until the 1820s that the Elizabethan-Renaissance style would be fully recognised on its own merits as one of the Revival styles.

John Nash was forty-four years of age when he visited Corsham in 1796 with Repton to consult about the intended alterations. Nash was six years younger than James Wyatt. While Wyatt had enjoyed a career of continuing success from 1770 onwards, when he established his professional reputation with his design of the Pantheon, Oxford Street, Nash's career was by contrast undistinguished. He was first employed in Sir Robert Taylor's office, and by 1777 had managed to establish himself as an architect and builder.[47] In 1783 he went bankrupt; he began another practice in Wales, where it appears he had relatives. Nash's stay at Carmarthen, Wales, from about 1783 to 1795, was very influential on his subsequent career because it brought him into contact with two important figures of the Picturesque Gothic movement, Richard Payne Knight and Uvedale Price. Nash knew the asymmetrical castle-mansion that Knight had built at Dowton (1774–78), a design he soon copied. The exterior asymmetry of Downton echoes the rugged Welsh landscape and contrasts the classical interior decoration of the mansion. Nash used similar contrasts in his own later work. It was through this circle of Picturesque landscape theorists that Nash met Humphry Repton,

---

[47] Sir Robert Taylor was one of the most accomplished architects of his day. Hardwicke commented that Taylor nearly divided the architectural practice with Sir William Chambers and James Paine until Mr Adams appeared. Colvin, *Dictionary of English Architects*, pp. 601–604.

before their attack on Brown's landscape designs. By March 1795, Nash had re-established himself in London, where he went into partnership with Repton.[48] In the following year Nash engaged Repton's eldest son, John Adey Repton, as a draughtsman in his Carmarthen Office.

John Adey Repton played an important role as the draughtsman at Corsham. His relationship with Nash, the architect, was much the same as that of Sir Charles Barry and A. Welby Pugin; the latter was largely responsible for the details of the Houses of Parliament. John Adey Repton had a keen interest in antiquities, especially in cathedral architecture. Before entering Nash's office, he had been a pupil of William Wilkins of Norwich; his deafness from birth kept him from leading an active architectural career. While in Norwich he began measured drawings of Norwich Cathedral for the Society of Antiquarians to be part of their *Cathedrals of Britain* series. Nash had employed him between 1791 and 1793 to make drawings for the restoration of St David's Cathedral. The drawings were inscribed with Nash's name as architect, and John Adey Repton and Augustus Charles Pugin as draughtsmen. Humphry Repton mentioned his son's knowledge and study of antiquities, crediting to him a 'full share of the general effects and proportions of the buildings' at Corsham.[49] Although John Adey Repton probably lavished much care in the drawings and research of the architectural detail at Corsham as his father seems to indicate, Nash was responsible for the specifications and the constructional work. The three persons engaged in the Tudor-Gothic remodelling of Corsham were not lacking in talent, but their enthusiasm outran their actual ability to direct the building operations.

A fairly accurate chronology has survived of preliminary visits to Corsham by Nash and Repton.[50] Both seem to have formulated plans for the alterations very quickly. Nash's first recorded visit was on 3 August 1796. He made two further visits in the autumn of the same year, on 18 October and 23 November,

---

[48] For a detailed account of the early career of John Nash, see Terence Davis, *John Nash The Prince Regent's Architect* (London: Country Life, 1966), pp. 15–31.

[49] Repton, *Observations*, p. 192. In a letter of 30 May 1812, to Paul Cobb Methuen, which includes an account for his fees for a visit to Corsham in 1810, Repton notes, 'the above includes also my son's visit [J. A. Repton], but his architectural designs and working drawings may either be considered as going on and hereafter to be settled as usual by a percentage when finished, or, if you prefer, the present settlement he desires me to put it at 15 guineas' (Corsham document 6082). This substantiates the claim made by Humphry Repton for his son.

[50] See Nash's account for professional services dated March 1798, and Humphry Repton's account of 23 January 1797 (Corsham document 6068).

when the first part of the projected interior alterations to the west wing were probably begun. A note on the estimate (Corsham document 6011) indicates that they were to be completed in 1797. It is not known precisely when Nash and Repton submitted their designs. They made joint visits on 7 July and 22 August 1797. Nash delivered his first estimate before 22 August, the date on which he charged a commission for his professional services. Included on this account is an item 'to a fair view in body colours fifteen guineas.' Repton delivered his Red Book during 1797, possibly in July. In it he set forth the principles for the alterations and his proposed designs for improving the grounds, illustrated by watercolour sketches with flaps to show the views before and after the proposed alterations.

Nash may have delivered his first estimate for the alterations to the house as early as the autumn of 1796.[51] The first section of this estimate covered the alterations to the west wing and included creating a new library, approximately twice the size of Brown's library, and extending the domestic premises; this work appears to have been completed toward the end of 1797.

The second section provided for the addition of new rooms to the north front, the central section of which was to be modelled after Henry VII's Chapel, for the remodelling of the east front, and for the provision of a grand hall in the centre section of the Elizabethan house.

A second series of estimates was delivered on 27 February 1798; it called for demolishing the old coach-house adjoining the kitchen building, erecting a Gothic dairy in its place, and providing windows for the south front podium. On 6 March 1798, Nash sent an estimate for a new coach-house to be located in the yard of the south front stable-block next to the ruin.

The principal feature of the alterations was the addition of a suite of rooms to the north front of the house.[52] It consisted of an octagonal salon, dining- and music-rooms on the ground floor, with bedroom accommodation on the first and second floors above the salon. The octagonal salon was joined to the flanking towers of the north front by a single storey, with the music-room on the east side and the dining-room on the west side of the salon (see **41**). The basic form of the north front is similar to Wyatt's rejected design, which showed a central tower-block linked to the corner towers by a slightly lower two-storeyed extension. For

---

[51] All the estimates are preserved at Corsham. The largest, document 6011, is undated, and covers the alterations to the house. It originally consisted of 27 pages; pages 12 to 16 have been lost.

[52] An accurate watercolour of the north front was commissioned from John Buckler by Sir Richard Colt Hoare, *c.* 1809 (see **65**).

Wyatt's massive crenellated towers at either end of the north front, Nash substituted the lighter more flamboyant Tudor-Gothic structures.[53] When the north front was destroyed by Thomas Bellamy in 1846, only the Gothic dairy and the remodelled east front were left, but these two remnants of Nash's work do provide some indication of the general effect of the former north front.

The Picturesque Gothic principle of asymmetry had become an increasingly important aspect of the Gothic style since Horace Walpole added the Round Tower at Strawberry Hill. Nash was aware of this important innovation and had visited Richard Payne Knight's Downton Castle, the first country residence wholly designed upon the principle of asymmetry.[54] But the influence of Downton does not appear in Nash's style until after Corsham. The symmetrical plan that Nash used followed Wyatt's solution to the problem posed by the projection of Brown's gallery 27 ft beyond Ireson's north front. Also, the centre section of Nash's proposed front—'Henry VII's Chapel,' needed to be balanced either side by a tower to be shown to its greatest advantage. Furthermore, the arrangement of the new rooms across the north front made some form of symmetrical plan desirable. The current fashion of using an asymmetrical design would have made the front awkward and lopsided. While Nash and Repton denied in theory the significance of the Renaissance elements of the Elizabethan style, Nash's and Wyatt's choice of a classically symmetrical plan implicitly admitted their importance. The so-called 'Gothic' house refused to submit to the most important principle of Gothic planning, although it remained for later architects to 'discover' the independence of the Elizabethan style.

Nash used only Tudor-Gothic architectural elements in his north front. No elements were taken from the Elizabethan south front of the house because they reflected the Renaissance influence which, according to Repton's definition of House Gothic, marred the Gothic qualities of the style. Only one design for the north front is known; it is an architectural drawing in watercolour executed by

---

[53] Summerson identifies the style of the north front with Nash's contemporary work at the Dulwich Casina (*c.* 1797) for Richard Shawe, solicitor to Warren Hastings, where Nash used a similar projecting centre section and flanking wings. Sir John Summerson, *John Nash: Architect to King George IV* (London: George Allen & Unwin, 1935), p. 62.

[54] In 1793 Nash worked for Thomas Johnes at Hafod, Wales. Johnes knew Uvedale Price who gave Nash his first commission to build Castle House, Aberystwyth, in the early 1790's. Its design was based upon the principles of the Picturesque movement. Mrs Johnes was a relative of Richard Payne Knight of Downton Castle, whose wife was Ursula Nash. Summerson suggests that Mrs Knight may have been a distant relative of John Nash. Davis, *Architecture of John Nash* (London: Studio, 1960), p. 10.

John Adey Repton (see **66**).[55] A comparison with John Buckler's watercolour of 1809 (**65**) confirms that the front was erected as shown in this design. The only important difference between the two drawings is in the design of the windows of 'Henry VII's Chapel.'

Nash seems to have drawn upon his repertoire of Gothic forms from his earlier work in designing the front. The octagon form of the chapel appears to have been one of Nash's favourite architectural shapes. He used it earlier in the library at Hafod, Wales, constructed for Thomas Johnes in 1793 (it was destroyed by fire in 1807).[56] This design may have influenced Nash's choice of the octagonal form at Corsham. The framework of the octagon and the flying buttresses were executed in Bath stone. The window-frames, probably considered too costly to execute in Bath stone, were made of wood and painted white.[57] The flying buttresses, characterised by an ogee-shaped finial, were a loose imitation of those used on Henry VII's Chapel. Repton may have suggested the choice of a pair of square towers crowned with octagonal turrets capped with ogee-shaped roofs. They show the influence of the north front of Cobham Hall where Repton had begun to remodel the grounds in July, 1790.[58] Here the towers are similar in style and placed at either end of the north front. The completed towers at Corsham had two windows, whereas the drawings show one. The north-east tower masked the north end of Brown's picture gallery, while the north-west tower provided an alternative entrance from the house to the gardens to the French windows of the salon. Gothic string-courses banded the north and east fronts at the level of the Elizabethan entablatures of the south front. Nash used crenellation around the parapets

---

[55] Vassar College possesses a watercolour ($4\frac{1}{2} \times 6\frac{1}{2}$ in.) by Humphry Repton showing a view of the north front that has the same architectural details as the architectural drawing in the Mellon Collection, especially the style of the windows. The measurements of the watercolour suggest that it may have come from the lost Red Book, which was submitted to Paul Cobb Methuen in 1797 at the same time as the architectural drawing. An engraving was made from the watercolour by Storer, and published 2 April 1801, by Verner and Hood, Poultry, London. It was also published by John Britton, *Beauties of Wiltshire* (London, 1801), II, 281. The Curator of the Vassar College Collection, Miss M. Delahoyd, informs me that the drawing formed a part of the original gift of Matthew Vassar in 1864, and it appears to have been acquired with other English watercolours from the Reverend Elias L. Magoon, a minister of New York City.

[56] For an illustration of Hafod, see Davis, *John Nash: The Prince Regent's Architect*, plate 3.

[57] Some remains of the wooden windows of the octagon still exist in the estate yard at Corsham.

[58] For an illustration of the north front of Cobham Hall, see Stroud, *Humphry Repton*, p. 44.

of both fronts. His Tudor-Gothic north front with its bold projections created a more graceful silhouette than the massive castle-like appearance of Wyatt's design.

Nash enlivened Brown's Palladian east front with Gothic architectural elements that harmonised with his north front and the Elizabethan south front (see **62**). He added four prominent crenellated octagonal turrets to the wall-surface in the same position as Brown's quoins.[59] The turrets gave a decided vertical emphasis to the front when added to Brown's flat wall-surface. Nash broke up the rows of single windows by adding more blank windows to the outer windows at both levels. Gothic drip-moulds replaced the classical pediments over the windows. A prominent oriel window (see **67**) at the mezzanine level further enlivened the variety of the wall decoration. A Gothic string-course replaced the entablature between the two window-levels. Nash cut away Brown's string-course connecting the lower window sills. Crenellation replaced the classical balustrade and stone urns. He clothed the east front in a Tudor-Gothic mantle, and through his use of turrets gave it a distinctive silhouette with a strong vertical emphasis that harmonised with the clumps of deciduous trees.

The Gothic decorative detail of the house was the responsibility of John Adey Repton, as his father tells us in his *Observations*, p. 192. Repton had made a study of Gothic windows; it was he who probably changed the design of those used at Corsham after the first design to the more authentic form we see today in the oriel window of the east front. This is the only example surviving *in situ* of Nash's larger windows at Corsham (see **67**). He inserted into this window a quatrefoil motif that he used for the larger windows of the north front. This common Gothic motif is found on the exterior of Henry VII's Chapel, Westminster Abbey. Through the use of this motif Repton gave the north front a more archaeologically authentic appearance than it had in his first design. He also inserted similar oriel windows overlooking the single-storey dining- and music-rooms, and added new gables over each window (see **66**). Repton and Nash probably used a shield motif in the clerestory of 'Henry VII's Chapel' for practical reasons to mask its division into two floors for bedroom space. Both fronts demonstrate John Adey Repton's familiarity with authentic Tudor-Gothic detail, so important at a time when draughtsmen had to rely upon their own knowledge in the absence of books of Gothic 'specimens.'

---

[59] The outer northeast turret was later removed by Thomas Bellamy. Nash used octagonal turrets later at Garnstone, Herefordshire *c.* 1806 (demolished), and Ravensworth Castle, Co Durham, 1808 (demolished). Davis, *The Architecture of John Nash*, plates 27, 28, and 11.

The interior remodelling of the house took part in two stages, the first from late 1796 to the end of 1797, when the west wing was remodelled, the second from 1797 to 1802, when Nash transformed the centre section of the Elizabethan house into a Grand Hall and decorated the new rooms of the north front. The first stage of the alterations was designed to convert Brown's library in the west wing into a breakfast-room and join the adjacent Elizabethan parlour and the staircase next to it to form a new library, approximately twice the size of Brown's library (see **68**). In the passage area outside of the breakfast-room a new staircase and light-well replaced the staircase which had been removed to form the new library. He remodelled the domestic premises and removed the 'chapel' building to make way for the west tower of the north front. The new domestic premises he erected on the west side of the house still exist. Much of the Rococo-Gothic decoration of Brown's library was destroyed during its conversion: the library was stripped of its Rococo-Gothic bookcases, the walls replastered and the Gothic overmantle of the chimney-piece removed. Nash created a new entrance in the middle of the north wall; the former entrance became a cupboard. A communicating door led into the new library from the south corner of the room on the fireplace wall. Fortunately, Nash retained Thomas Stocking's cornice and ceiling and also the coloured marble chimney-piece supplied by Prince Hoare of Bath.

The most completely preserved room at Corsham of Nash's alterations is the Gothic library. It is a room of impressive proportions, lighted by the two original Elizabethan windows on its east side and one bay-window on the south side. The coloured Siena panel marble chimney-piece was moved to the centre of the west wall.[60] A large rectangular area of space with recesses at the north and south ends of the room allows for the entrance ways and the bay-window area on the south side. In this way Nash created grand interiors. One of his favourite treatments of space, it is found in the picture gallery at Attingham Park in both the executed and the unexecuted designs (see **69**).

The Gothic decoration used in the Library gives some indication of the decoration of the Grand Hall (destroyed in 1846). A deep Gothic cornice fills the central area of the library ceiling; in the four corners clustered Gothic colonettes support the cross beams that retain the upper floor. Nash used similar colonettes for the archways of the Grand Hall (see **70**). Mahogany-edged bookcases reaching from the floor to the ceiling cornice line four sides of the room. The double doors that once opened directly into the Grand Hall have panels in the late Gothic

---

[60] This chimney-piece was supplied by Prince Hoare. For the reference in Nash's estimate for re-siting this chimney-piece see page 54, footnote 40.

Perpendicular style, similar to doors that existed in the Grand Hall. The wall-area and colonettes of the library were a dark green, with the cornice picked out in red and gold.[61] This library is probably one of the earliest surviving libraries designed by Nash, since his octagonal library at Hafod (1793) was destroyed by fire in 1806.

Nash's Grand Hall—providing such an imposing entrance to the house—was a design still novel at the time. The inspiration for such a hall may have come from Horace Walpole's gallery at Strawberry Hill, where the latter had revived the long-gallery form in the extensions to the house. But Nash's immediate influence may have come from James Wyatt, whose rejected designs for Corsham could have introduced a similar imposing hallway. The St Michael's and St Edward's galleries at Fonthill that Wyatt designed for William Beckford almost immediately after his discharge from the Corsham project suggest that he was already formulating such ideas and may well have recommended something similar at Corsham. In carrying out this scheme Nash had to demolish the centre lower floor of the Elizabethan house. The Elizabethan hall and staircase were removed together with the great chamber and the long gallery—if this was situated on the first floor—to make way for a new hall 110 ft long, 25 ft wide, and two floors high, with staircases at either end and a balcony running lengthwise on either side of the hall.

The Grand Hall symbolically expressed Repton's concept of the status of Corsham Court in relation to the town. Of course it was a show-place no longer serving the social function of the original Elizabethan and Gothic halls. Its baronial appearance impressed numerous visitors who said that it reminded them of the hall they romantically associated with Walpole's *Castle of Otranto*.[62]

The Tudor-Gothic decoration of the hall was largely the responsibility of John Adey Repton. Its decoration probably echoes to some extent that of the octagonal salon of the north front. Nash panelled the hall-ceiling around the

---

[61] A Gothic cornice similar to that used in the library at Corsham can be found in the dining room at Longer Hall, Shropshire, *c.* 1806. See Davis, *The Architecture of John Nash*, plate 88.

[62] Pierce Egan in his *Walks through Bath* (Bath, 1819), in his Walk (or Ride) XI, p. 249, describes the hall as impressing the visitor with its elegance: 'It does not exhibit any ancient trophies of war, shields, etc., like the renowned Castle of Otranto; but it has a few small bronzed busts, and other little ornaments; yet it possesses a sort of baronial appearance and maintains some of the character of former times.' The hall was converted into rooms again by Bellamy between 1846–1849.

border with stucco Gothic brackets corresponding to those supporting the balcony. Similar, although more elaborate, Gothic ceiling-brackets formed a part of Nash's design for the 'Gothick dining-room' of Carlton House in 1814.[63] He designed a balcony supported by carved wooden (oak) brackets, with flooring and handrails all executed in elaborate Gothic detail.[64] The north balcony led via a short flight of steps to the first-floor bedrooms above the salon. An open screen separated the staircases at each end of the hall. Both screens consisted of clustered colonettes which supported shallow Tudor arches with hanging pendants similar in design to those Nash inserted in the Gothic Bath house. An account survives for the balustrades of the double-return staircases at either end of the hall;[65] the balustrades were made of cast-iron with wrought-iron handrails; the walls of the hall were painted to imitate panels in the Late Perpendicular style. The hall was well lighted by the Elizabethan bay-windows on its south side, and by the oriel windows of the first floor overlooking the dining- and music-rooms.

Nash was especially concerned that the designs of the chimney-pieces should provide an appropriately Gothic effect, although they do not appear to have been the subject of the same archaeological research as those at Strawberry Hill. The chimney-piece in the centre of the north wall of the hall facing the front door had an ogee arch with a prominent finial and the Methuen coat-of-arms carved in the spandrel of the arch.[66] Nash made a rough sketch of this chimney-piece on the letter written to him on 19 January 1800 by William Walker, the clerk of works at Corsham (see **71**); it also appears in Neale's drawing of the hall (see **70**). The strong antiquarian movement in England resulted in the development of a greater

---

[63] For an illustration see *Pyne's Royal Residences* (London, 1819), plate 185, 'Carlton House: The Gothick Dining-room.' Also, Davis, *The Architecture of John Nash*, plate 188.

[64] Waagen, the director of the Royal Gallery, Berlin, visiting Corsham in August, 1835, mentions the hall: 'On entering the hall the eye is agreeably struck with a very elegant gallery of oak running all round it, from which the staircase leads to the first floor.' G. F. Waagen, *Works of Art and Artists in England* (London: John Murray, 1838), III, 88.

[65] The railings were supplied by William Stark, 19 May 1800, and they are described as '894 staircase railing in small Gothic panels and moulded with wrought iron top rails fitted with various ramps and curls with 4 turned ornamented newals, 28 pewter panels set in different sweeps, a variety of wood, pewter, brass and iron patterns, templates and moulds, and 250 strong screws, £625-16-0d.' The only surviving staircase at Corsham designed by Nash is found in the west wing. It has cast-iron balusters and a wooden handrail.

[66] During Bellamy's reconstruction the chimney piece was removed to the new servants' hall.

understanding of Gothic architectural detail by the end of the century; this is evident in Nash's handling of the interior Gothic decoration which shows a more authentic use of Gothic elements than Brown's Rococo-Gothic.

Corsham was amongst the first houses in the last decades of the 18th century to use structural cast iron, though it had been used since the first quarter of the 18th century for such decorative purposes as railings.[67] Isaac Ware comments upon the early uses of cast iron in his *Complete Body of Architecture:* '. . . cast iron is very serviceable to the builder and a vast expense is saved in many cases using it; in rails and balusters it makes a rich and massy appearance when it has cost very little.'[68] At this time the value of cast iron as a structural support was not appreciated: John Nash was one of the first architects to exploit its possibilities for building. Summerson suggests that Nash may have developed an interest in cast iron because he had relatives living at Broseley, where he could have studied cast-iron techniques at the foundries of Coalbrookdale and Bersham.[69] He constructed a bridge using cast iron in 1795.[70] By 1797 Nash was sufficiently confident to patent his use of cast-iron arches in bridge-building: he devised hollow voussoirs that could be filled with any kind of building material.[71] And so it is not surprising to find him attempting to explore further the new possibilities of this material at Corsham. Indeed, Summerson describes Nash 'as quite merciless in his use of cast iron as a general factotum.'[72]

Nash used cast-iron supports in the suite of three rooms on the north front which were intended to be a continuation of Brown's state rooms. There was a centre octagonal salon, a music-room between it and Brown's picture gallery on

---

[67] The first recorded cast-iron railings were those used for St Paul's Cathedral, London, and erected in 1714. Sir Christopher Wren disapproved of them. John Gloag and Derek Lawley Bridgwater, *A History of Cast Iron In Architecture* (London: George Allen and Unwin, 1948), p. 115.

[68] This quotation is taken from 'Of Iron'. Isaac Ware, *A Complete Body of Architecture* (London, 1768), I, xxvii, 89.

[69] Summerson, *John Nash*, p. 44.

[70] The first bridge Nash designed and erected across the River Teme at Stanford in 1795 for Sir Edward Winnington collapsed within hours of its completion. Undaunted, Sir Edward ordered a second bridge from Nash which was opened in September 1797, and stood until 1905. Gloag and Bridgwater, *Cast Iron in Architecture*, p. 100.

[71] See 'Bridge Foundations—New Westminster Bridge,' *The Builder*, 23 Aug. 1856, p. 454.

[72] Sir John Summerson, 'Records of an Iron Age,' *The Official Architect*, 5 May 1945, p. 235.

the east side of the house, and a dining-room on the other side of the salon adjacent to the kitchen. The music-room and salon were to house the balance of Sir Paul Methuen's collection; like the suite of state rooms provided by Brown, they were open to the public on certain days of the week.

No illustrations of their interiors are known to exist, but information about their decoration can be gleaned from Nash's estimate, the accounts, and brief descriptions recorded by various visitors.

The octagonal salon was of imposing dimensions, being 40 ft in diameter, and 24 ft high. (Brown's picture gallery is 24 ft wide.) It consisted of a single span to retain the clerestory area without an ambulatory or any form of columnar support. Nash's use of a cast-iron structure to span this distance was his first such innovation in a private house. According to Nash's estimate, the ceiling of the salon was supported by 'perforated flying Gothic brackets of cast iron' on which rested 'iron frames to support the inner octagon.'[73] The two floors of the inner octagon formed the clerestory area of 'Henry VII's Chapel.' Whether Nash could have produced such a spectacular structure without this cast-iron support is doubtful. His external flying buttresses were purely decorative. Nash's cast-iron structure at Corsham was a prototype for the structural supports he developed later for the vast rooms at Carlton House, the Royal Pavilion, Brighton, Buckingham Palace, and elsewhere.

The decoration of the salon exhibits the consistency with which Nash used certain motifs. Just as the pendants on the arch-rims of the Grand Hall re-occur in the Gothic Bath house, so the design of the cast-iron flying-brackets in the salon probably repeats that of the wooden brackets in the hall (see **70**). The ceiling of the salon had stucco Gothic mouldings, a Gothic cornice, perhaps similar to the library cornice, and Gothic panels in the spandrels of the windows and over the groins. The stucco Gothic ribs were painted in imitation marble.[74] The mahogany doors of all three rooms matched those of Brown's state rooms. The walls of the salon were papered for hanging the pictures. The three large Gothic windows with French doors and the window-shutters were also decorated with Gothic motifs taken from Tudor-Gothic architecture to conform with the style of Henry VII's Chapel. This archaeological interest was due to John Adey

---

[73] See Nash's estimate, Corsham document 6011, pp. 11 and 19. Nash also specified the use of 'girders in all floors of the north front except the ground floor' on page 17. The idea for the flying brackets may have come from the interior of Henry VII's Chapel, Westminster, where they spring from the side walls to support the fan-shaped pendants of the ceiling.

[74] Britton, *Beauties of England*, XIV, 512.

Repton, and did not extend to the materials used. Nash did not hesitate to replace traditional materials with cast iron if the latter would make a suitable cheap substitute; he also resorted to the use of painted plaster to imitate wooden panelling.[75] This detracted from the quality of his work, making it compare unfavourably with the craftsmanship of Brown's state rooms.

Nash gave particular attention to the chimney-piece of the salon because of its prominent position in his most important room. It was supplied by the builder, Thomas King of Bath, at a cost of £80 (see **72**).[76] Its dark green variegated marble background contrasts strikingly with the white marble ornamentation of colonettes, shelf and inlaid piping. The mantle-shelf is edged with a shield pattern, and the Gothic colonettes have feather capitals. The chimney-opening consists of a shallow concave Tudor arch edged with white marble, in the same shape as the centre archway of the hall screens. The Gothic design of Nash's chimney is more convincing than that of the Rococo-Gothic chimney-piece of Brown's library (see **48**). Nash's Gothic chimney-pieces frequently incorporated beautiful marble salvaged from those taken down during his remodelling.

The coved ceilings and classical decoration of the dining- and music-rooms followed a similar contrast between Classical and Gothic rooms at Downton Castle. Their dimensions were 36 ft × 24 ft × 18 ft high. Doors connected the rooms and led into the picture gallery. From the dining-room and music-room one entered the Grand Hall through double doors: an inner door of mahogany, and an outer door with Gothic panels similar to the library doors. There was no entrance to the Salon from the Grand Hall. The inner door-cases and architraves were executed in stucco, and window-surrounds also, in contrast to the carved wood used in Brown's rooms. The coved ceilings and cornices were heavily ornamented with pre-cast stucco decoration, such as guilloche, three-leaved ovolo, and rosettes.[77] The walls of the music-room were painted a dark brown.[78]

---

[75] On 8 December 1798, Farington refers to Nash's use of cast iron in his buildings, and he also quotes a short rhyme published by a Quarterly reviewer upon Nash's excessive use of plaster:

> 'But is not our Nash, too, a very great master,
> He finds us all brick and leaves us all plaster.'

Grieg, *Farington Diary*, I, 251.

[76] The chimney-piece was set up in the present dining room by Thomas Bellamy after Nash's extension was demolished (see **87**).

[77] These plaster casts were made in London by James Fletcher and delivered to Corsham.

[78] Egan, *Walks through Bath*, p. 249.

The chimney-piece for the music-room was supplied by Thomas King of Bath.[79] The dark green variegated marble and white colonettes of the dining-room chimney-piece, also supplied by King, was similar in style to the salon chimney-piece. The designs of both chimney-pieces harmonised with the decoration of his rooms. The repetition of the type of Tudor arch used in the former Grand Hall and the Bath House gave a sense of unity to the decorative scheme. However, Nash's work was marred by the inferior quality of his materials. This eye to economy compared unfavourably with the materials lavished on Brown's rooms, while the sombre decoration of Nash's suite must have been in sharp contrast to the sumptuous appearance of the state rooms.

Nash's most important innovation was in the design for the music-room, which was primarily intended as a picture gallery.[80] It was one of the first picture galleries to be specifically designed for top lighting through the use of cast-iron fittings. Nash's estimate provided for 'ye eating [dining] room covered with a lead flat as also ye music room ye latter to have a vertical and domical skylight and ye outside windows to be blanked' (Corsham document 6011, p. 11). The decoration of the ceiling, according to the same estimate (p. 19), entailed 'the fanlights to be surrounded with eliptical enriched spandrils [sic] and enriched frieze round the skylight, and mouldings, the fanlights to be hung with hinges and fastened outside.' The success of Nash's designs is confirmed by the Reverend Richard Warner of Bath, who visited Corsham in the year following the completion of the music room. He described the room as 'a particularly beautiful specimen of grand design, being coved, lighted with oval windows in the coving and glazed with coloured glass.'[81] Pierce Egan described the skylight that Warner

---

[79] This chimney-piece is described in Thomas King's account, now preserved at Corsham, as 'verd antique marble grounds, statuary slips and soffit, Siena columns with statuary Ionic capitals and bases, statuary bedmould and shelf of veined marble slab'. The account of forty guineas suggests that it was made from marbles salvaged from earlier chimney-pieces.

[80] Pierce Egan in 1819 described the Music Room as containing 'nearly twice as many pictures as any in the preceding apartments,' that is, the Cabinet Room and the Picture Gallery, although the Music Room pictures were smaller in size than those in Brown's picture gallery. Egan, *Walks through Bath*, p. 249.

[81] Warner, *Excursions from Bath*, p. 196.

may have overlooked 'as adding to the general appearance of this apartment, which is extremely curious, with stained glass partitions.'[82]

Nash submitted a similar design for a picture gallery to the second Lord Berwick of Attingham Park, Shropshire, *c.* 1810 (see **69**).[83] His first design, which was not executed, resembles the descriptions of the cast-iron coving and oval lights used in the music-room at Corsham. The Attingham design has a continuous ring of oval lights; the number used in the coving at Corsham is not known. At Corsham Nash may have punctured the coving with an intermittant series of oval lights as the skylight, absent in the Attingham design, would have provided additional lighting. In his second Attingham design Nash evolved a simpler method of using sheets of glass placed on the cast-iron half-arches of the coving. Through the use of overhead lighting at Corsham, Nash was able to exclude the side-windows used in Palladian galleries, thereby providing extra wall-space. The design evolved from inserting oval lights into the classical coving of the Palladian picture gallery ceiling, thus creating a clerestory—a device he further expanded and perfected at Attingham. Nash's design for the music-room represents a complete break with the traditional form of Brown's Palladian gallery. By introducing overhead lighting, an innovation made possible through his experimental use of cast iron and his contact with the Coalbrookdale Company, the leading iron founders in England, Nash was able to hang pictures on all four walls. This room was a prototype of the picture galleries erected in the 19th century with the increasing use of cast-iron, and later steel, girders. Nash's design shows an imaginative approach to the problem of gallery design, through what was then a relatively new building material.

---

[82] The term 'skylight' used by Egan may be synonymous with the oval windows in the coving described by Warner. In the absence of designs, Nash's description also leaves an element of doubt as to whether there were one or two different kinds of light fixtures. The cast-iron fittings were supplied by the Coalbrookdale Company (with whom Nash may have been associated, according to Summerson) between September 1798, and March 1799, for £279-3-0½d. Included in the account is an item of twelve guineas for 'drilling, cutting, and fitting the skylight.' Two accounts from the Coalbrookdale Company are preserved at Corsham. Correspondence with the Company does not reveal any records of surviving designs for the fanlight or the oval windows in the coving.

[83] I am indebted to Sir George Trevelyn, Bt., Warden of Attingham Park College, for supplying information concerning Nash's picture gallery. Sir George suggests that the watercolour illustrated in Davis' *The Architecture of John Nash*, plate 38, may possibly be attributed to Augustus Charles Pugin. Nash's second design as executed is illustrated on plate 37.

In a second series of commissions Nash set about to Gothicise the prominent out-buildings around the house, as originally suggested by Wyatt. He added a Gothic dairy to the northwest corner of the house and remodelled Brown's Gothic Bath house, as well as the stableblocks on the side facing the south front of the house; he erected a new coach-house in the Gothic style in the yard on the west side of the stable-blocks.

Among the surviving parts of Nash's work at Corsham are the Gothic dairy and a section of cloister used as a pantry. The cloister is located behind the crenellated north side of the domestic premises facing the pleasure-gardens. Both cloister and dairy originally joined Nash's northwest tower (see **65**). Repton was concerned that the style of the dairy should suit the principal style of the house, whether it be classical or Gothic.[84] The placement of the dairy at Corsham adjoining the Gothic north front accords perfectly with Repton's requirements, although it is more ornamental than utilitarian.

The octagonal design of the dairy was one of Nash's favourite forms. A one-storey structure, it is erected on the site of the former coach-house at the end of the cloister, separated from them by a pinnacle (see **65** and **73**). The communicating doors of the dairy allow one to pass from the south side of the house to the pleasure gardens on the north side of the house. In each section of the octagon, except for the doorways, is a single Gothic window framed with an ogee arch with crockets and finial; clustered colonettes and finials on the corners of the octagon link the arches. The meticulous but not very sculptural carving suggests the craftsman may have laboured on it from John Adey Repton's carefully prepared drawings.

The interior of the dairy, lighted by stained glass, has a plain form of stucco radial vaulting, one of Nash's favourite forms of ceiling decoration.[85] He used the same style of vaulting for the ground-floor ceiling of the Gothic Bath house being remodelled at the same time (see **74**). In the centre of the dairy is an octagonal pedestal holding a small, boat-shaped marble fountain[86] that has a snake's head

---

[84] Repton remarked, 'A Gothic dairy is now become as common an appendage to a place as were formerly the hermitage, the grotto, or Chinese pavilion. Why the dairy should be Gothic when the house is not, I cannot understand, unless it arises from that great source of bad taste to introduce what is called a pretty thing without any reference to its character, situation or uses. . . .' *Observations*, p. 151.

[85] Nash frequently used this form of ceiling for vestibules in his houses, a slightly more elaborate example can be found in the vestibule at Fynone, Pembrokeshire, 1793. See Davis, *The Architecture of John Nash*, plate 53.

[86] The fountain was supplied by Thomas King of Bath for twenty guineas (Corsham archives).

from which water trickled to cool the butter. The adjoining cloister has arches similar to the dairy, each crowned with a single pinnacle and a buttress and pinnacle between each window.

Nash's remodelling of the Gothic Bath house provides evidence of the form of archways that he used for the Grand Hall.[87] He substituted lighter, more graceful Tudor arches, similar to those used in the Grand Hall (see **70** and **74**), for Brown's ogee-shaped arches. The same pendants characteristic of Nash's style were used on the underside of the arches, and on the brackets supporting the Hall balcony. The colonettes supporting the arches were probably also modelled after those in the Hall. Nash removed Brown's arches, incorporating them into the ruin erected at the side of the new coach-house, but left untouched the side ogee arches from Brown's Bath house. The crude form of these ogee arches and the finials on the roof, compared with the more precise carving used on the Gothic dairy, supports the theory that Nash added the crenellation but not the finials to the Bath house (see **56** and **73**). The crenellation, which Nash used elsewhere to decorate parts of the main house, appears to be joined to the blocks carrying Brown's finials on the parapet, making them less prominent than originally intended (see **56**). The wedge-coping below the crenellation may also have been renewed at this time.

The surviving accounts show that Nash took several years to remodel the Bath house. In 1797 the roof was overhauled; this item appears on a statement prepared by Nash for work done that was not estimated. An account from the mason, James Rawlings, details the stonework executed in June, 1797, that included inserting new arches, grooved spandrels, bases for the colonettes and possibly the stringcourse. In October, 1802, the interior walls and ceiling of the ground floor were replastered and a radial form of vaulting installed. The Gothic Bath house is the only building at Corsham that incorporates two Gothic Revival styles in close proximity: the ogee arch, statue-niches, and finials (all of which have similar carving) belong to the earlier Rococo-Gothic of Brown, while the shallow Tudor arch, the crenellation, and radial vaulting are characteristic of Nash's Picturesque Gothic style. The Bath house allows us to compare the essential motifs through which two architects working in the same style achieved quite different effects. The changing motifs mark the evolution of the Gothic Revival style; the basis of Nash's work was more archaeological than the earlier Rococo-Gothic style of Brown.

---

[87] The Bath house erected by Brown (1761–1765), perhaps was in a dilapidated condition by the end of the century. Brown's pavilion had a triple-arched front using an ogee form of arch like those he designed for Tong Castle in 1765.

In the course of Gothicising Corsham, Nash added false gables with a pinnacle above the Elizabethan windows of the stable-blocks facing the house, and a buttress and pinnacle between each window (see **75**). He modelled the Gothic cloister adjoining the dairy on the north side of the house in the same way, adding a Gothic string-course above the level of the stable-block ground-floor windows; it has a profile similar to the one used on the east front. It is not known whether Nash had submitted any plans to Gothicise the main entrance as recommended by Wyatt. The picturesque silhouette of the newly Gothicised stable-block harmonises with the Gothic spire of St Bartholomew's to the east of the main entrance.

An estimate dated 6 March 1798 for the erection of a new coach house for £337-7-10d., marked the last step in the programme to Gothicise the outbuildings. It was to occupy the corner of the western stable-block courtyard next to the 'ruin.' The coach-house, which still exists, is built of cut Bath stone in a very simple design. The front consists of three Tudor arches with double doors and a parapet wall above. The double eagle of the Methuen coat-of-arms stands over a gable above the centre arch.

The unsatisfactory quality of the work executed under Nash's building programme was partially due to the change in methods of contracting from the time when Lancelot Brown enlarged the house. Nash resorted to sub-contracting all the work because it seems that by the end of the century the estate labour-force was not large or skilled enough to carry out any major building-operations. He employed a clerk of works, William Walker, to supervise the contract labour; payments were made by the solicitor, Daniel Clutterbuck of Bradford-on-Avon. Paul Cobb Methuen does not appear to have taken the same close personal interest that his father did in controlling the building operations. Paul Cobb Methuen belonged to the first generation of the family to be brought up at Corsham, and so may have considered it beneath his dignity to engage in such activities. Towards the end of the long Georgian period the members of the new Whig society began to forget that their ancestors themselves had worked to establish the positions the descendants enjoyed.

The end of the century was also a period of inflation in the English economy. The migration of skilled craftsmen from the country to the cities as the Industrial Revolution progressed caused rising wages and a scarcity of skilled labour. The Napoleonic Wars also created a shortage of imported wood and caused prices to rise. The estimates that Nash gave were soon exceeded. There seemed to be difficulty in getting ready money from the solicitor Clutterbuck to pay the labourers, who soon became discontented. Apparently Clutterbuck had been embezzling money from the estate for many years, but was not found out until later.[88] Although Nash made regular visits to Corsham, he had a reputation for lack of attention to detail; inferior materials were used, and he delegated his responsibility to Walker, a person less competent than himself.

The nature of the building did not help. It was flimsy in its conception and hurried in its construction. The contract labourers hired by Nash did not have the skill to build a complex structure like Henry VII's Chapel. For the sake of economy and to lighten the weight of the clerestory windows, wood was substituted for stonework. The woodwork began to shrink and allowed water to enter, spoiling the decorations of the salon below. Also, incorporating cast-iron into the structure was expensive at this time, and does not seem to have been successfully accomplished. As parts of the Elizabethan house were gutted, some of the timber was found to be rotten and had to be replaced. The combination of all these factors resulted in such inferior work that by 1846 the suite of rooms on the north front had become so dilapidated that they had to be demolished.

A chronological account of the building operations will give some indication of the difficulties experienced, especially by Nash's clerk of works, William Walker, who had the unenviable task of trying to coordinate the work of the sub-contractors. Between the autumn of 1796 and December, 1797, Nash remodelled the west wing and realised various minor works. He fitted the new library into the Elizabethan west wing, remodelled the domestic premises and transformed Brown's library into a breakfast-room. He renovated the library and breakfast-room floors. He also carried out repair work on the hothouse; this may have been the greenhouse erected by Brown. After repairing the roof of the Bath House he began to build the ruin located on the west side of the stable-block.

In 1798 the principal work began on the north front and some of the out-buildings. On 17 February Nash left a note at Corsham for Paul Cobb Methuen to apologise for breaking an engagement because he had to visit the Magistrates of Hereford concerning their new gaol (Corsham document 6012). But he did provide a report upon the state of the work, in which he promised to put the new Gothic dairy in hand, make windows in the south basement, demolish the old coach-house, erect a new one near the stable-block, and furnish estimates for all this work. The first thing to be done to the north front would be to shut off the north front wall from the rest of the house, and to enclose enough ground from the north lawn to begin building-operations. In a postscriptum Nash mentioned that 'his clerk will deliver the new plans with this letter in exchange for the old

---

[88] In a letter dated 20 June 1812, written by Lady Christian Boston (Methuen) to her sister-in-law, Mrs Paul Cobb Methuen, a reference was made to the solicitor, Clutterbuck, 'I daresay he has thousands [of pounds] that ought to be Mr Methuen's' (Corsham archives).

ones.' It is not known what this change of design involved. On 31 May, Nash wrote promising to visit Corsham between 10 and 20 June, when 'he hopes to find the dairy and coach house done with, and the new work very forward' (Corsham document 6010). Nash was indeed at Corsham from 17 to 19 June. The construction of the north front must have proceeded rapidly, because the skylight of the music-room was fitted by an employee of the Coalbrookdale Company in December.

Work on the north front continued through 1799. On 17 September, Nash wrote from 28 Dover Street, London, his home and office, that he would visit Corsham after calling at Attingham and Downton Castle. He arrived at Corsham on 9 October (Corsham document 6016). In his acknowledgement to Nash's letter Paul Cobb Methuen complained about the work being carried out in excess of Nash's estimate. In October, Nash was sued by one of his sub-contractors, Whitford the plasterer, for the non-payment of an account. They eventually settled the case by arbitration when Nash wrote to Clutterbuck on 30 January 1800, asking 'to stop the suit so that both solicitors can work out a settlement out of court' (Corsham document 6020). On 30 December 1799, Nash wrote to Paul Cobb Methuen from Glower Castle, 'I propose being at Corsham on Monday next in order to sett on the work in consequence of our new arrangements, and you may depend upon my doing the utmost to forward it' (Corsham document 6017).

In 1800 work started to convert the centre section of the Elizabethan house into the Grand Hall but practical difficulties, unforeseen at the time, followed owing to the structural weakness of the Elizabethan house. Nash visited Corsham on 6 January to supervise the building arrangements for the new Grand Hall. Nevertheless the clerk of works, Walker, wrote to Nash on 19 January about the difficulties he was experiencing with this work (Corsham document 6018). Walker complained that the cellar-joists, too high for the intended stone paving above, had collapsed because of the rubbish falling on them from the first floor. He suggested the timber from the first floor be used for replacements. Also, the width of the hall would have to be reduced by four inches from the drawings submitted, or otherwise cutting into the main walls might weaken the roof-beams. The work proceeded rapidly; upon fixing the hall balconies, Walker asked whether wooden or stone steps should be used for the staircases in order to erect sufficient supports. He recommended the local Painswick stone for paving the hall and use as steps, which Nash approved. Nash neglected to make sufficient structural preparation for carrying heavy loads such as the hall-floor and the staircases despite Walker's timely reminders. The many unexpected complications added considerably to the cost of the alterations.

On 13 May, Nash again wrote to Clutterbuck complaining about the slow payment of accounts, the subject of numerous letters by both Nash and Walker (Corsham document 6028). Shortly afterwards the workmen fixed the staircase railings in the Grand Hall on 19 May. The masons completed the stonework of the north front in May and began to clean the walls. On 8 July, Nash complained again about insufficient funds: the workmen could not be paid and might have to be discharged (Corsham document 6032).

The year 1801 saw most of the interior decoration completed. During February and March workmen erected scaffolding in the Grand Hall and the new suite of rooms in preparation for the stucco-work and painting. The plasterers had substantially completed the stucco-work by 12 August, while the painters were at work until December. The labourers dismantled the scaffolding in August, and Thomas King's masons fixed the chimney-pieces in the salon, dining- and music-rooms. The dairy was plastered at this time. The fast pace of the work combined with the perennial shortage of money to pay the workmen led to discontent: on 22 April 1801, Walker wrote to Nash complaining about his labour troubles and Clutterbuck's negligence (Corsham document 6034). The plasterers were especially rebellious, although their wages had been raised to a guinea and a half per week. The labour situation had deteriorated considerably by 2 May, when Walker wrote to Nash threatening to leave his post; the men were discontented, especially the carpenters, who were resentful because of the plasterers' rise in wages (Corsham document 6036). Nash discharged most of the labour-force in September, leaving a small number of craftsmen to complete the work. On 24 December, he made his last visit in connection with the new work, when he was paid his commission and fees for the year. Accounts for contracting work continued to be discharged by Clutterbuck for work done in 1802, and on 12 November 1803, Nash received the final balance of his account amounting to £924-11-0d. (See Appendix F for a statement of the expenditures on Nash's extension.) Nash's building operations at Corsham were fraught with trouble from the beginning. The dilatory way in which Clutterbuck paid the labourers led to much discontent. Nash made widely-spaced visits to Corsham but left Walker to cope with the daily management of the work. No one represented Paul Cobb Methuen's interest as Boucher had done in the 1760s.

While Nash was engaged upon the architectural improvements at Corsham, Humphry Repton supervised the remodelling of the park, and the construction of the new lake Brown had planned but did not execute. Work on the new lake began in 1797. Repton wrote to Clutterbuck on 25 January, asking him to enter into an agreement with a man Repton had interviewed to build the dam. The engineer, Dudley Clarke, surveyed the site on 23 February and provided a specification. On 25 March, Clutterbuck signed an agreement with James Sharp and John Holmes to build the lake. Repton originally planned islands for the new lake but this idea was later dropped. The lake was completed by 7 May 1798, when Dudley Clarke submitted Sharp's account for payment. Difficulties had arisen in calculating the quantity of earth excavated, the very basis of the contract, but the problem was settled by arbitration. A watercolour design by Repton showing the contour of the embankment is preserved at Corsham. Repton drained the ponds Brown had enlarged as a temporary measure and partially filled in to form a shallow depression.[89] The total cost of this work amounted to £1662. Between October 1798 and May 1799 Repton further increased the surface-area of the lake to 13 acres at an additional cost of £448.

Repton enlarged the western boundary of the park known as the Mynte Wood by 110 acres. He diverted the London to Bath turnpike-road beyond the perimeter of the new enclosure, re-laying it roughly parallel with the North Avenue. The new section of road amounted to 1091 yds. He broke up the old road-surface and planted a screen of trees around the new perimeter of the park that enclosed several large fields. That part of the Mynte Wood lying between the North Avenue and the old turnpike-road was also enlarged, an operation which involved building new boundary-walls and gateways, and laying a new drainage system.

Repton made extensive tree-plantings in the park and pleasure-gardens, mostly deciduous trees to compliment the Gothic silhouette of the house. The accounts from local nurserymen show that Repton planted approximately 2,700 oaks, 1,550 Spanish chestnuts, 600 English elms, 1,450 beeches, 100 sycamores, and a variety of willow-leaved, ilex-leaved, and scarlet oaks.[90] The local nurseries were scoured to provide trees, many of them supplied by Miller and Sweet of St Michael's Hill, Bristol. Writing to Humphry Repton from Grosvenor Street on 26 January 1798, at the conclusion of this operation, Paul Cobb Methuen commented, 'Corsham is no doubt considerably improved in your hands, and we are much pleased, with what you have done there' (Corsham document 6062). Repton's relations with the Methuen family remained friendly despite the later estrangement between them and Nash.

---

[89] On an account from James Sharp, the contractor who excavated the new lake, there is an item 'to excavating and filling in the late poole and forming a valley . . . £261-7-6d.' Corsham archives 6075a; the account is dated 3 April 1797 to 15 June 1799. An aquatint published 1 October 1792, shows a distant view of the east front of the house from the far side of Brown's lake (see **50**).

[90] This list of trees planted by Repton, which does not include all the species purchased at the time, is taken from Stroud, *Humphry Repton*, p. 96.

Repton took the layout that Brown had made in the early 1760s as the basis for his work at Corsham. The park had already begun to assume a mature appearance in the intervening 40 years. Repton improved Brown's plantings by replenishing trees which had died off and adding new clumps and belts of trees. Repton always planted trees of one variety in his clumps, avoiding Brown's frequent practice of using different species in the same clump to obtain a variegated effect. By grouping trees of a single specie, each group a different shade of green, Repton wished to create an effect of separate masses whose silhouettes would distinctly contrast with the turrets, pinnacles and buttresses of the house.

Several visitors to Corsham recorded their impressions of the park following Repton's improvements. The Reverend Richard Warner, who visited Corsham on 14 September 1800, soon after the lake was completed, was reminded of the landscapes of Poussin. Warner's observation indicates how strongly Poussin's paintings influenced the minds of English landscape enthusiasts even at the beginning of the 19th century when the Picturesque movement was fashionable. Warner did not approve of the approach to the south front, 'through an avenue as wide as the front formed by two lofty clipped hedges, embedded in which are bad vases and tasteless statues, extremely incongruous to the Gothic edifice.'[91] Repton often retained old hedges to add an air of antiquity to a building, which was particularly the case with Corsham.

Waagen also paid tribute to Repton's tree-planting when he visited Corsham on a Sunday afternoon in August, 1835:

Wearied with seeing so much [that is, the picture collection], I went at five o'clock to take a walk in the beautiful grounds, where again I enjoyed the noblest southern vegetation, cedars and uncommonly large tulip trees. The rays of the sun, which already began to fall obliquely, produced the most decided masses and the most beautiful effects of light and shade, and the house, seen from the park looked extremely well.[92]

The unmistakably pastoral aspect of the park in the golden evening sunset is reminiscent of the landscapes of Claude. The carefully ordered arcadian setting transposes the idyllic world of Claude's and Poussin's compositions into terms of Gothic architecture and vegetation suited to an English climate.

A visitor to comment exclusively upon the architecture was Sir Richard Colt

---

[91] Warner, *Excursions from Bath*, p. 197.

[92] Waagen, *Works of Art and Artists in England*, III, 109. Commenting upon Dr Waagen, B. Denvir says, 'Not until the advent of the industrious Dr Waagen in the 1830s was there anyone to rival Walpole himself in the expertise of country house viewing.' B. Denvir, 'Visiting Country Houses 200 years ago,' *Country Life*, 25 Oct. 1956, 934–936.

Hoare, the noted Wiltshire antiquarian and owner of the famous gardens at Stourhead, who called at Corsham on Sunday 12 April 1801. Then Nash's north front was gleaming in all its new splendour with no trace yet of its inherent faults in design. Sir Richard noted that 'The front of the mansion is in the Old English style, the other is now finishing in the Late Gothic style under the direction of Mr Nash, an architect who has shown much taste in buildings he has erected of that description.'[93] The 'Old English Style' described the mixed qualities of Elizabethan architecture, which did not fit into the Tudor-Gothic or the Palladian style of Inigo Jones. Sir Richard's comment probably reflected a well informed contemporary opinion of Nash's work.

The Gothic style used at Corsham was very fashionable at this time, especially when we remember that Fonthill, an even larger mansion situated in Wiltshire, represented the very pinnacle of Gothic Revival aspirations. The picturesque exterior of Nash's work and the imposing Grand Hall and Salon must have seemed especially attractive to the Gothic Revival enthusiast. The innovative design of the Music Room must have impressed the connoisseurs who could now view the pictures under conditions unknown to the traditional Palladian gallery of Brown. Corsham at this time was the very acme of contemporary taste. Nash's work at Corsham laid the foundation for his larger commissions for the Prince Regent.

John Nash appears in the role of innovator at Corsham with his use of cast iron for structural and decorative purposes. He was able to design a salon of impressive proportions, carrying two upper floors, which would have been impossible by traditional methods. But his inexperience in handling structural cast iron led later on to difficulties in the music-room that were not easily remedied. Cast iron also provided attractive decorative possibilities, particularly for intricate Gothic moulding. It was highly competitive in price and could be produced more cheaply than hand-craft work in wood. This came at a time when the rising wages of skilled craftsmen made the type of decoration produced in Brown's state rooms almost prohibitive. The effect of the Industrial Revolution was already being felt in displacing the traditional methods of building and craftsmanship by the manufacture of cheaper mass-produced items. The fine quality of Brown's interior decoration is in marked contrast to the 'massy appearance,' as Isaac Ware called it, of Nash's cast iron and painted plaster walls.

Nash's most important contribution was the design of the music-room, which

---

[93] Cardiff City Library, MSS 3.127, Journal of Tours, 1793–1810. Luscombe, Devonshire was erected for Charles Hoare the Banker, a relative of Sir Richard Colt Hoare, by John Nash *c.* 1800. It was one of Nash's most accomplished Picturesque Gothic houses.

we have been able to partially visualise from the architect's estimate and Warner's description. This description confirms beyond doubt that the Corsham design preceded that of Attingham, hitherto regarded as one of the earliest picture galleries to be designed with overhead lighting.

In his Tudor-Gothic design for the north front at Corsham, Nash was content to follow Wyatt's symmetrical solution to the problem of Brown's gallery. Nash was shortly to abandon the principle of symmetry under the influence of Knight's asymmetrical design of Downton Castle; Corsham was one of the last of Nash's designs to preserve a strictly symmetrical form. He seems to have taken little interest in the architectural detail or the theoretical aspect of the alterations. He gave John Adey Repton, who probably worked under his father's guidance, a free hand with the decorative detail.

Humphry Repton's additions and improvements to the park really perfected the skilful layout of Lancelot Brown. Repton's theory of relating the shape of the trees to be planted to the architecture was something Brown never practised. At Corsham Repton was able to use this theory to admirable effect.

Repton's important contribution to the history of English architecture was his theoretical writings. His definition of the Elizabethan style as 'House Gothic,' in 1803, was adopted by contemporary architectural theorists, and not seriously challenged before the Elizabethan Revival in the 1830s. Repton had already formulated this principle in 1796, in his Red Book for Corsham. Repton's definition preserved the south front at Corsham, and must have influenced later Revival architects to retain Elizabethan facades, rather than ruthlessly remodel them in the Gothic style, which had become fashionable for older houses.

Repton provided a theoretical basis for the scheme to Gothicise Corsham, but the suggestion to do so belongs to James Wyatt. Behind Repton's decision to preserve the walls and stables surrounding the south front was a theoretical consideration of the social relationship between the landowner and tenant. Repton wanted to emphasise the social relationship which we know existed during the Tudor period between the country landlord and his tenant. But during the 18th century a growing isolation had emerged between landlord and tenant. The Methuens, lords of the manor, did not encourage the same social contacts with their tenants as had existed in the Tudor period. Nash's Grand Hall was but an empty symbol of a relationship that no longer existed. Repton's theory anticipates a growing nostalgia in English society, as the alienating effects of the Industrial Revolution became more widely felt, for the 'idyllic' social relationship that once subsisted in the countryside during the Tudor period. This mood was expressed in the upsurging Elizabethan Revival in the 1830s, which tried to recapture the florescence of a golden age.

CHAPTER FOUR

Thomas Bellamy's Extension

THE REPAIRS TO NASH'S WORK

The faultiness of Nash's work led in 1846 to the demolition of all of the north front except for Brown's picture gallery and the tower at the west end. Although Nash's extension showed signs of deterioration before 1807, a collapse of a part of the music-room ceiling in that year necessitated immediate repairs. The surveyors, Price, Masters and Stock of Bath and Bristol, surveyed the damage between December 1807 and September 1808, and reported their findings to Paul Cobb Methuen, who had appointed Edward Boodle, a lawyer, to negotiate a settlement with John Nash on the cost of repairing the damage. When Boodle was in London in August 1808 trying to contact John Nash, he also left a note at James Wyatt's London address asking him to visit Corsham and survey Nash's work. Wyatt ignored this request. When in July Lady Boston, Mrs Paul Cobb Methuen's sister-in-law, explained the accident at Corsham to George III, the King replied, 'It was too much the way now to build with unseasoned wood.'[1]

Clutterbuck reported to Paul Cobb Methuen on 25 May 1809, that Nash would arrange to repair three major defects, and agreed to pay for any costs in excess of £200 (Corsham document 6046). The flat roof of the music-room was repaired first. Because the roof was not inclined enough, pools of water formed on it. Water had seeped through the joints of the lead-sheeting and caused the

---

[1] This remark is contained in a letter from Lady Christian Boston (Methuen), Paul Cobb Methuen's sister, to Mrs Methuen, written from Hedsor Lodge, near Windsor, 9 July 1808 (Corsham archives).

ceiling to collapse. Defects and limitations of the skylight and the oval windows set into the cast-iron covings probably contributed to the dampness. After the defective woodwork had been replaced the plasterer, Francis Bernasconi, came from London in 1808 to repair the stucco ceiling and replace the defective mouldings. The timbers of the dining-room and salon roofs were also found to be defective, having been treated originally with a roofing composition that made the deal boards damp. Although this was scraped off and both roofs then covered with sheet-lead, the boards were not permitted to dry out thoroughly before being re-covered with lead, thus hastening the decomposition of the timber. In the Grand Hall the weight of the stone paving laid over the wooden joists caused a part of the flooring to sink. The western staircase settled because insufficient support had been given to a cast-iron pillar carrying the weight of the staircase landing. The surveyors and Nash agreed that brick arches should be erected in the cellar to provide additional support; Paul Cobb Methuen agreed to pay for this addition.

Negotiations for the settlement of the claim dragged on for six years. On 27 November 1812, John Nash submitted his bill for the extra work; he asked £790 for the repairs carried out in 1808 and 1809 (Corsham document 6051). Some items had been replaced with better materials at an additional charge. For arching the cellar he asked £138; for his and his foreman's time he asked £172. On 29 May 1813, Nash, after further negotiations, accepted £300 from Paul Cobb Methuen as a final settlement for his extra work at Corsham (Corsham document 6055).

Nash's initial repairs did not remedy the defect in the music-room ceiling, perhaps because of the inexperience at this time in using structural cast iron. The inherent weakness in the design of the roof-structure and skylight of the music-room still continued to exert pressure to bear upon the ceiling-joists and forced the plaster to crack and collapse. This defect may have been brought about by Nash's ignorance of the properties of cast iron in its rate of expansion, and the resulting pressures exerted upon the adjoining wood and stonework. Although the final discharge had been made in May, 1813, Paul Methuen wrote to Nash on behalf of his father in September, 1815, to complain that the music-room ceiling was collapsing again (Corsham document 6053). Paul Methuen and his father both agreed that this must be attributable to a structural defect rather than poor workmanship. They appealed to Nash's professional integrity to have it put right. In his reply of 22 September Nash remarked, 'I hope my professional character after 26 years is not easily shook,' and continued, 'Architects are responsible for designs and for construction, but not for the knowing or neglect of workmen' (Corsham document 6054). Here again, as in the earlier repairs of 1808–9, Nash sought to shift the responsibility for the defects elsewhere, although he did agree to accept the blame if he were found to be responsible. Nash apologised for being unable to come to Corsham personally on the dates Paul Methuen suggested because he was sitting on committees of the Board of Works and the Forestry Commissioners, but he promised to send the foreman who had supervised the repairs in 1808–9. By now Nash had climbed to a high position in the English architectural profession. It is not known how long this latest defect took to repair.

When Paul Cobb Methuen died in 1816, the latest repairs to the music-room were probably being carried out. The building programme that he had begun after his father's death 21 years earlier had plagued him ever since. Mrs Paul Cobb Methuen, while acknowledging the receipt of an aquatint of Corsham House he had dedicated to her, reiterated to John Britton the family's sentiments towards the disappointing outcome of Nash's extension: 'The large plate is a most beautiful specimen of a miniature drawing, but I fear it is a good deal of a flattering likeness more as we should wish the place to be than it is.'[2] She no doubt felt bitter after spending over £25,000 erecting and restoring Nash's work.

Paul Methuen, who was created a Baron in 1838, inherited Corsham upon the death of his father, Paul Cobb Methuen. Nash's extension steadily deteriorated during the next eight years until Lord Methuen had the north front demolished in 1846, and ordered a new and more substantial stone structure built. He lived long enough to see the completion of this work in 1849. Thomas Bellamy was commissioned as the architect to carry it out. He remodelled the north front in the Elizabethan style, submitted a design for the east front of the house and decorated the interior.

THE HISTORICAL DEVELOPMENT OF THE ELIZABETHAN REVIVAL STYLE

A fashionable taste for the Elizabethan Revival style did not develop until the late 1820s. Isolated examples occurred during the 18th century, but they were not instrumental in creating an interest in the style, partially because the Elizabethan style was considered to be late Gothic without any decided characteristics of its own. The earliest examples of a revival of Elizabethan architecture and decoration have been cited by Pevsner in the work of Vanbrugh and Kent.[3] Pevsner refers to

---

[2] John Britton's correspondence, Devizes Museum, Wiltshire. The aquatint is after a drawing by C. V. Fielding from a sketch by John Britton, published by Robert Havell the Elder, in *A Series of Picturesque Views of Noblemens' and Gentlemens' Seats* (London, 1823).

[3] Nikolaus Pevsner, 'Good King James's Gothic,' *Architectural Review*, 107 (1950), 117–122.

Vanbrugh's plan of Seaton Delaval (1720–29), as the earliest record of a conscious attempt to understand what the Elizabethan and Jacobean styles were about. Summerson also considers Vanbrugh's own house at Esher as purely Jacobean with such Tudor characteristics as octagonal corner-towers.[4] In 1732, Kent provided Jacobean ceilings for the upper rooms of his Tudor gateway erected for George II in the Clock Courtyard, Hampton Court. Later, Brown also built an Elizabethan summer-house at Burghley, *c.* 1756, and his Bath house at Corsham (1761–66), as we have seen, is Elizabethan in form with surviving Rococo-Gothic decoration (see pp. 66–68). Brown's duplication of the south front at Corsham in the original Elizabethan style clearly shows that he recognised the distinctive qualities of the style, although he told Lord Dacre that his Elizabethan work at Burghley was 'Gothick.' The isolated examples of the Elizabethan style in the work of Vanbrugh, Kent and Brown were not sufficiently influential to create a fashionable taste.

The second phase of the Elizabethan Revival might be said to begin with an illustration in Richard Payne Knight's 'Landscape' (1794).[5] The engraving by Thomas Hearne, most probably at Knight's express request, illustrated an Elizabethan house after the style of Hardwick Hall situated in a picturesque landscape. This was to contrast the picturesque landscape with the arcadian landscape and classical architecture of the Brown School with its 'shaven and defac'd lawns and timid clumps of trees' (see p. 83). Knight does not specifically mention the Elizabethan style in his poem, which he probably considered as late Gothic or a 'mixed' style, but it is significant that he should have preferred to illustrate an Elizabethan rather than a Gothic house. Pevsner attributes this choice to the stout vitality of the Elizabethan style as more appropriate for a 'picturesque' landscape than the less robust Rococo-Gothic style of Kent and Walpole, although we do not know Knight's real intention in choosing the Elizabethan style.

A few isolated buildings in the Elizabethan style were erected in the first quarter of the 19th century before the style rose in popularity during the 1830s. Between 1801 and 1811 Sir Jeffry Wyattville, James Wyatt's nephew, added the stable-block to Longleat House in the Elizabethan style. Later, between 1825 and 1827, a Mr Webster of Kendall erected Eshton Hall, Yorkshire, in the Elizabethan style. Peter Frederick Robinson (1776–1858), also designed several large Elizabethan houses in the late 1820s.

---

[4] Summerson, *Architecture in Britain*, p. 168.

[5] Pevsner, 'Good King James's Gothic,' 122.

In the 1830s several important country houses were built or remodelled in the Elizabethan style. In 1835 Anthony Salvin (1799–1881) began the construction of Harlaxton Hall, Lincolnshire (1835– *c.* 1855); its design was based upon Burghley House, Northamptonshire. In 1837 Sir Charles Barry, who also practised in the Gothic and Renaissance styles, remodelled the Georgian Highclere House, Hampshire, in the Elizabethan style for the Earl of Carnarvon. Barry, using Wollaton Hall as his model, refaced the external walls of the house, added a tower to each corner and a higher tower over the main entrance. Highclere, with its bold silhouette and a skyline of balustrades and obelisks dominated by the massive central tower, was more influential than Harlaxton Hall.

During the 1830s the Elizabethan style rivalled the Gothic as the emerging national style of the new Victorian era. For example, the Elizabethan style was an alternative choice designated by the Select Committee which sat in 1835 to draw up rules for the competition to rebuild the Houses of Parliament (destroyed by fire on 12 October 1834).[6] But certain limitations in the Elizabethan style prevented its widespread application to various types of buildings. It was essentially a domestic style of architecture whose range of architectural elements was unsuited for church designs. The Elizabethan style had no ecclesiastical architecture, because church-building had practically ceased after the Reformation in 1537, when the construction of large country mansions was emphasised. The style could not provide a suitable form of church architecture for the series of church-building programmes in the 19th century. Hitchcock also points out that the Elizabethan style did not develop into a major cultural influence throughout the world as had the earlier Greek Revival.[7] The persuasive influence of John Ruskin's *Seven Lamps of Architecture* (1849), and *The Stones of Venice* (1851–53), contributed to the decline of the Elizabethan style from the challenging position it had begun to assume during the second quarter of the 19th century.

THE ARCHITECTURAL THEORY OF THE ELIZABETHAN REVIVAL

The architectural theorists in the 1830s attempted a more precise definition of the Elizabethan-Renaissance style than had earlier theorists of the Gothic Revival. They defined it as the Early Renaissance style of architecture in England, in

---

[6] Charles Robert Cockerall (1788–1863), submitted an Italianate–Elizabethan design for the competition while Anthony Salvin produced a Tudor design. See John Steegman, *Consort of Taste 1830–1870* (London: Sidgwick & Jackson, 1950), p. 122.

[7] Henry Russell Hitchcock, *Early Victorian Architecture in Britain* (New Haven: Yale University Press, 1954), I, 16.

contrast to the current architectural theory that held it to be essentially Late Gothic with some Renaissance elements added. The Elizabethan style was acknowledged a separate identity as a result of their theoretical writing, and from a growing public interest in Elizabethan and Jacobean architecture.

Repton, in his *Observations* of 1803, had placed the Elizabethan style under his third category of 'House Gothic,' claiming that 'the general character and effect of those houses [Elizabethan] is perfectly Gothic.'[8] His reason for doing so was that no domestic models existed in the earlier phases of Gothic architecture suitable for building country mansions. Repton acknowledged a mixture of both Gothic and Renaissance elements in the Elizabethan style, but he rejected the latter as corruptions of the Gothic style. Repton and his sons, John Adey and George Stanley, in 1808, reiterated this theory in their description of the Elizabethan style: 'It is in reality the only Gothic style that can be perfectly characteristic of a palace.'[9] Repton's theory had found a general acceptance among Gothic Revival architectural writers until the 1830s, when several architectural theorists who had become interested in Elizabethan architecture repudiated Repton's argument.

Thomas Warton's description of the Elizabethan style in 1762 was one of the few unbiased definitions. He described it quite logically as one in which neither Gothic nor Renaissance elements predominated: 'However, most of the great buildings of Queen Elizabeth's reign have a style peculiar to themselves, both in form and finishing; where, though much of the Old Gothic is retained and a great part of the new taste is adopted, yet neither predominates.'[10] John Carter (1748–1817) thought it sufficiently important to quote in the introduction to his *Specimens of Gothic Architecture and Ancient Buildings in England* (1786).[11] Carter's *Specimens*, reprinted in 1824 when the Elizabethan Revival was becoming fashionable, was probably influential in making other architectural theorists aware that Repton's principles were debatable.

Humphry Repton was not the only Gothic Revival theorist who made a strong case against the Renaissance qualities of the style to justify copying it for domestic Gothic Revival architecture. Gothic Revival theorists rejected the

---

[8] Repton, *Observations*, p. 190.

[9] As cited in Repton, *Designs for the Pavillon at Brighton*.

[10] Thomas Warton, *Observations on the Fairy Queen of Spenser*, 2nd ed. (London, 1762), II, 186.

[11] John Carter, *Specimens of Gothic Architecture and Ancient Buildings in England* (1786; rpt. London: E. Jeffrey & Son, 1824), I, 5.

Renaissance elements in the Elizabethan style because they felt it created in their aesthetic judgment an undesirable mixture which detracted from their conception of domestic Gothic architecture. In his 'Remarks on the Gothic Architecture and of Modern Imitations,' which accompanied A. W. Pugin's *Specimens of Gothic Architecture* (1821), Edward James Willson drew a sharp distinction between the Gothic and Renaissance styles. He condemned the Elizabethan style for its mixture of Gothic and Renaissance elements, stating that 'nothing could be more barbarous than mixtures for the leading forms of both Gothic and Renaissance where very different manners of building became violated by their being brought into contact.'[12] Willson cited Longleat House as a particular example of this mixture, and argued that when the 'specimens' of different ages became better known the impropriety of blending ornaments of different styles would become less widespread. Willson, who subscribed to a general eclectic and archaeological approach to architecture that developed in the last decade of the Georgian era, saw little merit in Elizabethan architecture because it was neither decidedly Classical nor Gothic. He supported his contention by noting that many modern Gothic mansions are spoiled because their windows were not in the 'true Gothic style,' referring to the use of the Elizabethan form of bay-window in a Gothic house. We see, then, that with the notable exception of John Carter, who had resurrected Thomas Warton's description of the Elizabethan style, architectural theorists in the 1820s generally regarded it as Gothic or at the most an undesirable mixture of Gothic and Renaissance. Repton's definition of the Elizabethan style as House Gothic in 1803 was very influential in formulating this principle at a crucial time in the development of Gothic Revival theory. Repton's theories influenced Pugin and Willson whose *Specimens* provided the major direction of the Gothic Revival theory before Ruskin's *Seven Lamps of Architecture* in 1849.

Opposing Repton and Willson was James Hakewill, a contemporary theorist, who attempted to identify the Elizabethan style in precise terms by rejecting the Gothic elements in the style which they considered its principal qualities. Hakewill's most definitive statement on the Elizabethan style appeared in his *An attempt to determine the exact character of Elizabethan Architecture* (1835). Hakewill defined the Elizabethan style as: 'The pure Elizabethan style is the Cinquecento of Italy, unmixed with Gothic forms or Gothic enrichments.'[13] Thus, according to

---

[12] Augustus Welby Pugin and E. J. Willson, *Specimens of Gothic Architecture, selected from various edifices in England* (London: J. Taylor, 1821), I, i.

[13] James Hakewill, *An attempt to determine the exact character of Elizabethan Architecture* (London: J. Weale, 1835), p. 10.

him, the Elizabethan style was essentially a form of Early Renaissance architecture derived directly from Italy. Working from this theory, Hakewill endeavoured to fix some general rules for the Elizabethan style, as well as 'to relieve it from some of the barbarism [Gothic] with which it was overloaded.' His was the first architectural theory to separate the Elizabethan from the Gothic style, although it was based upon a mistaken assumption.

Hakewill argued that the style of Somerset House and Longleat is derived directly from the cinquecento in Italy rather than, as has been subsequently proved, from French Renaissance architecture.[14] As models for the Italian influence in England he cites Bramante's Palazzi delle Cancellaria (1495) and Giraudi (1504). Hakewill concluded that the Elizabethan style 'admits of no feature of Gothic in its composition; and its elements are entirely drawn from Roman examples, and every moulding is essentially Roman in its curvature,'[15] although he conceded that there were 'exceptions to the true character of the style,' in which Gothic elements are mixed. This statement contradicts Repton, who, in his *Observations* (1803), rejected Renaissance elements as inconsistent with the Gothic style, and cited Somerset House and Longleat as Gothic-style houses where Renaissance elements are found. The latter example was also cited by Willson in 1821 as a mixture of Gothic and Renaissance styles. Both the Elizabethan and Gothic Revival theorists cited the same buildings as important examples to justify their principles, but both tended to place undue emphasis upon decorative detail while lightly passing over more basic elements of planning and proportions. This preoccupation with archaeological detail, which seemed to overshadow planning in aesthetic importance, is attributable to the variety of Revival styles offered in pattern and specimen books. The failure of the late Georgian and Early Victorian periods to develop a contemporary style of architecture created a void which was filled by the Revival styles. Vischer described the eclecticism of the period in 1852[16] as a time 'which knows, respects, and repeats all styles, and can build in any except its own.'

Hakewill also cited other authors whom he thought were mistaken in their attributions, including James Dallaway who had described Somerset House and

---

[14] Girouard, *Robert Smythson*, p. 65.

[15] Hakewill, *Elizabethan Architecture*, p. 7.

[16] Paul Frankl, *The Gothic* (Princeton, N.J.: Princeton University Press, 1960), p. 581. Friedrich Theodor Vischer (1807–87), *Aesthetik oder Wissenschaft des Schonen* (Reutlingen & Leipzig, 1846–57), 6 vols. The volume on architecture appeared in 1852.

Longleat as 'mixed' in style.[17] He also charged that Thomas Pennant in his *London* (London: Faulder, 1790) showed the same ignorance and carelessness in describing Somerset House as 'a mixture of Grecian and Gothic, when at the time the proportions of Greek art were scarcely known . . . the large mezzotint [Somerset House] published by Moss in 1777 will show that, as at Longleate, the arrangement and detail are purely Roman.'[18] The authors who considered the style a mixture usually recognised the presence of Renaissance elements but considered the buildings as Gothic in form.

Hakewill also drew particular attention to the use of the symmetrical plan in Elizabethan architecture. He noted that the buildings were universally square in plan, using pilasters to terminate the angles of the facades. Dallaway in his *Discourses* (1833) also mentioned the importance of symmetrical planning in the Elizabethan house, pointing out 'that no building of consequence was undertaken without a plan previously regulated.'[19] These references to symmetrical planning are important, because it was one of the principal innovations of Elizabethan architecture, derived from contemporary French Renaissance influences and also from such treatises as those of du Cerceau and Serlio. The restatement of this principle was fundamental in designing Elizabethan Revival-style houses, especially as the use of asymmetry had been fashionable since Horace Walpole introduced the Round Tower at Strawberry Hill in 1759, and the castle-mansion designed by Richard Payne Knight (Downton Castle, 1774–78). It would be incompatible for an Elizabethan Revival mansion to follow Gothic Revival planning, once symmetry had been recognised as an important principle of design introduced during the Elizabethan era.

The mistake that Hakewill made in formulating his theory of 1835 was based upon a generally held belief that the architect John of Padua was responsible for the Italian influences at Somerset House and Longleat. Such an attribution may seem strange to us today in view of the scholarship upon both buildings. It was based upon the mistaken assumption that John of Padua was an Italian; Summerson has traced the origin of this misconception to Horace Walpole.[20] The office

---

[17] James Dallaway, *Discourses upon Architecture in England* (London: Samuel Bentley, 1833), p. 106.

[18] Hakewill, *Elizabethan Architecture*, p. 14.

[19] Dallaway, *Discourses*, p. 355.

[20] Horace Walpole, *Anecdotes of Painting in England with some Account of the Principal Artists*, Ralph H. Wornum ed. (London: Chatto & Windus, 1876), I, 128–129. Summerson, *Architecture in Britain*, p. 347, n. 4.

that John of Padua held under Henry VIII was described as 'architectus."[21] In spite of its faults Hakewill's theory was important because it liberated the style from its Gothic bondage and recognised its intrinsic value. The theory justified the use of Elizabethan decorative elements in designs for Elizabethan Revival houses. Hakewill's pioneering work was soon taken up by other architectural theorists, and the result was finally to separate the Elizabethan-Renaissance style from its former Gothic association, and provide it with its own books of 'specimens.'

Among those who published specimen books the most important was Charles James Richardson (1806–71), a fellow of the Royal Institute of British Architects (1838–68) and a colleague of Thomas Bellamy. Richardson was a pupil of Sir John Soane, and between 1845 and 1852 was the master of the architectural class in the school of design at Somerset House. In his *Observations on the Architecture of England during the reigns of Elizabeth and James*, published in 1837, he attributed the change from the Tudor, or Perpendicular, style to the Elizabethan-Renaissance to a taste for classical literature and travelling for pleasure, when men 'viewed with astonishment and delight the splendid works of Italian art, and on their return, could ill-tolerate the gloomy mansions which had sufficed their paternal dwellings.'[22] Richardson and Hakewill both subscribed to the influence of John of Padua on Somerset House and Longleat, where, according to Richardson, the Paduan architect exhibited 'fewer impurities in his design than English architects in later works.'[23] In discussing Somerset House Richardson agreed with Hakewill that its 'arrangements and details are purely Roman.'[24] Although Richardson mentioned contemporary French Renaissance architecture, he did not connect its influence with Somerset House.

Richardson also advanced theories for the most appropriate use of the Elizabethan style. He wrote, 'Whatever merit the style may appear to possess, I

---

[21] John of Padua was first mentioned in 1543 on the court lists of Henry VIII, and his last known date is 1557. Many important Elizabethan buildings have been attributed to him at various times. Summerson considers that Somerset House facade is wholly un-Italian in character. Summerson, *Architecture in Britain*, pp. 6 and 17, n. 2. Walpole, in addition to Somerset House and Longleat, attributes the Gate of Honour, Caius College, Cambridge, to John of Padua. *Anecdotes*, I, 129, n. 1.

[22] Charles James Richardson, *Observations on the Architecture of England during the Reigns of Queen Elizabeth and James I* (London: J. Weale, 1837), p. 3.

[23] Richardson, *Observations*, p. 4.

[24] Richardson, p. 4.

do not desire it should be extensively adopted.'[25] He did not recommend the style for general use; it was more suitable for domestic architecture than public. Richardson's concern for the appropriate country setting for the style, which Hakewill did not share, reflects the influence of Repton's landscape principles. Richardson thought the Elizabethan style most suitable in the countryside 'for the parsonage house, the rural and sequestered villa, amidst coppice and gardens, the Elizabethan style is not only admissable, but in accordance with the genius loci.'[26] Richardson was captivated by the silhouette of the Elizabethan house— its quaint gables, fantastic pinnacles and intricate parapets—much as Repton was with the south front of Corsham. Both would have agreed that the Elizabethan style blended harmoniously with the surrounding countryside. The use of Elizabethan architecture at Corsham conforms with the theories of Repton and Richardson. If the more solid central tower substituted by Bellamy does not catch the sunlight in quite the same way as Nash's octagonal turrets, the silhouette of receding balustrades and pinnacles and the boldly projecting masses of the facade, fulfil Repton's requirements.

ELIZABETHAN REVIVAL 'SPECIMEN' BOOKS AND THE 'OLDEN TIME'
The Elizabethan Revival style was widely disseminated through the publication of books of architectural 'specimens' similar to those of the Gothic Revival, in which important examples of the Elizabethan and Jacobean styles and details of their decoration were illustrated. Two publications that appeared in the 1820s were Peter Frederick Robinson's *Rural Architecture*, 1822 and *Designs for Ornamental Villas*, 1827 in which he illustrated Tudor parsonages that soon became as popular as the Rustic cottage and the Italian villa. Although Robinson's books were Late Georgian pattern books of cottage and villa designs, and not books of architectural 'specimens,' they contributed towards a revival of interest in the Elizabethan Period.[27] Among the most important of these publications were Charles James Richardson's three volumes of architectural details, published between 1837 and 1848. Perhaps the most influential publication for the Elizabethan Revival was Joseph Nash's *Mansions of England in Olden Time* (1839), which was almost exclusively devoted to Elizabethan and Jacobean architecture. In his *History of the Gothic Revival* (1872), Charles Eastlake (1833–1906), acknowledges the popular appeal of Nash's work and credits it with 'reviving a taste for

[25] Richardson, p. 8.

[26] Richardson, p. 8.

[27] Hitchcock, *Early Victorian Architecture*, I, 16 and 30.

that old manorial style of domestic architecture.'[28] Eastlake believed that Joseph Nash had made the public aware of the old national style of building which was neither so gloomy nor uncomfortable as it had once been considered. Steegman points to the unsettling effect of the Industrial Revolution upon late Georgian and early Victorian society when a nostalgia developed for the past, clearly implied in the title of Joseph Nash's *Mansions of England in Olden Time*.[29] Nash included no fewer than 53 houses among his 'mansions' that were either Tudor or Jacobean. The illustrations of people in period-costume created a sense of realism which gave the book its strong sentimental appeal. In literature, Disraeli wrote admiringly of the Tudor Mr Millbank of Hellingsley, one of the characters in *Coningsby* (1844). But Disraeli's novel, like those of other authors who mentioned the Elizabethan Revival, circulated only among a highly educated class of reader. Their writing never won the widespread popular appeal necessary to formulate a supporting literary revival sufficient to create an international influence.[30]

The Industrial Revolution was to have a marked impact upon English architecture in its creation of a new class of wealthy entrepreneur. The established aristocracy, and the working classes who had migrated from the countryside, felt confused by the changing social conditions. The first Lord Methuen's awareness of these social transitions is evidenced by the active part he played in the promotion of the Reform Bill of 1832, which earned him his elevation to the peerage in 1838. Elizabethan architecture reminded the aristocracy and the working classes of an era that reflected the qualities which seemed to have been lost with the changing economic circumstances of both landowner and tenant. The significance of the traditional social position of the landowner had already been discussed by Repton in 1796 in his remodelling of Corsham. This sentimental indulgence was the public's way of escaping from the harsh realities and competitive spirit of the Industrial Revolution to the pleasant idea of an earlier and more hospitable golden age. This concept was created partially by Sir Walter Scott's novels which stimulated a general interest in the medieval period. An event that helped to foster public interest in the medieval world was the Eglinton Tournament, Ayrshire, held on 28 August 1839 and attended by 80,000 people.[31] That it was spoiled by torrential rain did not diminish the enthusiastic publicity

---

[28] Charles L. Eastlake, *A History of the Gothic Revival* (London: Longmans, Green and Company, 1872), p. 237.

[29] Steegman, *Consort of Taste*, p. 90.

[30] Steegman, p. 100.

[31] Steegman, p. 92.

it received in the national press. It so impressed Disraeli that he described it 40 years later in his *Endymion* as the Monfort Tournament.

The taste for a 'Baronial' style, developing in the 1830s, found its medium in the Elizabethan and Jacobean Revival architecture. This revival reached its most enthusiastic pitch in the 1840s, when it mingled with a general sentiment for all things medieval. At this time it co-existed with Gothic Revival style architecture. The publication of John Ruskin's *Seven Lamps of Architecture* in 1849 put an end to this brief spell of popularity. In his Seventh Lamp of Obedience, Ruskin called for a national style, the Gothic, to be used universally, which meant the application of the style to all forms of architecture, both ecclesiastical and secular. Ruskin virtually ousted the Elizabethan style from the popularity it had enjoyed by his insistence upon the use of Gothic in all types of architecture. Later, architectural critics like Charles Eastlake continued to denounce the Elizabethan Revival as a kind of vulgar phenomenon. Although Ruskin had dealt the virtual death-blow, S. C. Hall in 1858 published *Baronial Halls and Ancient Edifices of England*, which has 70 Tudor and Jacobean houses, compared with 53 similar houses illustrated by Joseph Nash. In a few illustrations he depicted people in contemporary Victorian dress, something that Nash had never allowed. Although the Elizabethan Revival was not finally extinguished, Hall's publication failed to recapture the popular sentiment that Nash had aroused in 1839.

Hall's publication was one of a large number of illustrated books of specimens available to architects working in the Elizabethan Revival style. Familiarity with these specimens tended to create a greater uniformity and authenticity in Elizabethan Revival architecture than the Gothic Revival had known, especially since most of the buildings erected were country mansions. The Elizabethan 'Specimen' books were used by the leading architects, including Sir Charles Barry for Highclere in the 1830s.[32] Relying upon 'specimen' books had now become a part of the normal architectural practice for the architectural details of an appropriate Revival style. But while the large number of surviving prototypes led to greater authenticity of detail, the Elizabethan style still lacked the variety of architectural forms necessary for a more general application to public and ecclesiastical architecture, and so could not fulfil Ruskin's demands for a universal style.

When Eastlake wrote his influential book in 1872, the eclectic phase of the Elizabethan Revival had already lost its appeal as a fashionable style with leading architects of the day. Although Eastlake comments upon the widespread influence of Joseph Nash's *Mansions of England*, he ignored the theories of Hakewill,

---

[32] Hitchcock, *Early Victorian Architecture*, I, 187.

Dallaway, and Richardson, and upheld the earlier opinions of Repton and Willson that the Elizabethan style was a 'mixed' form of architecture essentially Gothic in spirit. Eastlake wrote 'Even down to the Reign of James I, the domestic architecture of England, as exemplified in the country houses of the nobility, was Gothic in spirit, and frequently contained more real elements of a Medieval character than many which have been built in modern times by the light of archaeological orthodoxy'.[33] His advocacy of the Gothic influence is confirmed when he writes of Willson's contribution to Pugin's *Specimens*: 'It is to be feared that Mr Willson's share in the preparation of this work has never been thoroughly appreciated . . . he was thoroughly master of his subject both in the antiquarian and artistic aspect.'[34] With this support for Willson it is not surprising that Eastlake thought Nash's illustrations of value only for their pictorial quality. He did not regard them as contributing to our understanding of any architectural theory when he wrote that the Elizabethan style 'appeals at once to the taste and sympathies of many an amateur who may be unable to discriminate nicely between Tudor [Gothic] and Elizabethan work.'[35] He also criticised Joseph Nash for illustrating 'many specimens of the Elizabethan and Jacobean periods which possessed sufficient architectural merit to satisfy a half educated taste but, as models of decorative treatment, were models of all that should be avoided.'[36] Here Eastlake refers to the Renaissance elements in Elizabethan architecture which had led Willson to define the Elizabethan style as 'mixed.'

The architectural theory of the Elizabethan Revival was most influential in the 1830s and 1840s when Bellamy worked at Corsham. Ruskin's plea for a national Gothic style eclipsed the Elizabethan Revival style in popularity. The Ruskinian phase of the Gothic Revival, which created a fashionable taste for Venetian Gothic—vulgarly known as 'the streaky bacon style'— also contributed to the decline of the Elizabethan-Renaissance movement. Interest in Elizabethan architecture took a different course in the 1850s under the influence of Norman Shaw, who introduced asymmetry in his Elizabethan work; because of this the theories of Hakewill, Dallaway and Richardson based upon Renaissance principles and an archaeological approach to the style lost their authority. This strictly eclectic phase of the Elizabethan Revival style, that centred around a small group of Elizabethan mansions, paved the way for the development of the

---

[33] Eastlake, *Gothic Revival*, p. 5.

[34] Eastlake, p. 90.

[35] Eastlake, p. 238.

[36] Eastlake, p. 239.

more informal use of the style in the second half of the century. For a period of two decades the Elizabethan-Renaissance style enjoyed a separate identity from the Gothic Revival. This recognition of the Elizabethan Revival style for its own intrinsic merits fostered an interest in its Renaissance decorative motifs ignored by Gothic Revival purists. Henceforth the Elizabethan-Renaissance style became more eclectic than the Gothic Revival in domestic architecture in the application of its planning and architectural detail.

THOMAS BELLAMY AND THE ALTERATIONS AT CORSHAM COURT

Thomas Bellamy (1800–76), engaged by the first Lord Methuen to reconstruct the north front at Corsham, was a Revival style architect who practised principally in the London area. He was one of the founders of the Royal Institute of British Architects in 1834, of which he was vice-president from 1848 to 1850. He designed and erected public and ecclesiastical buildings in different Revival styles. His churches are the Emanuel, Camberwell Road (which Pevsner describes as a poor effort in the Romanesque style), and St Anne Brookfield, Highgate West Hill (1855) in the Early English Gothic style.[37] His public buildings include King's College Hospital, London, and the Law Fire Insurance Office, Chancery Lane.[38] Bellamy also exhibited designs at the Royal Academy for a Casino, 36 King Street, Covent Garden, in 1816; the Fishmongers' Hall, Albany, Piccadilly in 1832; the National Naval Monument, in 1835; the front of the Fitzwilliam Museum, Cambridge, in 1836; and the Old Well, Cheltenham, in 1837.[39]

The Methuens' reason for choosing Thomas Bellamy as the architect to carry out the alterations at Corsham are not known. Although Bellamy's work was the last major extension to the house, fewer documents have survived concerning it than from the previous extensions of Brown and Nash. Only a few plans and watercolours are preserved at Corsham and in the R.I.B.A. library. Most of the accounts and correspondence were deposited with the solicitors as evidence in a lawsuit brought by the first Lord Methuen's heirs to decide which part of the estate should bear the extra cost of Bellamy's work.[40]

---

[37] Nikolaus Pevsner, *Buildings of London* (Harmondsworth: Penguin Books, 1952), pp. 75 and 358.

[38] For Bellamy's obituary notice, see *The Builder*, 34 (1876), 600.

[39] Graves, *Royal Academy Exhibitors* 1769–1904, I, 176.

[40] The first Lord Methuen died on 11 September 1849, and his second son, Frederick Henry Paul Methuen (1818–1891), succeeded to the title; the second Lord Methuen's elder brother Paul Mildmay Methuen, had died as a young man while in the Diplomatic Service in St Petersburg on 16 July 1837.

The Elizabethan was the most appropriate Revival style for remodelling the exterior of Corsham because the original Elizabethan south front of 1582 had survived intact. The facade was structurally sound; it also presented an imposing appearance as one entered the main gateway. The south front provided Bellamy with an authentic model on which to base his design of the north and east fronts. His extension was not to be a restoration of the plain gabled appearance of the former Elizabethan north front (see **6**), but the creation of a new front using a wall articulation and architectural elements partially derived from the existing Elizabethan south front. Bellamy's problem of designing a new north front and refacing the existing east front was comparatively simple because he was not faced with a conflict of Revival styles as were Brown and Nash.

The scheme to re-model both the north and east fronts of Corsham in the Elizabethan style evolved after Bellamy had submitted his first designs in which only the north front was to be Elizabethan. Bellamy's attitude towards the Elizabethan-Renaissance style is disclosed in a letter 11 December 1849, concerning the choice of chimney-pieces. Towards the end of the building programme Bellamy wrote to the second Lord Methuen, who had recently succeeded to the title, reminding him of this object:

I need hardly remark how important a feature the chimney piece is always found to be in the works of the Elizabethan Age, and what care was bestowed by their architects to render them fitting accessories . . . in the Designs for those at Corsham Court, I have caught the spirit of the Old Architecture and made them to harmonise with that of the respective rooms.[41]

Bellamy's letter indicates that he may have been familiar with Richardson's *Observations*, who also stressed the prominence given by the Elizabethans to their chimney-pieces:

I cannot leave the interior of the house without alluding to the principal feature of every room—the fire place. Certainly, the Elizabethan period was that of its glory, for it exhibited a front imposing as that of an ancient temple, frequently reaching to the ceiling, in two stories, which were alike profusely decorated. It must be in justice admitted, that many of these mantel pieces displayed more skill and taste than the heavy pedimented erections we meet in the rooms of a later period.[42]

The statement in Bellamy's letter that he had caught the spirit of the 'Old Architecture' reflected the current taste for the architecture of the 'Olden Time' of the Elizabethan and Jacobean periods that Joseph Nash had helped to foster. This style was at the height of its popularity in the 1840s when the first Lord Methuen decided to have Corsham remodelled. His decision may have been influenced by

---

[41] Corsham archives.

[42] Richardson, *Observations*, p. 15.

fellow members of the House of Lords who were having their country seats remodelled.[43] The Elizabethan Revival had captured the imagination of the aristocracy and the landed gentry as well as the *nouveau riche* entrepreneurs of the Industrial Revolution. The Methuens were hardly *nouveau riche*; in remodelling Corsham they were probably influenced more by the current taste of some of their fellow peers than by a need to provide a new 'baronial' home for themselves. This decision provided an opportunity to give the exterior a unified appearance in the fashionable Elizabethan style.

THE DESIGNS FOR THE NORTH AND EAST FRONTS

The remains have survived of two sets of designs that Bellamy produced for remodelling the house. In both he preserved the 'symmetrical' design of the Elizabethan house, the importance of which Dallaway and Hakewill had stressed in their writings. The symmetrical plan of the Elizabethan house still survived within the extensions of Brown and Nash. Bellamy substituted for Nash's Grand Hall a system of corridors, and created a new staircase hall projecting from the north side of the house, replacing the staircase at either end of the Grand Hall. To take the place of Nash's recently demolished front, his plans show a new corridor 10 ft wide and 120 ft long running parallel to the exterior of the north wall of the original Elizabethan house. The new staircase hall leads from the centre of the ground-floor corridor to the first floor (see **76** and **84**). In place of Nash's Grand Hall on the south side of the house Bellamy provided a dining- and a billiard-room on the ground floor and bedroom-space on the first floor (the billiard-room was later converted into a music-room). Between the music- and dining-rooms Bellamy inserted a tunnel-vaulted corridor leading from the main entrance on the south side of the house to the new north corridor. In the space formerly occupied by the staircases his first design substituted wide corridors leading to the original Elizabethan east and west wings (see **76**). In this design Bellamy intended to preserve the octagonal ante-room that formed the entrance to Brown's suite of state rooms. In his second design as executed (**79**), Bellamy increased the length of the dining- and music-rooms, reducing the width of the side corridors. This insensitive alteration spoiled the shape of Brown's octagonal room for the sake of the rigid symmetry he imposed in replanning the house.

In his first design Bellamy intended to remodel in the Elizabethan style

---

[43] They included: Lord Holland for whom Barry prepared designs for enlarging Holland House; the Earl of Carnarvon at Highclere House, Hampshire, which Barry remodelled from 1837 to *c.* 1855, and Lord Francis Egerton, the heir to the Duke of Bridgwater, at Worsley Hall, 1840 to 1845, designed by Edward Blore.

Tudor-Gothic towers erected by Nash at either end of the north front (see **65** and **78**). They were built of Bath stone, and were probably structurally sound. On the east front, Bellamy proposed to dismantle Nash's octagonal turrets at either end of the facade and the one on the southwest corner of the west wing. The east front would still have retained its Gothic appearance.

At this stage of the planning Lord Methuen approved an important change in the projected design of the north and east fronts partially due to a decision to provide additional cloakroom and corridor space. The effect of this alteration was to change both fronts into the Elizabethan style. Bellamy made a sketch of a part of the suggested alterations to the north front on his first design for the first floor (see **77**).

From this sketch we can see that he proposed to extend the side corridors to the end of Brown's picture gallery, permitting the use of the existing doorway that formerly led from the picture gallery into Nash's music-room. He also inserted windows at the end of the corridor and provided cloakrooms. To preserve the strict symmetry of the ground-plan, Bellamy placed a similar corridor and cloakrooms on the west end of the north front, as well as a similar arrangement of corridors and cloakrooms on the first floor.

A watercolour has survived (see **78**) which shows Bellamy's first design for the north front. The centre of the facade is occupied by Bellamy's staircase-tower and at either end are Nash's towers remodelled in the Elizabethan style. He intended to dismantle the octagonal turrets and ogee-shaped roofs to the attic level, and terminate the towers with fan-shaped pediments. All Gothic windows were to be replaced with Elizabethan windows, including the oriel windows over-looking Nash's former dining- and music-rooms, though the gables above them were to be retained.

On the east side of the house Bellamy planned to cover the existing facade with three rows of windows. The lower row, and the upper row forming the mezzanine level, were to have Elizabethan cross-shaped mullion windows like those on the north and south fronts. The middle row, which would have corresponded with the coving of the picture gallery, was to be blank with ornamental panels similar in design to the one above the Doric order of the south-front porch (see **13** and **78**). He also intended to add Elizabethan square bay-windows, similar in design to those on the south front, set into slightly projecting wings at either end of the front. Bellamy proposed to remove Nash's crenellation, turrets, oriel window, and all vestiges of Gothic decoration, and to add an elaborate stone balustrade like the one that had originally linked the projecting wings of the Elizabethan south front.

This watercolour does not agree precisely with the first set of plans, and must mark an interim stage between the decision to retain Nash's towers and a proposal to encase the east front in the Elizabethan style.

Another watercolour, now preserved at the R.I.B.A. (**80**), shows the final design of the north front. Nash's towers have been refaced and incorporated into the projecting wings and his gables, which appeared in the earlier watercolour, have been removed. The additional side corridors appear from the exterior as two-storeyed wings surmounted by fan-shaped tympanums. In making the side wings wider in relation to the centre tower, Bellamy's final design has given the north front a greater sense of volume. The design for the east front remains the same. Because of the high cost of the work, the scheme to remodel this front was abandoned, and it was left as Nash had remodelled it, except for the dismantling of the northeast turret (see **62**). Other illustrations supplied by Bellamy, but not illustrated, include a watercolour of the South front with an oblique view of the East front (R.I.B.A. collection), and a watercolour of the North front, second design, as seen in (**80**); the latter watercolour is preserved at Corsham.

Bellamy's design for the north front at Corsham embodied the Elizabethan-Renaissance principle of symmetry to be found in Elizabethan facades. The front consists of a centre tower-block, which is its prominent feature, and projecting side wings. The staircase hall takes up the ground and first floors of the centre tower, its shallow barrel-vaulted ceiling corresponding to the attic level. Above it are two large rooms reached by a staircase from the attic storey. The room overlooking the north front, which has windows on three sides, might be regarded as a 'prospect room,' a distinctive characteristic of Elizabethan architecture.[44] In creating this design, Bellamy followed the same solution as his predecessors, Wyatt and Nash, balancing the projecting north end of Brown's gallery with a similarly projecting wing on the west side. As well, Bellamy created an effect of solidity by his use of compact forms and plain wall-surfaces similar to those in the earlier crenellated design of Wyatt, quite removed from the elegance of Nash's Tudor-Gothic front (see **65**).

The problem posed by the projection of Brown's picture gallery may have led Bellamy to find an Elizabethan example of a similar front with projecting wings. In the absence of documentary evidence we may speculate upon the influence of Burghley House (1577–85).[45] One of the important and prestigious

---

[44] These rooms were often located in towers rising from the centre of the mansion above the main roof level. Important examples occur at Wollaton Hall (1580–88) Gawthorpe Hall (1600–1605), and Hardwick Hall (1590–1597).

[45] For an illustration of the courtyard at Burghley House, Northamptonshire, see Summerson, *Architecture in Britain*, plate 19B.

specimens of the Elizabethan style, it was illustrated by both Nash and Richardson. The courtyard at Burghley resembles Corsham, having a similar disposition of masses: the prominent central tower at Burghley is surmounted by a smaller stone clock-tower and a short steeple. Burghley, in turn, reflects the influence of French Renaissance architecture in its use of the centre-block and side pavilions. Bellamy's design for Corsham seems to be a free adaptation of architectural masses from the Burghley courtyard, chosen to give an authentic Elizabethan appearance to the north front.

Two other houses, both examples of contemporary Elizabethan Revival style, probably also influenced Bellamy's design for the north front. Harlaxton Hall, Lincolnshire, begun by Anthony Salvin in 1835, was modelled after Burghley House (construction continued until around 1855). In 1837, Barry began to remodel Highclere House, Hampshire, in the Elizabethan style, using Wollaton Hall as the model for his alterations. He added four corner-towers to the house, refaced the external walls with rows of mullion windows, and added a high tower on the side containing the main entrance. A like disposition of side-towers and a higher centre-tower was to be the basic element of Bellamy's north front. Architects using the Elizabethan Revival style in the Early Victorian period, like Barry and Bellamy, adopted a very eclectic and archaeological approach towards the designs of their buildings. This attitude was similar to Gothic Revival architects, who considered it desirable to base their designs upon a specific building as Repton had recommended (*Observations*, p. 190).

In the exterior decoration at Corsham Bellamy used authentic Elizabethan-Renaissance architectural elements, some taken directly from the south front. But most of the detail he derived from contemporary books of Elizabethan architectural decoration. The Elizabethan Revivalists, when they separated the style from the late Gothic, published a wealth of Renaissance architectural detail. The publications of Charles James Richardson, Joseph Nash and others provided 'correct models for imitation' just as Pugin's *Specimens* was the copy book for Gothic architectural detail. In 1837, Richardson published his influential *Observations on the Architecture of England during the reigns of Elizabeth and James*. The book included John Adey Repton's engraving of the former Elizabethan screen from the hall at Corsham (see **21**), and illustrations of other Elizabethan houses in the vicinity of Corsham: Claverton Manor (now remodelled); The Hall, Bradford-on-Avon; and Montacute House.[46] A stylistic analysis of Bellamy's decorative

---

[46] Richardson presented copies of his publications to the R.I.B.A. library. He presented a copy of his *Studies of Ornamental Design* (London, 1848) to the Institute on 12 January 1852, according to the note in the front cover of the presentation copy.

motifs at Corsham indicates that he derived them principally from this group of local houses. Bellamy depended mainly on Richardson's illustrations and to a lesser degree on those of Joseph Nash, whose details were not so accurate as Richardson's. Bellamy, as vice-president of the R.I.B.A. from 1848 to 1850, must have known Richardson, who was a member of the Institute. With their common interest in Elizabethan architecture, Bellamy was probably aware that Richardson had published an illustration of the hall screen at Corsham in 1837. Bellamy copied some of the Renaissance motifs from the south front, but what little interior decorative detail had survived from the Elizabethan rooms was destroyed by John Nash in 1800 when he created the Grand Hall.

Bellamy's archaeological treatment of the north front is partially due to the initiative of the stone-mason, Brewer, who testified in the Methuen Family lawsuit that he was delayed because Bellamy did not supply working-drawings on time. Consequently, Brewer himself copied the old stonework of the heavy cornices for the exterior of the north front. The strong horizontal emphasis of the north front was created by the entablatures which were to extend across the east front to join those of the south front. The profiles of the north front windows were also copied from those of the south front.

It seems that Bellamy wished to achieve a sense of unity by using the same decorative motifs on the exterior and interior of the house, a practice also followed by Elizabethan architects. He used consoles for the upper entablatures of the tower, for the piers of the parapet that support the finials, and for the cornice of the stair hall (see **80, 82** and **84**). The parapets are surmounted by balustrades; the design of the balusters is repeated in the balustrade of the main staircase. The roof balustrades have pyramidal finials similar to those used at Montacute House and Burghley.[47] The roof balustrade was used at Somerset House and by Sir John Thynne at Longleat. Bellamy probably derived this motif, and the shell niche, from 'specimen' books, because we have no evidence of their use in the original Elizabethan house at Corsham. However, the shell niches that he introduced externally and internally at Corsham were a common decorative feature of Elizabethan houses. He used them at the corners of the balustrades in the piers that support the finials (see **82**). More prominent niches appear on the first-floor level on the side of the centre tower (see **81**). For the interior he used niches in the north corridor, and in the dining- and music-rooms. Examples of exterior niches can be found at Montacute, Cranborne Manor, and Burghley.

---

[47] For illustrations of the balustrade at Montacute, see Charles James Richardson, *Studies from Old English Mansions, their furniture, gold and silver plate, etc., by an architect* (London, 1841), plate 'Terrace in Garden, Montacute, Somerset.' The facade at Burghley is illustrated in Joseph Nash, *Mansions of England*, III, plate I.

The fan-shaped pediment or tympanum was another important Elizabethan decorative element Bellamy introduced into his designs. He used them on the north front, in his design for the proposed east front, and in the interior for the single doorways of the corridors (see **85**). He took this motif from the porch of the south front.[48] Its use on the exterior at Corsham is an exception among Elizabethan houses, although it was frequently used for interior decoration. Bellamy did not repeat its design; instead he used radial fluting with a baron's coronet in the centre. He could have taken a similar design with radial fluting (without a coronet) from the tympanum of the wooden porch leading into the great chamber at Montacute (illustrated by Richardson, see **83**).[49] Bellamy used three pediments on the north front, all on the same level, one above the window of the north entrance, and the other two over the side wings. The design for the proposed east front shows the bay-windows surmounted by fan-shaped pediments in place of the triangular form of the south front bay-windows. Bellamy made this unique fan-shaped pediment a prominent feature of his design, thus demonstrating that he had given the 'old architecture' of the south front careful study, rather than merely repeating details from a facade at Wollaton, or Burghley, for example.

Bellamy's familiarity with Elizabethan architecture is also shown in the careful attention he gave to the entrance to the north front (see **78**). He used a round arch with a prominent keystone, and side piers or pilasters, variations of which are to be found in other Elizabethan houses, among them The Hall, Bradford-on-Avon, and Wollaton Hall; they come initially from the Strand front of Somerset House.[50] The archway is enframed with attached double Doric columns, having a pilaster on the outer edge. Bellamy's design is a variation of the Doric order of the south porch, where free-standing triple-clustered columns have been used (see **13**). In both cases the entablature is broken forward over the leading

---

[48] The origin of this motif can be traced to French Renaissance architectural treatises such as du Cerceau's *Le premier volume des plus excellants Bastiments de France* (Paris, 1576); the motif had appeared in French architecture as early as 1565.

[49] Richardson illustrates the porch in his *Studies from Old English Mansions*, plate 'Doorway in Great Chamber, Montacute,' now the library. Richardson's original watercolour is preserved in the Victoria and Albert Museum, No. 3304/4.

[50] For illustrations of the entrance to Wollaton Hall, The Hall, Bradford-on-Avon, and the Strand Front of Somerset House, see Girouard, *Robert Smythson*, plates 20, 119, and 120.

columns.[51] This archway set the scale for the archways of the corridors, and for the entrance to the dining- and music-rooms, creating a harmonious relationship between the exterior and interior design.

THE STAIRCASE HALL AND CORRIDORS

Bellamy's design for the staircase hall and corridors at Corsham combined both Elizabethan and Italian Renaissance forms. In it we detect the influence of the 'Anglo-Italian' style introduced by Sir Charles Barry in the 1830s. Barry's first design in this style was the Travellers' Club, Pall Mall (1831), based upon Roman Renaissance palaces.[52] The club established Barry's reputation as the leading English architect in the International Renaissance Revival. In 1839 a monograph by W. H. Leeds on the club helped to disseminate the design among the architectural profession. The interior decoration of this and later Italianate buildings erected by Barry is characterised by elaborate stone-balustraded staircases, corridors partitioned by Roman arches, and stone ashlar walls that reflect the influence of the Italian Renaissance palazzo. Bellamy used these forms in the decoration of the staircase hall at Corsham, combining these Roman Renaissance architectural elements with Elizabethan plasterwork, window profiles, and ceiling panelling. In view of Bellamy's letter to Lord Methuen on 11 December 1849 (see p. 132), we do not know to what extent Bellamy was being consistent in his use of the Elizabethan Revival style at Corsham. However, if Bellamy was aware of Hakewill's theory, possibly through his connections with Richardson, he could justify his design for the staircase hall as Elizabethan-Renaissance, for Hakewill's theory specifically related the Elizabethan-Renaissance style to a direct influence of the Roman Renaissance palaces of Bramante. Barry's style was derived from slightly later Roman Renaissance palaces such as Raphael's Vidoni Caffarelli, *c.* 1515–20, and Antonio da Sangallo the Younger's Farnese (begun *c.* 1535 and completed by Michelangelo *c.* 1548). To accuse Bellamy of mixing his architectural styles at Corsham would be to overlook contemporary architectural theory in the 1840s regarding the source of the Elizabethan-Renaissance style.

The precise origin of Bellamy's design for the staircase hall is not known. The staircase is of the double-return form, and executed in Bath stone, with balusters similar to those of the north parapet. The staircase-landing leading to the

---

[51] In place of the normal Doric entablature there is a plain frieze carved with the Methuen motto 'VIRTUS INVIDIAE SCOPUS.' Bellamy later designed a very similar main entrance for King's College Hospital, London (1856–1860).

[52] For a detailed discussion of the Travellers' Club and illustrations, see Hitchcock, *Early Victorian Architecture*, I, 38–41, and plate II, 19.

first-floor corridors was also executed in Bath stone, and is supported by brackets.[53] The first design (**77**) shows a balcony in front of the triple archway on the first floor, but was altered in the execution by the removal of the balcony to create a greater sensation of spaciousness from the ground floor (see **79**). The walls of the hall and the ground-floor corridors, plain except for a dado moulding, are executed in cut Bath stone, creating an effect of monumentality and permanence quite the opposite of the painted Gothic panelling of Nash's plaster walls. The scale of the hall is reminiscent of Sanderson Miller's Gothic hall at Lacock Abbey, also executed in stone with a similar shallow barrel-vaulted ceiling. In view of the close proximity of Corsham to Lacock (three miles), Bellamy might have taken the Lacock hall as his model. Although Sanderson Miller's hall has a shallow classical barrel-vaulted ceiling covered with a veneer of Gothic fretwork stucco decoration, Bellamy may have interpreted the form of the hall as Renaissance, despite its Gothic decoration, for the purpose of designing a similar one for his staircase at Corsham. Despite his professed intention of creating the 'spirit of the Old Architecture,' he altered the traditional form of the Elizabethan great hall in order to provide a magnificent setting for the principal staircase, probably considering his design 'Elizabethan-Renaissance' under the influence of Hakewill's definition, (see **84**).

The system of archways that Bellamy used for the intersection of hall and corridors, and in the corridors themselves, has a monumentality of form and simplicity of design that we can readily associate with Italian Renaissance architecture. Bellamy combined the round arch and pier in the manner that Alberti preferred in his later architecture.[54] One of the earliest examples of the round arch and pier (with a keystone) in English Renaissance architecture occurred in the principal doorway of the Strand front, Somerset House (1547–52). This use of the archway does not appear consistently in Elizabethan interiors. Similarly, Bellamy's treatment of the corridors can only be explained within the context of Hakewill's definition of an Early Renaissance influence, if we are to regard Bellamy's work at Corsham as an Elizabethan Revival design. Otherwise, his work appears to be a series of eclectic borrowings as a solution to a particular problem of designing a country mansion.

Bellamy's subdivision of the corridors with archways gave them a greater

---

[53] Bellamy used a similar method of supporting the grand staircase of King's College Hospital, a drawing of which is preserved in the R.I.B.A. Collection, No. U8/3.

[54] Rudolf Wittkower, *Architectural Principles in the Age of Humanism* rev. ed. (1962; rpt. New York: Random Press, 1965), pp. 33–37.

sensation of monumentality. The intersections of the hall and north corridor are supported at both levels by three archways (see **79**).[55] The north corridor on both floors is subdivided into three sections by archways, and a pair of archways mark the junction of the north corridor with the east and west corridors. Bellamy inserted shell-niches in the blind archways facing either end of the north corridor, similar in design to those on the exterior of the north tower. The east and west corridors are also subdivided by two archways. The system of archways performs an important function in Bellamy's interior decorative scheme, unifying his extension with the Elizabethan centre-section of the house, (see **86**).

The archways divide the corridors into units of space based upon a modular system associated with Early Renaissance architecture. This arrangement is governed by the ceiling-design of the north corridor, which is subdivided into three sections by the archways. The ceiling of each section has three square coffered designs, similar to the door of the great chamber at Montacute (see **83**).[56] This forms a modular system that Bellamy used to subdivide the side corridors with archways into sections of one, two and three units. The single unit is used at the intersection of the side corridors with the north corridor; two square panels are used for the ceiling compartment at the north end of the side corridors, and three panels at their south ends leading into the former Elizabethan wings.

To what extent the Elizabethan Revivalists were aware of the Renaissance modular system, or whether they were more than superficially interested in Elizabethan proportions and planning, is not certain. Their writings seem to indicate that these problems did not especially interest them. Their main concern was to distinguish the Elizabethan style from its late Gothic association, and to relate the style to the Early Italian Renaissance influence. This was achieved most easily by emphasising the Renaissance architectural detail which appeared to be a more concrete expression of the style than planning and proportions. Their publications concentrated upon decorative detail; plans were rarely discussed or illustrated. Hakewill, identifying the Elizabethan style as dependent upon the direct influence of Early Italian Renaissance architecture, seems to have disregarded or ignored the concepts of Early Renaissance planning. Writing of the drawings of the Elizabethan architect John Thorpe, Hakewill comments, 'no

---

[55] The arches have prominent rims and sunken panels on their undersides, and the piers are edged with semi-circular moulding, and have prominent cornices (see **85**). At the first-floor level the arch rims and mouldings are executed in stucco. Bellamy designed similar piers and arches at King's College Hospital.

[56] The sections of the corridor are not perfect squares, but Bellamy's design gives them an illusion of being square.

principle of beauty of form appears to have guided his compositions [Thorpe's], and the quaint learning of his time seems to have decided the form of his buildings.'[57] Hakewill refers to the architecture of Longleat where 'the arrangement and detail are purely Roman,' but although he may have been aware of the architectural principles of its design, he does not specifically mention them. Dallaway, in his *Discourses* (1833), shows some awareness of proportions in Elizabethan architecture, but does not develop his ideas: 'Domestic architecture had assumed a more scientific character. No building of consequence was undertaken without a plan being previously regulated.'[58] Dallaway also refers to the architectural treatises of John Shute, *The First and Chief Groundes of Architecture* (London, 1563), and Philibert de l'Orme's treatise (1576), but he does not discuss their contents.[59] The references to Italian Renaissance proportions by the Elizabethan Revival theorists were vague. Although there is no tangible evidence, it seems that Bellamy's use of a modular system came from his own knowledge of Renaissance architecture, and the contemporary influence of Barry's Renaissance Palace style. Bellamy probably did not realise that Elizabethan architects only imperfectly understood Renaissance architectural theory.

THE INTERIOR DECORATION

The dining- and music-rooms are the best examples of Bellamy's handling of Elizabethan revival decorative detail. Bellamy formed these rooms from the ground-floor area of Nash's Grand Hall that occupied the centre section of the Elizabethan house. Their ready-made proportions provided an authentic scale upon which to decorate the rooms. They are approximately the size of the original Elizabethan hall, excluding the entrance-corridor that lay behind the screen (see **2**). Today, this area forms the corridor leading from the main entrance on the south front to the north corridor. Bellamy's decorative detail can be identified with such local houses as The Hall, Bradford-on-Avon, and Montacute House, and with other illustrations from Burghley and Hatfield. Bellamy may have assumed that in choosing motifs from local houses erected contemporaneously with Corsham he was introducing authentic local influences. But he does not appear to have used any motifs from Longleat, probably because he was unaware

---

[57] Hakewill, *Elizabethan Architecture*, p. 14.

[58] Dallaway, *Discourses*, p. 355.

[59] Dallaway, *Discourses*, p. 388, n. 8. Lord Burleigh had Philibert de l'Orme's *Nouvelles Inventions* (Paris, 1561) purchased for him in Paris, when the construction of Burghley was nearing completion. Summerson, *Architecture in Britain*, p. 23.

of any stylistic association between the two houses. There is no evidence to suggest that Bellamy visited these houses, but in all probability he took their details principally from the publications of Joseph Nash and Richardson, just as Barry took his detail for Highclere from books of specimens. The reliance upon specimen books at this period to reproduce authentic Elizabethan detail, rather than attempting to use these elements in a new way as we find in the Queen Anne style of the 1860s, reflects the architectural stagnation of the second quarter of the century.

Bellamy paid careful attention to his selection of Elizabethan decorative detail for the dining- and music-rooms—the two principal rooms for which he was responsible. His source for the detail must have come from Elizabethan 'specimen' books, because nothing had survived from the interior decoration of the original house which he could copy. In the dining-room Bellamy used a more elaborate cornice with alternate consoles and strapwork panels than the cornice of the staircase hall (see **87**).[60] He designed the ceiling with an overall pattern of raised circular and square-shaped stucco panels; a source for this design can be found on the staircase archways at Burghley House.[61] On the doors he used raised diamond panels set in rectangular frames; similar panels can be found at The Hall, Bradford-on-Avon, and in designs drawn of the former Elizabethan house at Claverton, near Bath.[62] Set in the stone doorcases of the corridors over the single doorways, Bellamy has placed fan-shaped tympanums similar in design to those used on the north front (see **85**). At the west end of the dining-room is an arched doorway the same height as the corridor archways. This doorway has double rectangular doors beneath a semi-circular wooden tympanum. Similar doors are found in the gallery at Hatfield House.[63] Bellamy inserted a shell-niche in the north and south walls of the dining- and music-rooms on either side of the double doorways; these are shown in the ground-floor plan (see **79**). The shell motif occurs in the interior decoration of such Elizabethan houses as Burghley, Montacute, and The Hall, Bradford-on-Avon. There is no evidence to suggest that Bellamy copied all of his decorative detail from any specific room or house, but his close attention to detail reflects a characteristic of Revival style architects

---

[60] The strapwork panels are similar in design to three pulpit panels from North Cray Church, Kent, in Richardson's *Observations*, plate XXXIV.

[61] For an illustration see Joseph Nash, *Mansions of England*, III, plate II.

[62] Richardson, *Observations*, plate XII, The Door (Claverton Manor). A similar design is found in the panelling at The Hall, Bradford-on-Avon.

[63] For an illustration see Joseph Nash, *Mansions of England*, III, plate XIV, 'The Gallery, Hatfield House.'

in general: their use of authentic detail wherever possible to give their houses an archaeological correctness, even though the structural design, as in the staircase hall, may not be true to the particular Revival style.

It was the choice of chimney-pieces for the dining- and music-rooms, to which reference has been made (p. 132), that provides some indication of Bellamy's intentions in using Elizabethan decorative detail at Corsham. Although his designs for the chimney-pieces have been lost, they were most probably in the elaborate double-tier form that Richardson cited in his *Observations* (p. 15), similar to the Corinthian chimney-piece at Claverton Manor that Richardson recommends as a particularly beautiful example. Claverton Manor, near Bath, was one of the sources for the diamond-shaped door-panels Bellamy used; he may also have taken his chimney-piece design from this house on Richardson's recommendation. Because of the impending lawsuit over the excessive expenditure upon Bellamy's extension, the proposed chimney-pieces were not ordered, and instead Nash's Tudor-Gothic chimney-piece from the salon was installed in the dining-room. This mixture of Gothic and Elizabethan decoration has spoilt the character of the dining-room, and would hardly have met with Repton's approval.

We do have some indication of the type of chimney-pieces Bellamy had in mind for the dining- and music-rooms, since two different examples of his chimney-pieces survive in the corridors. One opposite the dining-room doorway in the west corridor has an elaborate Elizabethan strapwork design containing the Methuen coat-of-arms (see **88**).[64] A pair of less ornate chimney-pieces are situated at either end of the north corridor on the first floor. These chimney-pieces, executed in Bath stone, are not on such a magnificent scale as those proposed for the dining- and music-rooms.

THE BUILDING OPERATION AND LAWSUIT

The circumstances under which the contract was awarded provides some information concerning the building operation. We read in the family lawsuit testimony related to the construction of the extension, and the apportionment of the costs. Bellamy's extension was erected between July 1846 and December 1849 but some of the interior decoration was still incomplete upon the death of the first Lord Methuen in September 1849. Bellamy received estimates from four contractors in

---

[64] A similar form of chimney-piece with strapwork designs formerly in the hall at Claverton Manor was illustrated in Richardson, *Observations*, plate XIV.

the Spring of 1846: William James Brewer of Corsham, Mr Curtis of Streatford, a Mr Mansfield, and Henry Charles Holland of London. The contract for the erection of the new extension was awarded to Holland in July, 1846. At Lord Methuen's request, Bellamy had written to Brewer, who was a builder and mason of Corsham, in May 1846, asking him to submit an estimate, but the estimate was not accepted. On 18 June, Brewer's son entered into an agreement with Holland, without his father's permission, to construct the stonework and make other alterations to the house. Brewer subsequently recognised this agreement and worked as a sub-contractor under Holland. He demolished Nash's extension, and started to excavate the foundations and to erect the new stonework. In April 1847, Holland asked Brewer to terminate the agreement; Brewer complied on 13 April. After paying £2,058 for the work done and for the stock of building materials, Holland took over the building operations himself.

Some details of the building operation occur in the testimony arising from the lawsuit brought by the heirs of the first Lord Methuen over the settlement of the account due to Holland. Brewer stated in testimony that half of the contracted work was completed by April 1847, while the second half, except for some of the internal decoration, had only just been completed (December 1849). According to Brewer, unnecessary excavations into rock and hard clay had increased the cost of building. In his report of June, 1854, the arbitrator for the lawsuit stated that the increase was due to two factors: the first, additional work had been contracted although the amount was not specified at the time; the second, an estimate was submitted of work to be done, in which the omission of certain items of work raised the price. The bills submitted by Holland amounted to £23,000. The cash paid on account (£12,923) left a balance of £10,077 due, of which the arbitrator considered £8,500 should be paid from the estate to Holland.

In other correspondence the Methuens' complained about Bellamy's infrequent visits to Corsham. In December 1848 a dispute broke out between Lord Methuen's steward, Joseph Manning, and Bellamy's clerk of works, Fenton, over the latter's burning sound timber salvaged from the mansion roof over the picture gallery. Intervening in the dispute Lord Methuen's son, the Hon. Frederick Methuen, wrote to Bellamy expressing surprise that the architect should leave the undertaking entirely in the hands of his clerk of works, remarking that Bellamy had visited Corsham only once in the previous eight months. In reply to this letter, which also asked for Fenton's dismissal, Bellamy said he would have difficulty in finding another clerk of works. Later, Bellamy wrote in a letter to Charles Bailey, Lord Methuen's solicitor:

I shall only say that there is no portion of the work for which a drawing and special directions are not given by me, that my visits are timed with reference to the state of particular parts of the work

. . . I have never sought praise in respect of Corsham Court, if it should ultimately be accorded, then I shall be proud of it.[65]

Bellamy's opinion of his own work at Corsham regarding its quality is amply justified by the careful integration ot his design to the existing house, and the attention given to the decorative detail. The stonework of the north front has a permanence and monumental appearance lacking in Nash's work. One weakness of Bellamy's north-front design is the intrusion of the tower with its balustrades and pinnacles above the roof-line of the Elizabethan south front. However, it is easy to forget that Nash's towers and the pinnacles of 'Henry VII's chapel' also pierced the skyline although to a lesser extent.

CONCLUSION

We have seen that Bellamy's choice of design for the north front at Corsham, like those of Wyatt and Nash, was restricted by the projection of Brown's picture gallery. Bellamy's design with its centre tower and projecting side-wings shows the influence of Burghley House. Salvin had earlier modelled his Harlaxton Hall after Burghley, and Barry chose a free adaptation of Wollaton Hall for the more influential design of Highclere, which Bellamy probably knew. Had Bellamy's projected design for the east front at Corsham been executed, it would have given the exterior of the house a unity of style on its three principal fronts it had not possessed before on such a grand scale.

Bellamy's handling of the architectural detail reflects a typical archaeological approach of the Early Victorian period. He used Renaissance elements found on the south front both for the exterior and interior of his extension. When suitable motifs were not available, Bellamy turned to books of Elizabethan Revival 'specimens,' where he seems to have chosen examples principally from nearby Elizabethan houses erected contemporaneously with Corsham. The Elizabethan Revivalists were essentially interested in the decorative elements of the style, for it was the important visible form of the style that expressed its emancipation from the domination of the Gothic Revival style, and Bellamy's use of 'specimen' books was typical of the architectural practice at this time. In domestic architecture the Elizabethan Revival could be more eclectic than the Gothic Revival, for a number of Elizabethan mansions had survived to provide more authentic detail than had been available to Gothic Revival architects in Gothic domestic architecture, forcing them to use ecclesiastic decorative motifs.

It is in the interior of the house that we detect that Bellamy's style is not

---

[65] Corsham archives.

purely Elizabethan Revival. His design for the staircase hall and corridors show the influence of Barry's Anglo-Italian style drawn principally from Roman Renaissance palaces. Examples of this style were to be seen in the newly rising London clubs, and such private houses as Bridgwater and Dorchester House. It was fortuitous that this style should have coincided with the Elizabethan Revival, thereby adding another ingredient to it. Bellamy's work appears as a mixture of two styles, because he introduced an Italian Renaissance modular system nowhere used in Elizabethan architecture in such a logical and sophisticated manner.

This confusion of styles in Bellamy's work is partially accounted for by the Elizabethan Revival theorists who had developed a theory that the Elizabethan style was attributable to a direct Early Italian Renaissance influence upon Elizabethan architecture. We do not know whether Bellamy regarded his design for the staircase hall and corridors as purely Elizabethan within Hakewill's definition of Elizabethan architecture. If he did subscribe to Hakewill's mistaken theory, it would go a long way towards explaining the inconsistency between Bellamy's reference to preserving the Elizabethan character of the house in his chimney-piece designs, and his treatment of the staircase hall.

Bellamy's reference to catching 'the spirit of the Old Architecture' in his letter concerning the chimney-pieces shows his awareness of the popular taste for the Elizabethan period partially attributable to the social disruptions of the Industrial Revolution. He must have read Joseph Nash's popular *Mansions of England in Olden Time*, and probably knew Charles James Richardson through their connections with the R.I.B.A.

Bellamy's extension at Corsham was executed when the Elizabethan Revival style was at the height of its popularity. Ruskin's *Seven Lamps of Architecture*, published in the last year of Bellamy's work at Corsham, was to hasten the end of the strictly archaeological phase of the Elizabethan Revival of which Bellamy's extension at Corsham is a product. The theories of Hakewill, Dallaway and Richardson, upon which Bellamy's work was based, lost their authority when a more asymmetrical form, the Queen Anne style, evolved in the 1860s.

CHAPTER FIVE

Conclusion

In their solutions to the problems posed in the alterations and remodelling carried out on the Elizabethan House, the successive Revival architects who worked at Corsham Court between 1749 and 1849 made a significant contribution to English architectural history. The important aspects of their work at Corsham are revealed in this study. It advances our knowledge of this complex period both from the point of view of actual construction and the theories that governed the designs, and it throws considerable light upon the interaction of patronage and taste.

In this concluding chapter, I will comment on various implications of the study that can be made of Corsham Court because of the surviving elements in the building and the existence of documentary sources: the increasing importance attached to Gothic Revival architectural theory, and the effect of the dual nature of the Elizabethan-Renaissance style upon it, which ensured the preservation of the south front and symmetrical plan at Corsham; the reasons for the growing eclecticism during this period (1749–1849); the implications of John Nash's experimental work in cast iron at Corsham; the eclecticism inherent in the architectural theory of the Elizabethan Revival; and, finally, the social and cultural reasons leading to changes in national taste in architecture as indicated by the patronage and taste of the Methuen Family in their improvements at Corsham.

This study has shown how Gothic Revival architectural theory became an important factor in the preservation of the Elizabethan south front at Corsham at a time when a theoretical controversy hinged around the dual nature of the Elizabethan style with its Gothic and Renaissance elements. In the 1760s, when Brown was commissioned to enlarge the house, no specific theory had been formulated for the Elizabethan style. He recognised the character of the south front, and in doubling the wings made one of the few truly Elizabethan extensions of the century, although he considered the style to be Gothic. In the late 18th century and early 19th century, Gothic Revival architects preferred instead to Gothicise a mansion and the outbuildings. Wyatt advocated this at Corsham in accordance with a method he had formulated through his extensive country-house practice, no doubt influenced by his sweeping restorations of cathedrals. However, Repton's definition of the Elizabethan style as 'House Gothic' ensured at Corsham the preservation of the south front, though the north and east fronts were remodelled in the Tudor-Gothic style, and his definition had an important influence on later theorists such as Pugin. The alterations at Corsham in the last decade of the 18th century reflected an increasing national concern by architects with the application of Gothic Revival theory. By the second quarter of the 19th century this had led to a more authentic use of Gothic architectural detail.

The study of Corsham indicates that the symmetrical plan of the original Elizabethan house survived throughout the alterations within the wall-system. Each successive architect observed the original arrangement in his interior planning. None of the architects, as far as we know, submitted any asymmetrical plans for the alterations of the house; this indicates a persistent regard for the classical symmetry of the original throughout the period of the Gothic Revival. Even Nash, who was elsewhere influenced by the asymmetry of Knight's Downton Castle, followed Wyatt's symmetrical design. Although Walpole had introduced the principle of asymmetry at Strawberry Hill in 1759, many other important Gothic Revival buildings were symmetrical, including the most famous Gothic Revival landmark, the Houses of Parliament, which has a symmetrical river frontage. The preservation of the symmetrical plan at Corsham was an important consideration leading to the integration of Bellamy's design into the existing building.

There was from 1749 to 1849 a growing eclecticism in the use of architectural elements. Brown drew upon a stock of Palladian motifs without undue regard for their archaeological correctness. But with Walpole's Rococo-Gothic innovations at Strawberry Hill, an antiquarian approach to the use of Gothic detail developed. This conception was also stimulated by a national interest in the extensive restorations being made to some of the cathedrals.

The employment of John Adey Repton brought to Corsham a draughtsman with a keen sense for authentic Gothic detail. Repton's work anticipates the concentration upon Gothic architectural motifs which in the 1820s, with Pugin's *Specimens*, contributed towards the eclecticism of the Early Victorian Era. The architectural theory of the Revival styles placed more stress upon the quest for decorative correctness than on planning and design. This eclecticism was even more pronounced in the Elizabethan Revival because a greater number of Elizabethan and Jacobean than Gothic houses survived to provide authentic models. Salvin based his design for Harlaxton, begun in the 1830s, directly upon the Elizabethan Burghley House.

An important innovation in Nash's work at Corsham was his use of cast iron. This study has demonstrated that Nash's experimental work in this media for the coving in the music-room at Corsham preceded the earliest surviving example— the picture gallery at Attingham. Although the structural defects of Nash's design unhappily led to its demolition in 1846, it provided a valuable experience for his subsequent use of cast iron elsewhere. Cast-iron decoration provided a cheap and attractive substitute for the more costly handcraft work at Corsham. By the 1860s a general decline in the quality of industrial design in such work as this led to the movement initiated by William Morris and Philip Webb to reinstate handcraft to improve aesthetic standards of manufactured products.

Most Revival movements in architectural history have been supported by their own body of architectural theory. This study has pointed to the existence of a small corpus of Elizabethan Revival theory. The Elizabethan Revival was one of the last to emerge; it only gradually gained popularity during the late 1820s in competition with the well established Palladian, Rococo and Picturesque Gothic Revivals and the Greek Revival following at the very beginning of the 19th century. The duration of the Elizabethan Revival was relatively short and it did not develop a large body of architectural theory. Nevertheless, what theory it produced is important, because the theorists emancipated the Elizabethan Revival style from its hitherto late Gothic connotations, which had been formulated partially by Repton's theory of the 'House Gothic.'

The small collection of Elizabethan Revival theory stimulated the production in the 1830s of a succession of 'specimen' books in the Elizabethan and Jacobean styles, similar to Pugin's *Specimens* for the Gothic Revival. It led to new concepts of the style by permitting Renaissance decorative detail to be used, with the result that Elizabethan Revival mansions and extensions such as the one at Corsham were more authentic than contemporary Gothic examples. The Elizabethan Revival, despite its popularity, was relatively short-lived, soon eclipsed by Ruskin's persuasive writing upon Gothic architecture and his call for a 'national' style to give some coherent direction to the architecture of the Victorian Era.

With the waning of the Elizabethan Revival style in the 1850s, its principles and values were disregarded by succeeding generations of architects and architectural theorists. But the Elizabethan Revival was the path that led to the new ideas in domestic architecture introduced by W. Eden Nesfield, Norman Shaw and Philip Webb in the 1860s. Between 1853 and 1862, both Nesfield and Shaw worked in the office of Nesfield's uncle, Anthony Salvin, one of the leading architects of the Elizabethan Revival during the 1820s. Their appreciation of the plainer structures and simple masses of Elizabethan architecture enabled them to break decisively with the eclecticism of the Elizabethan Revival and the Gothic Revival and to create what has been subsequently called the 'Queen Anne' style.

They combined Elizabethan and medieval forms with the conventional asymmetrical plan of the Gothic Revival; this had the effect of neutralising the theories of the Elizabethan Revivalists. Symmetrical planning, which had been such an important feature of the Elizabethan Revival style and given prominence by its theorists, no longer had any practical application. In disregarding these rules for domestic planning and using Elizabethan elements in a new way, Nesfield, Shaw, and Webb went beyond Hakewill's Revival theories, and emancipated domestic design from the rigid observation of rules and use of detail associated with the Revival.

The eclecticism of the Early Victorian period is apparent in Bellamy's design for the staircase hall at Corsham. The hall reflects the contemporary taste for sumptuousness to be found in the grandiose interior planning of Barry's Italian Renaissance London clubs. Bellamy does not appear to have shown the same concern to design an authentic Elizabethan hall that he showed towards the chimney-piece designs for the dining- and music-rooms, when he assured the second Lord Methuen of his desire to capture the spirit of the 'old architecture' that is, Elizabethan. Unfortunately, we cannot say to what extent Bellamy was aware of this mixture of closely related Revival styles in his work at Corsham. Both of them were introduced in the 1820s. By the 1840s, unless an architect was attempting to produce an authentic Elizabethan design, Italian Renaissance decorative motifs and forms could easily become incorporated into his building. In this respect, Hakewill's theory of a direct Italian influence in Elizabethan architecture was misleading, because in fact the influence came from the French Renaissance. Elizabethan Revival architectural theory unwittingly contributed towards the mixture of Elizabethan-Renaissance and Anglo-Italian styles which made the Early Victorian Era so characteristically eclectic.

Between 1749 and 1849 a complete reversal of national taste occurred. In 1747, Paul Methuen regarded Wollaton Hall as old-fashioned, whereas in 1846 his grandson, the first Lord Methuen, chose to remodel Corsham in the Elizabethan style. The decision reflects the interaction of changing social conditions upon national styles. In 1749 the Whig landowning class, to which the Methuens belonged, formed their taste for the Palladian style on the Grand Tour. The fashionable taste for the Rococo-Gothic style is attributable to a literary influence that developed within essentially aristocratic circles; it does not reflect a significant change in the social structure. But the established position of aristocratic society from the late 18th century onwards was crumbling before the dynamic impact of the Industrial Revolution. A shift in patronage to a wider section of the public occurred, both of industrial and middle-class origin. At this time the aristocracy and the working-classes both felt insecure and looked back to the social intercourse existing between the landlord and tenant in the countryside during the Elizabethan Era as a kind of Golden Age. Already when Repton discussed this association in his Red Book the spirit persisted although the institution did not.

The architectural preferences current in the Early Victorian Era reflect the ideals and aspirations of a newly industrialised society, one in which the cultural outlook of the Georgian landowning class had been thoroughly subverted. The influence of Sir Walter Scott's Waverley novels acted upon a wider section of the public than Walpole's work and created a nostalgic sentiment for the Medieval Period. The Elizabethan 'specimen' books with their emphasis upon the architecture of the 'Olden Times' catered for this association in architecture. The new patronage preferred an English style of architecture. In the 1830s the Elizabethan style competed with the Gothic to become the national style of the new Victorian Age. There was also a keen interest on the continent in Early Renaissance national styles in which England led the way in the 1820s with the Elizabethan Revival. In France in the 1830s a similar phenomenon occurred when the Early Renaissance style of Francis I became fashionable. The same thing happened slightly later in Germany.

At Corsham, we have seen both the use of discriminating Georgian taste, reflecting the active participation of the first owner in the choice of decoration and styles, and also a rather passive response by later owners who acquiesced in their architect's judgment to the changes in fashion. Paul Methuen's taste had been formulated by the 'national taste' of Burlington's Palladian followers, and their use of the 'right models of perfection.' We are very much aware of Methuen's discerning judgment in the decoration of the state rooms, his employment of Brown and slightly later Robert Adam, and the successful effect that was accomplished. Although Brown was not the most fashionable architect of the day, he showed a correct regard for the existing Elizabethan style in his treatment of the south front and in blending his design for the east front with that of the existing north front. Wyatt and Nash were both architects who built in the fashionable Picturesque Gothic style. Nash's taste in decoration would appear somewhat vulgar to us today, especially his use of cast-iron ornamentation, his substitution of stucco for wood carving, and his painted-plaster walls. Bellamy's extension was fashionable; his design emulated those of Barry and Salvin who were among the initiators of the Elizabethan Revival, and who formulated a national taste for the Elizabethan style. Bellamy's extension, executed in the best quality materials, a hall-mark of Victorian country mansions, somehow seems to lack the convincing taste of Brown's extension. Bellamy's detail seems too correct, and while he was careful to achieve a harmony between the exterior and interior forms, the authentic Elizabethan atmosphere is missing.

With the passing of the Reform Act of 1832 the long reign of Georgian taste ended, giving way to an uneasy eclecticism that Russell Hitchcock has detected in the Early Victorian Era. Perhaps Bellamy's defects are the result of his being unaware of the stylistic influence of Longleat upon Corsham. He might have chosen an harmonious design that was in character with both houses; instead, he drew upon Burghley and Wollaton Hall, erected when Elizabethan architects were more assured in handling their masses.

This study dramatises the changing relationship between the architect and his patron during the century from 1749 to 1849. This is partially attributable to a change in the status of the architect. The man who had in the 18th century depended upon aristocratic commissions became the established professional of a rapidly expanding industrial society. This change led to a more impersonal relationship between the architect and his client. Paul Methuen emerges as a much more cultured and knowledgeable patron than his son and grandson. He was responsible for introducing both Palladian and Rococo-Gothic influences to Corsham. His decision to employ Brown, who was much sought after as a family guest, to landscape the park and add the picture-gallery has given Corsham the principal characteristics we see today. Paul Cobb Methuen did not take the same close interest in Nash's alterations. The Methuens were on friendly terms to some extent with Repton and expressed their pleasure with his work in remodelling the park. On the contrary their relationship with Nash was strained because of his shoddy work. The first Lord Methuen does not seem to have maintained any social relationship with Bellamy. The Industrial Revolution having placed the architect in a secure position with lucrative business in industry and commerce, he did not have to ingratiate himself to the same extent as in the 18th century, and could delegate more of his responsibilities to the clerk of works.

There was also a change in building practice during the same period. The boom in speculative building that accompanied the Industrial Revolution made necessary a more technical organisation of the building industry. Brown's extension in the 1760s was carried out principally by the estate labour-force supervised by Boucher. The organisation of the labour-force was almost a medieval craft tradition. Specialists came from Bristol and London only to do the final work. Under Nash in the late 1790s all construction and decoration was hired out to sub-contractors whose work was supervised by his clerk of works.

In 1846, Bellamy awarded the principal contract to Henry Charles Holland, who was entirely responsible for the construction of the extension, engaging his own sub-contractors. Bellamy's procedure had become the normal building-practice for this kind of work, having evolved in the early 19th century from the speculative method of contracting. These changes resulted in a deterioration in the quality of workmanship of the sub-contractors, who did not have the same personal interest in their work as the craftsmen employed in Brown's state rooms.

The landscape improvements carried out by Brown and Repton reflect the general development in this sphere of activity in the 18th century. Many parks like Corsham were landscaped from an existing field-system and further improvements were often made upon the initial layout. The study has shown the importance given to the relationship between the architecture and the landscape in the theoretical writing of Repton. The choice of the Tudor-Gothic style with its decided vertical emphasis for Nash's extension also fulfilled Repton's requirements for tree-planting. Visitors to Corsham associated the setting of the park with the landscapes of Poussin, which had directly inspired the early work of Brown's, master Kent. The Methuens' choice of landscape-gardeners to carry out or advise upon the architectural extensions indicates the importance attached to the environs of the house. Eighteenth-century landowners were concerned with creating an overall pictorial effect when improving their property, in which every part was subordinate to the whole—the picture collection, furnishings, architecture and landscape. In fact, the earliest anticipation of the Elizabethan Revival was a landscape illustration of an Elizabethan house in Richard Payne Knight's *Landscape* of 1794.

The *raison d'être* for the additions of Brown and Nash was the provision of suitable picture-galleries to house Sir Paul Methuen's picture collection. This study has shown the important change that took place in design from the Palladian style of Brown's gallery to Nash's gallery, a prototype of the later galleries of the Victorian Era which used overhead lighting. With this change in style came a divorce between the association of the gallery and the landscape that appealed to the Georgian sense of taste. Nash's design ushered in a new conception of the picture-gallery to be used solely for viewing the pictures, excluding any vistas across the parkland.

The dominant contribution of this study has been to reveal how the dual nature of the Elizabethan Renaissance style was able to accommodate successive Revival style additions to Corsham Court. Despite the major alterations within the original core of the house, and the additions and modifications to its exterior, the south front and the symmetrical plan continued to exert a powerful influence upon successive architects. Many Elizabethan houses were altered beyond recognition in the 18th century, making it very difficult to add an extension to them in the original style. Bellamy was able to do so at Corsham in 1846, because these two features had always been respected here. Although the present house incorporates Palladian state rooms, a Tudor-Gothic library, and the Elizabethan Revival extension, the essential plan of the house and its two major fronts (north and south) are Elizabethan or in the Revival style. The east front remains an historical record of the alterations of Brown and Nash sandwiched between two monumental Elizabethan facades. The exterior of the house has retained an unmistakable Elizabethan character, although Bellamy was not permitted the remodelling of the east front that would have united the whole, though perhaps to the detriment of Brown's picture gallery.

A related factor in the survival of the Elizabethan house was the increasing importance attached to the definition of the Elizabethan-Renaissance style as 'House Gothic' in Gothic Revival architectural theory. The evidence of a small body of Elizabethan Revival theory contributes to our understanding of the movement, and partially explains the eclectic mixture to be seen in Bellamy's work. Few country houses can provide such a panorama of Revival styles illustrating the complete reversal of taste from the Palladian Revival of the 1740s to the Elizabethan Revival of the 1840s where the alterations were executed within and around the framework of an Elizabethan house.

APPENDIX A

A Genealogy of Members of the Methuen Family

A Genealogy of Members of the Methuen Family who have
owned Corsham Court from 1745 to 1891

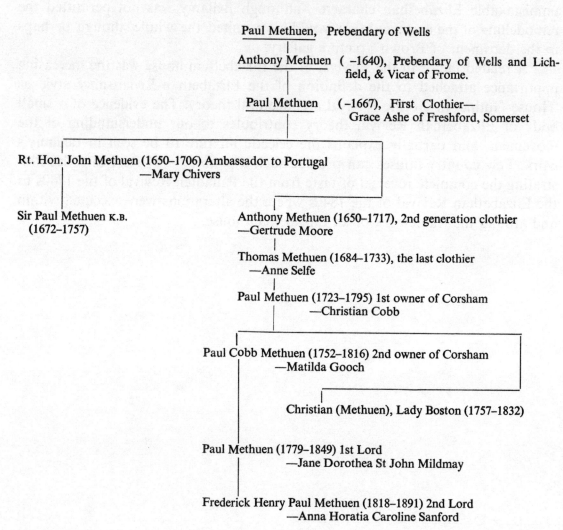

Paul Methuen,   Prebendary of Wells

Anthony Methuen (–1640), Prebendary of Wells and Lichfield, & Vicar of Frome.

Paul Methuen   (–1667), First Clothier—
Grace Ashe of Freshford, Somerset

Rt. Hon. John Methuen (1650–1706) Ambassador to Portugal
—Mary Chivers

Sir Paul Methuen K.B.
(1672–1757)

Anthony Methuen (1650–1717), 2nd generation clothier
—Gertrude Moore

Thomas Methuen (1684–1733), the last clothier
—Anne Selfe

Paul Methuen (1723–1795) 1st owner of Corsham
—Christian Cobb

Paul Cobb Methuen (1752–1816) 2nd owner of Corsham
—Matilda Gooch

Christian (Methuen), Lady Boston (1757–1832)

Paul Methuen (1779–1849) 1st Lord
—Jane Dorothea St John Mildmay

Frederick Henry Paul Methuen (1818–1891) 2nd Lord
—Anna Horatia Caroline Sanford

Sir Paul Methuen's important Architectural Treatises still at Corsham

Barbaro, Daniel. *La Pratica della prespettive*. Venice, 1569.

Barriere, Dominique. *Villa Pamphilia*. Rome, c. 1650. Purchased at Thomas Coke's sale, 52/6d.

Bellori, Giovanni Pietro. *Veteres Augustorum triumphis insignes ex religuiis quae Romae etc.* Rome, 1690. Coke's sale 31/6d.

Borromino, Francesco. *Opera . . . la chiesa, e fabrica della sapienza di Roma con le veduta in prospettiva etc.* Rome, 1720. Coke's sale 25/-.

Bosse, Abraham. *Traite des manieres de dessiner les orders dell' architecture antique en toutes leurs parties etc.* Paris, n.d.

Campbell, Colen. *Vitruvius Britannicus.* 3 vols. London, 1715-1725. Sir Paul Methuen's subscription copies.

Cataneo, Pietro. *L'architettura.* Venice, 1567. Purchased at Thomas Coke's sale, item no. 446.

Desgodetz, Antoine. *Les Edifices antiques de Rome.* Paris, 1682. Coke's sale, item no, 458, 73/6d.

Dosio, Giovanni Antonio. *Urbis Romae aediciorum illustium etc.* Rome, 1569.

du Cerceau, Jacques Androuet. *Livre d' architecture.* Paris, 1561.

——. *Livre d' architecture.* Paris, 1582.

——. *Livres des edifices antiques Romains.* Paris, 1584.

Falda, Giovanni Battista. *Il nuovo teatro delle fabriche etc.* Rome, 1665.

——. *Romanorum fontinalia, etc.* Nuremburg, 1685.

Felibien, Andre. *Recueil historique de la vie et des ouvrages des plus celebres architectes.* Paris, 1687. Coke's sale, item no. 437.

Ferrerio, Pietro. *Palazzi di Roma de piu celebri architetti etc.* Rome, c. 1650.

Fontana, Carlo. *Templum Vaticanum et ipsius origo etc.* Rome, 1694.

——. *Utilissimo tratto dell'acque correnti etc.* Rome, 1696. Coke's sale, item no, 445, 28/-.

Fontana, Domenico. *Della Trasportatione dell'-obelisco Vaticano et delle Fabriche di . . . Papa Sisto V.* Rome, Coke's sale, item no. 448, 45/-.

Kent, William, ed. *The Designs of Inigo Jones consisting of plans and elevations for publick and private buildings, publish'd by William Kent with some additional designs.* London, 1727.

L'Abacco, Antonio. *Libro appartenente a l'architettura, nel qual si figurano alcune notabili antiquita di Roma.* Rome, 1552. Coke's sale, item no. 463, 19/-.

Le Muet, Pierre. *Maniere de bastir pour toutes sortes de personnes.* Paris, 1623. Coke's sale, item no. 457. 11/6d.

Lomazzo, Pado. *Trattato del Arte della pittura scoltura ed architettura.* Milan, 1585. Coke's sale, item 436.

L'Orme, Philbert de. *Ouvres.* Paris, 1626. Coke's sale, item no. 340 (?), 7/6d.

Los Santos, Francisco de. *Description del real monasterio de Lorenzo del Escorial, fabric del . . . rey Filipo II, re edificada por nuestro rey . . . Carlos II, etc.* Madrid, 1681.

Marot, Jean. *Views, plans, elevations & sections of Les Invalides, etc.* Paris.

Montano, Giovanni Battista. *Architettura con diversi ornamenti cavti dall'antico.* Rome, 1636.

Nardini, Famiano. *Roma antica.* Rome, 1666.

Neve, Richard. *The city and country purchaser, and builder's dictionary, or the compleat builders guide etc.* 2nd ed. London, 1726.

Overbeke, Bonaventura von. *Reliquiae antique urbis Romae quarum singulas Innocentio XI, Alexandro VIII, & Innocentio XII, etc.* Amsterdam, 1708. Purchased October 1727, 6 guineas.

Palladio, Andrea. *I Quattro Libri dell'architettura etc.* Coke's sale, item no, 451, 70/-.

Palladio, Andrea. *The Architecture of Andrea Palladio in four books to which are added several notes . . . by Inigo Jones, revis'd by Giacomo Leoni.* 5 vols. London, 1715. Coke's sale, item no. 460, 150/-.

——. *Fabbriche antiche disegnate da Andrea Palladio* (intagliata da P. Fourdrimier), London, 1730.

Le Pautre, Jean and Silvestre, Irael. *Fountains & ornaments in the gardens of Versailles.* Paris, c. 1670-1685.

Perrault, Charles. *Paralle des anciens et des moderns, en ce qui regarde les arts et les sciences.* Nouvelle edition. 2 vols. Paris, 1693.

Perrault, Claude. *Ordannance des cinq especes de colonnes selon la methode des anciens.* Paris, 1683.

Pozzo, Andrea. *Rules and examples of prespective proper for painters and architects etc.* . . . by John Stuart, done into English from the original . . . 1693, by John James. London, 1707. Purchased from Mr Payne, 1743/44, for one guinea.

Rossi, Gio Jacomo. *Belle Fabriche et edifici in prospettivo Roma Moderno, sotto il felici Pontificato di N.S. Papa Alessandrovii.* 1 vol. in 4 pts. Rome, 1665–1669.

Ruggieri, Ferdinando. *Studio d' architettura civile sopra gli ornamenti di porte, etc. di Firenze.* 2 vols. Florence, 1722–1724. Coke's sale, 35/–.

Sadeler, Egidio. *Vestigi delle antichito di Roma, Tivoli, Pozzuolo et altri luochi.* Prague, 1606.

Scammozi, Vincenzo. *Les cinq ordres d'architettura (traduits) par Augustin Charles d'Aviler.* Paris, 1685.

Serlio, Sebastiano. *L'architettura da Sebastiano Serlio.* Venice, 1545. Coke's sale, item no. 454.

Severani da S., *Severino Giovanni, Roma sotterranea: opera postuma . . . compita, disposta & accresciuta del Giovanni Severani de S. Severino* . . . etc. Rome, 1632.

Shaftesbury, Anthony Ashley Cooper. *Characteristicks of men, manners, opinions, times.* 3 vols. 2nd ed. London, 1711.

Vasari, Giorgio. *Vite de'pui eccellenti pittori, scultori e architetti.* 3 vols. Florence, 1568.

Vasari, Giorgio. another ed. Bologna, 1647. Coke's sale, item no. 424, 32/–.

Vignola, Giacomo da. *Les cinque ordini d'architettura et aguintade l'opere etc.* Venice, 1603.

——. *De Columna imperatoris Antonini Pii dissertatio.* Rome, 1705.

Vitruvius, Pollio Marcus. *De Architectura: libra decem etc.* Amsterdam, 1649.

——. *Les dix livres d'architecture etc. avec des notes & des figures par (Claude) Perrault.* 2nd ed. Paris, 1684. Coke's sale, item no, 459, 40/–.

——. An abridgement of the architecture of Vitruvius . . . Studio now Englished. London, 1692.

——. 5th edition. London, 1703.

Wotton, Sir Henry. *Reliquiae Wottonianae: or a collection of . . . characters of sundry personages etc.* 4th ed. London, 1685.

APPENDIX C

Mr Brown's Plans

No. 1 Boucher[1] Elevation of Anti-Room [Octagon Room]

2 Boucher Cieling [sic] of Anti-Room and Dressing Room [Cabinet Room]

3 Boucher Cieling or Bedchamber [State Bedroom]

4 Boucher Mouldings and Margins for Anti-Room, and Dressing Room

5 Boucher Cornice to Dressing Room, fireplace and Plint[h] Base to ditto, and Entablature for Doors in Bedroom and Dressing Room

6 Brown Elevation of Alcove Bedchamber [State Bedroom]

7 Brown Elevation of the Dressing Room [Cabinet Room]

8 Brown Elevation of the Gallery

9 Brown Sketch of Cieling for dit[t]o

10 Boucher Principal storey for Corsham

11 Boucher Plan of the North Front

12 Boucher Dit[t]o of the East or Gallery Front

13 Chimney piece Dressing Room

14 Chimney piece Bedchamber

15 Brown Cold Bath, Room over and Drawings of dit[t]o

---

[1] Dorothy Stroud suggests that either 'Brown' or 'Boucher' appearing against all but two entries indicates who held the drawings when the list was prepared. Stroud *Capability Brown* (new ed. 1975). p. 88.

APPENDIX D

Stocking's Estimate delivered (a note in Paul Methuen's handwriting)

Nov. 11th 1763
    Cornice for Vestibule [Octagon Room] and Cove Bedchamber [State Bedroom] the same as the Hall

No. 5 Cornice for the Dressing [Cabinet Room]— 5 Enrichments at 2s & 2d.

No. 2 The Dressing [Cabinet] Room Cieling [ceiling] Ornaments and mouldings included £38-9-6d.

No. 2 Vestibule [Octagon] Room Cieling [ceiling] ornaments & mouldings £27-19-7d. (Here Paul Methuen seems to have quoted the wrong design number.)

No. 3 The Cove [State] Bedchamber Cieling [ceiling] £18-18-0d. Mr. Brown's valuation of above

Sat. Jan^{ry} 7th 1764
    Dressing [Cabinet] Room Cieling [ceiling] £30-0-0d.

    Vestibule [Octagon Room] Cieling [ceiling] £25-0-0d.

N:B: An Alteration is proposed in the Bedchamber [State] Cieling [ceiling]: when it is fixed it shall be sent.

APPENDIX E

Articles of Agreement between Mr Skeemaker and
Mr Methuen, 22 April 1763

Mr. Skeemaker agrees to finish in the most masterly manner a chimney piece for his Great Room at Corsham of the dimensions of Mr. Brown's plan and according to a model made by the said Mr. Skeemaker and that the whole shall be highly polished and richly carved.

The Chimney piece to be the clearest and best statuary marble as free from flaws as possible, the slabb likewise to be furnished by Mr. Skeemaker of the same statuary marble and to be of a proper proportion to the size of the chimney piece, the coves to be black marble, the boxes, packing it up, sending men to Corsham and charges in setting it up, to be at Mr. Skeemaker's expense. And in consideration of Mr. Skeemaker performing the above Agreement, Mr. Methuen agrees to pay the said Mr. Skeemaker the Sum of Three Hundred and Twenty five pounds and to be at no other expense but for the carriage of the Chimney Piece to Corsham. In witness thereof we have here unto set our hands.

P. METHUEN
P. SCHEEMAKERS

APPENDIX F

*A Provisional Summary of Expenditure of the Building
carried out by John Nash at Corsham*

Expenditure upon John Nash calculated on his commission of 5 per cent.

To January	1798	2,997-19- 3½
31 December	1798	3,163- 0- 0
13 December	1799	4,281-13-11
23 December	1800	4,800- 0- 0
December	1801	4,977- 4- 4
		£20,219-17- 6½

Add: Expenditure summarised by Daniel Clutterbuck for

1802	2,115-13- 3
1803	1,317- 8- 1
1804	67-13- 5
	£23,720-12- 3½

Add: Fees, commission and travelling expenses charged by John Nash

1796–1797	445-12- 6
1798	272- 8- 6
1799	336- 4- 0
1800	371-15- 6
1801	341-19- 6
	£25,488-12- 3½

Add: Humphry Repton's fees, etc.

1795–1797	142-14- 0
1801–1803	31-10- 0
	£25,662-16- 3½

This statement of expenditure for the architectural work carried out is provisional. It would require an accountant to arrive at a precise amount from the bills, receipts, and statements available, some of which duplicate the same items.

Bibliography

Primary Sources: Books

Brayley, Edward Wedlake and John Britton. *The Beauties of England and Wales (Wiltshire)*. Vol. 15. London: Vernor & Hood, 1814.

Britton, John. *The Beauties of Wiltshire*. 3 Vols. London: Vernor & Hood, 1801.

———. *An Historical Account of Corsham House*. London: Joseph Barrett, 1806.

———. *The Autobiography of John Britton*. London, 1850.

Campbell, Colen. *Vitruvius Britannicus*. 3 Vols. London, 1715–1725.

Clark, Lord Kenneth Mackenzie. *The Gothic Revival, an essay in the history of Taste*. 3rd ed., 1928; rpt. London: John Murray, 1962.

Colvin, Howard Montagu. *Biographical Dictionary of English Architects 1660–1840*. London: John Murray, 1954.

Dale, Antony. *James Wyatt*. Oxford: Basil Blackwell, 1956.

Dallaway, Rev. James. *A Series of Discourses upon Architecture in England*. London: Samuel Bentley, 1833.

Davis, Terence. *The Architecture of John Nash*. London: Studio Books, 1960.

———. *John Nash The Prince Regent's Architect*. London: Country Life, 1966.

Eastlake, Charles Lock. *A History of the Gothic Revival*. London: Longmans, Green & Co., 1872.

Egan, Pierce. *Walks through Bath*. Bath, 1819.

Farington, Joseph. *The Farington Diary by Joseph Farington RA*, ed. James Greig, 8 Vols. London: Hutchinson & Co., 1922.

Francis, Alan David. *The Methuens and Portugal 1691–1708*. Cambridge: Cambridge University Press, 1966.

Girouard, Mark. *Robert Smythson and the Architecture of the Elizabethan Era*. London: Country Life, 1966.

Hakewill, James. *Attempt to determine the exact character of Elizabethan Architecture: illustrated by parallels of Dorton House, Hatfield, Longleate, and Wollaton in England*. London: J. Weale, 1835.

Hitchcock, Henry Russell. *Early Victorian Architecture in Britain*. 2 Vols. New Haven: Yale University Press, 1954.

Hussey, Christopher Edward Clive. *English Country Houses: Early Georgian 1715–1760*. London: Country Life, 1955.

Jourdain, Margaret. *The Work of William Kent*. London: Country Life, 1948.

Loudon, John Claudius, ed. *The Landscape Gardening and Landscape Architecture of the Late Humphry Repton*. London: Longman & Co., 1840.

Methuen, Lord Paul Ayshford. *Corsham Court*. Bath: Harding & Curtis, 1951.

———. *Corsham Court*. 1st ed. 1958; 2nd imp. 1965; 2nd Rev. ed. Bristol: Holloway & Son, 1971.

Nash, Joseph. *Mansions of England in Olden Time*. 4 Vols. London: T. M. Lean, 1839–1849.

Pevsner, Nikolaus. *The Building of England—Wiltshire*. Harmondsworth: Penguin Books, 1963.

Pugin, Augustus Welby and Edward James Willson. *Specimens of Gothic Architecture Selected from Various Edifices in England*. 2 Vols. London: J. Taylor, 1821.

Repton, Humphry. *Sketches and Hints on Landscape Gardening*. London: W. Bulmer & Co., 1794.

——. *Observations on the Theory and Practice of Landscape Gardening: Including some Remarks on Grecian and Gothic Architecture.* London: J. Taylor, 1803.

——. *An Enquiry into the Changes in Taste in Landscape Gardening.* London: J. Taylor, 1806.

——. assisted by John Adey Repton. *Fragments on the Theory and Practice of Landscape Gardening: and Remarks on Grecian and Gothic Architecture.* London: J. Taylor, 1816.

Repton, Humphry, Esq., with the assistance of his sons, J. A. Repton and G. S. Repton, Architects. *Designs for the Pavillon at Brighton.* London: J. C. Stadler, 1808.

Richardson, Charles James. *Observations on the Architecture of England during the Reigns of Elizabeth and James I.* London: J. Weale, 1834.

——. *Architectural Remains of the Reigns of Elizabeth and James I.* London: the author, sold by Ackerman & Co., 1840.

——. *Studies from Old English Mansions, their Furniture, Gold, and Silver Plate, etc., by an Architect.* 4 Vols. London: T. McLean, 1841.

Steegman, John. *Consort of Taste 1830–1870.* London: Sidgwick & Jackson, 1950.

Stroud, Dorothy. *Capability Brown.* London: Country Life, 1950. New ed. London: Faber & Faber, 1975.

——. *Humphry Repton.* London: Country Life, 1962.

Summerson, Sir John Newenham. *John Nash: Architect to King George IV.* London: George Allen and Unwin, 1935.

——. *Architecture in Britain 1530–1830.* 5th ed. Harmondsworth: Penguin Books, 1969.

Turnor, Reginald. *James Wyatt.* London: Art & Technics, 1950.

Waagen, Gustav Friedrich. *Works of Art and Artists in England.* 3 Vols., trans. H. E. Lloyd. London: John Murray, 1838.

Warner, Rev. Richard. *Excursions from Bath.* Bath and London, 1801.

Primary Sources: Periodicals

Brakespear, Sir Harold. 'Corsham,' *Wiltshire Archaeological and Natural History Society,* 43 (1927), 511–539.

Gray, H. St George. 'Nathaniel Ireson, Master Builder and Potter.' *Country Life,* 12 April 1939, 423–424.

——. 'Nathaniel Ireson of Wincanton: Master Builder,' *Proceedings of the Somerset Archaeological and Natural History Society,* 87 (1941), 81–84.

Hussey, Christopher Edward Clive. 'Corsham Court, Wiltshire,' *Country Life,* 20 Nov. 1937, 516–521; 27 Nov. 1937, 548–554.

Lang, S. 'The Principles of the Gothic Revival in England,' *Soc. Arch. Historians,* 25 (1966), 240–267.

Pevsner, Nikolaus. 'Good King James's Gothic,' *Architectural Review,* 107 (1950), 117–122.

Stroud, Dorothy. 'The Architectural Works of Lancelot Brown,' *Country Life,* 6 Jan. 1940, 14–18.

Primary Sources: Manuscripts

The Marquess of Bath's Archives, Longleat House, Wiltshire

6711 'The Survey of Mr Henry Smythe's Lands at Cossham,' 1602.

6712 A receipt for the purchase of the Corsham Estate from Thomas Lewis for £11,607, dated 1707.

6713 A letter from the Rev. Francis Richard Greene to the First Viscount Weymouth, dated 18 January 1706/7.

The Bristol Municipal Library, Bristol

222111 Diary of an unknown traveller to Bath and Bristol in 1745.

The Bristol University Library, Bristol

180/4 A letter addressed to an unknown correspondent by Humphry Repton, 13 February 1796.

The British Museum, London

BM add 28,570

Osborne, Francis Godolphin, 5th Duke of Leeds. Tour of the West, 1791.

The Cardiff City Library, Cardiff, Wales

3.127 Hoare, Sir Richard Colt. 'Journal of Tours, 1793–1810.'

The National Trust—Stourhead House Archives, Wiltshire

Correspondence I (1736/37–1835) Two letters from Henry Flitcroft (1697–1769) to Henry Hoare the Younger, dated 18 and 25 August 1744.

Secondary Sources: Books

Adam, Robert. *Ruins of the Palace of Diocletian.* London, 1764.

Allen, Beverly Sprague. *Tides in English Taste.* 2 vols. Cambridge, Mass.; Harvard University Press, 1937.

Angus, William. *Seats of the Nobility and Gentry in Great Britain and Wales in a Collection of Select Views engraved by W. Angus.* London: W. Angus 1787.

Aubrey, John. *The Natural History of Wiltshire,* ed. John Britton. London: Wiltshire Topographical Society, 1847.

——. *Wiltshire: The Topographical Collections of John Aubrey . . . Corrected and Enlarged by John Edward Jackson,* ed. Rev. John Edward Jackson. Devizes: H. Bull, 1875.

Baker, Charles Henry and Muriel Isabella Baker. *The Life and Circumstances of James Brydges, First Duke of Chandos. Patron of Liberal Arts.* Oxford: Clarendon Press, 1949.

Beckford, William Thomas. *Memoirs of William Beckford of Fonthill.* 2 Vols. ed. Cyrus Redding. London: C. J. Skeet, 1859.

Belcher, John and Sir Mervyn Edmund Macartney. *Later Renaissance Architecture in England.* 2 Vols. London: B. T. Batesford, 1901.

Bentham, James and Willis Brown. *History of Gothic and Saxon Architecture in England, Exemplified by Descriptions of the Cathedrals, etc.* London: C. Boydel & Co., 1798.

Bolton, Arthur Thomas. *The Architecture of Robert and James Adam.* 2 Vols. London: Country Life and George Newnes, 1922.

Boorde, Andrew. *A Dyetary of Helth,* ed. F. J. Furnivall. London: Early English Text Society, 1870.

Borenius, Carl Tancred. *A Catalogue of the Pictures at Corsham Court (The Methuen Collection).* London, 1939.

Bowden, Peter J. *The Wool Trade in Tudor and Stuart England.* London: Macmillan, 1962.

Boyce, Benjamin. *The Benevolent Man—A Life of Ralph Allen of Bath.* Cambridge, Mass.: Harvard University Press, 1967.

Brayley, Edward Wedlake. *The History and Antiquities of the Abbey Church of St Peter, Westminster.* 2 Vols. London, 1818.

Britton, John. *The Architectural Antiquities of Great Britain.* 5 Vols. London: Longman & Co., 1807–26.

Burke, Edmund. *A Philosophical Enquiry into the Origin of our Ideas of the Sublime and Beautiful.* 5th ed. London, 1767.

Burnett-Brown, Janet. *Lacock Abbey, Wiltshire.* Bolton: Tillotsons, 1969.

Buxton, John. *Elizabethan Taste.* London: Macmillan, 1963.

Carter, John. *Views of Ancient Buildings in England Drawn in Different Tours and engraved by John Carter.* 6 Vols. London: J. Carter, 1786–93.

——. *Ancient Architecture of England, Part I.* 2 Vols. London, 1795.

——. *Specimens of Gothic Architecture and Ancient Buildings in England.* 4 Vols. 1786; rpt. London: E. Jeffery & Son, 1824.

Castle, Sydney Ernest. *Domestic Architecture of the Tudor Period.* New York: International Casement Co., 1927.

Cerceau, Jacques Androuet du. *Le Premier Volume des plus excellents Bastiments de France.* Paris, 1576.

——. *Architecture pour les Champs.* Paris, 1582.

——. *Livre d'Architecture.* Paris, 1582.

Clarke, Thomas Hutchings. *The Domestic Architecture of the Reigns of Queen Elizabeth and James the First. Illustrated by a Series of Views of English Mansions.* London, 1833.

Climenson, Emily J., ed. *Mrs Philip Lybbe Powys. Passages from the Diaries of, Hardwicke House, Oxon AD 1756 to 1808.* London, 1899.

——. *Mrs Elizabeth Montages. 'The Queen of the Blues.'* London, 1906.

Coke, Thomas. *A Catalogue of Thomas Coke's Auction.* London, 1727/28.

Cook, Olive. *The English House Through Seven Centuries.* London: Nelson, 1968.

Cooke, Robert. *West Country Houses.* Bristol: The Author, 1957.

Cottingham, Lewis Nockalls. *Plans, Elevations, Sections, Details and Views of the Most Magnificent Chapel of King Henry the Seventh at Westminster Abbey Church, with the History of its Foundation and an Authentic Account of its Restoration.* London: Priestley & Weale, 1822.

Cowper, Mary. *Diary of Mary Countess Cowper,* ed. Hon. C. S. Cowper. London: John Murray, 1864.

Dart, Rev. John. *The History and Antiquities of the Cathedral of Canterbury, etc.* London: J. Cole; J. Hoddle, 1726.

——. *Westmonastorium. Or the History and Antiquities of the Abbey Church of St Peter's, Westminster.* London: T. Bowles; J. Bowles, 1742.

Dickins, L. and M. Stanton. *An Eighteenth Century Correspondence.* 8 Vols. London: John Murray, 1910.

Dodsley, Robert. *London and Its Environs Described.* 3 Vols. London: R. & J. Dodsley, 1761.

Evans, Joan. *A History of the Society of Antiquaries.* Oxford, 1956.

Ferriday, Peter, ed. *Victorian Architecture*. London: Johnathan Cape, 1963.

Field, Horace and Michael Bunney. *English Domestic Architecture of the 17th and 18th Centuries*, Rev. ed. London: George Bell & Sons, 1928.

Fleming, John. *Robert Adam and his Circle*. London, 1962.

Frankl, Paul. *The Gothic*. Princeton, New Jersey: Princeton University Press, 1960.

Garner, T. and A. Stratton. *Domestic Architecture of England During the Tudor Period*. 2nd ed. rev. 2 Vols. London: B. T. Battsford, 1929.

Gay, John. *The Poetical Works*. ed. John Underhill, 2 Vols. London: Lawrence and Bullen, 1893.

Gilpin, William. *Observations Relative Chiefly to Picturesque Beauty Made in the Year 1772, on Several Parts of England, Particularly in the Mountains and Lakes of Cumberland and Westmorland*. 2nd. ed., 2 Vols. London, 1788.

——. *Observations on the Western Parts of England, Relative Chiefly to Picturesque Beauty*. 2nd ed. London: T. Cadell and W. Davis, 1808.

Gloag, John Edwards. *Victorian Taste*. London: Adam and Charles Black, 1962.

Gloag, John Edwards and Derek Lawley Bridgwater. *A History of Cast Iron in Architecture*. London: George Allen & Unwin, 1948.

Goodwin, Francis. *Rural Architecture—Second Series of Designs*. London: John Weale, 1835.

Gotch, John Alfred. *Architecture of the Renaissance in England*. 2 Vols. London: B. T. Batsford, 1891–94.

——. *Early Renaissance Architecture in England*. London: B. T. Batsford, 1901.

——. *The English Home from Charles I to George IV*. London: B. T. Batsford, 1918.

Graves, Algernon. *Royal Academy of Arts. A Complete Dictionary of Contributors and their Work from its Foundation in 1769–1904*. 8 Vols. London: Henry Graves & Co., and George Bell & Sons, 1905–6.

Green, Mowbray Aston. *The Eighteenth Century Architecture of Bath*. Bath: George Gregory, 1904.

Grose, Francis. *Antiquities of England and Wales*. 4 Vols. London, 1773–87.

Hall, Samuel Carter. *The Baronial Halls and Picturesque Edifices of England*. London, 1848.

Hartshorne, Emily Sophia. *Memorials of Holdenby*. London and Newcastle-upon-Tyne, 1868.

Harvey, John Hooper. *An Introduction to Tudor Architecture*. London: Art & Technics, 1949.

Havell, Robert the Elder and Robert Havell the Younger. *A Series of Picturesque Views of Noblemen's and Gentlemen's Seats*. London, 1823.

Hearne, Thomas. *Antiquities of Great Britain*. 2 Vols. London: T. Hearne & W. Byrne, 1786.

Heath, Sidney. *The Romance of Symbolism*. London: Francis Griffiths, 1909.

Hervey, Lord John. *Some Materials towards Memoirs of the Reign of King George II*. ed. Romney Sedgwick. London: Eyre & Spottiswoode, 1931.

Holme, Charles, ed. *Old English Mansions Depicted*. New York: Studio, 1915.

Hussey, Christopher Edward Clive. *The Picturesque: Studies in a Point of View*. London: G. P. Putman's Sons, 1927.

——. *English Country Houses: Mid-Georgian, 1760–1800*. London: Country Life, 1956.

——. *English Gardens and Landscapes, 1700–1750*. New York: Funk & Wagnalls, 1967.

Hutton Stanley (pseud. Albert Edward Tilling). *Guide to Arnos Castle, Brislington, Bristol*. Bristol, undated.

Jekyll, Gertrude. *Garden Ornament*. London: Country Life and George Newnes, 1918.

Jordan, Robert Furneaux. *Victorian Architecture*. Harmondsworth: Penguin Books, 1966.

Jourdain, Margaret and Anthony Ayscough. *Country House Baroque*. London: Heywood Hill, Ltd., 1940.

Kendrick, Thomas Downing. *British Antiquity*. London: Methuen & Co., 1950.

Lamb, Edward Buckton. *Studies of Ancient Domestic Architecture, Principally Selected from Original Drawings in the Collection of Sir W. Burrell*. London: J. Weale, 1846.

Langley, Batty and Thomas Langley. *Gothic Architecture Improved by Rules and Proportions in Many Grand Designs*. London, 1742.

Latham, Charles. *In English Homes*. London: Country Life and George Newnes, 1904–09.

Leland, John. *The Itinerary of John Leland the Antiquary*. 9 Vols. ed. Thomas Hearne. Oxford: J. Fletcher, 1745.

——. *Leland's Journey Through Wiltshire AD 1540–42*. ed. Rev. John Edward Jackson. Devizes: H. Bull, 1875.

Manwaring, Elizabeth Wheeler. *Italian Landscape in Eighteenth Century England*. New York: Oxford University Press, 1925.

Martyn, Thomas. *The English Connoisseur. Containing an Account of Whatever is Curious in Painting, Sculpture, etc., in the Palaces and Seats of the Nobility and Principal Gentry of England, both in Town and Country*. 2 Vols. London, 1766.

Meade, Richard Dr. *Bibliotheca Meadiana, sive catalogus librorum*. London, 1754–55.

Methuen, Paul Cobb. *Catalogue of the Books . . . at Corsham House*, 1799. Manuscript.

Methuen, Thomas Anthony. *The Autobiography of Thomas Anthony Methuen*. London: Hatchards, 1870.

Milne, James Lees. *Tudor Renaissance*. London: B. T. Batsford, 1951.

Moir, Esther. *The Discovery of Britain: The English Tourists, 1540 to 1840*. London: Routledge & Kegan Paul, 1964.

Montagu, Lady Mary Wortley. *Works*. ed. Lord Wharncliffe. London: Richard Bentley, 1866.

Morris, Rev. F. O. ed. and Francis Orpen. *A Series of Picturesque Views of Seats of the Noblemen and Gentlemen of Great Britain*. 2 Vols. Leeds, 1855.

Neale, John Preston. *The History of the Abbey Church at Westminster*. 2 Vols. London: J. P. Neale; Hurst, Robinson & Co., 1818.

——. *Views of the Seats of Noblemen and Gentlemen in England, Wales, Scotland and Ireland*. 6 Vols. London: W. H. Reid, 1818–23.

Neve, Richard, ed. *Builder's Dictionary or Gentleman's and Architect's Companion*. 3rd ed. London, 1736.

Oliver, Dr William. *A Practical Dissertation on Bath Waters*. London, 1707.

Oswald, Arthur. *Country Houses of Dorset*. 2nd ed. London: Country Life, 1959.

Overton, Thomas Collins. *The Temple Builder's Most Useful Companion, Being Fifty Entire New Original Designs for Pleasure and Recreation Consisting of Plans, Elevations, and Sections in the Greek, Roman and Gothic Taste*. London, 1766.

Palladio, Andrea. *The Four Books of Architecture*. Trans. Isaac Ware. 1738; rpt. New York: Dover Publications, 1965.

Papworth, Wyatt, ed. *The Dictionary of Architecture*. 8 Vols. London, 1852–92.

——. *Renaissance and Italian Styles of Architecture in Great Britain*. London: B. T. Batsford, 1883.

Pevsner, Nikolaus. *Buildings of London*. Harmondsworth: Penguin Books, 1952.

Ponting, K. G. *History of West of England Cloth Industry*. London: Macdonald, 1957.

Pope, Alexander. *The Correspondence of Alexander Pope*. 5 Vols. ed. George Sherburn. Oxford, 1956.

Pyne, William Henry. *The History of Royal Residences*. 3 Vols. London, 1819.

Ramsay, George Daniel. *The Wiltshire Woollen Industry in the Sixteenth and Seventeenth Centuries*. London: Oxford University Press, 1943.

Repton, Humphry. *Odd Whimes and Miscellanies*. 2 Vols. London, 1804.

Repton, John Adey. *Norwich Cathedral at the End of the Eighteenth Century with Descriptive Notes by William Wilkins*. Ed. Pierce S. Rowland. London: Gregg Press, 1965.

Richardson, Charles James. *The Workman's Guide to the Study of Old English Architecture, etc.* London, 1845.

——. *Studies of Ornamental Design*. London: J. Weale, 1848–52.

——. *Picturesque Designs for Mansions, Villas, Lodges, etc.* London: Atchley & Co., 1870.

——. *The Englishman's House*. London: J. C. Hotten, 1871.

Richardson, Sir Albert Edward. *Georgian England*. London: B. T. Batsford, 1931.

Richardson, Sir Edward Albert and C. Lovett Gill. *Regional Architecture of the West of England*. London: E. Benn, 1924.

Rickman, Thomas. *Attempt to Discriminate the Styles of English Architecture*. London: Longman & Co., 1819.

Robertson, Archibald. *A Topographical Survey of the Great Road from London to Bath: Bristol with Historical and Descriptive Accounts*. 2 Vols. Ed. Horace Walpole. London, 1792.

Robinson, Peter Frederick. *Designs for Ornamental Villas*, 3rd ed. London: H. G. Bohn, 1836.

Serlio, Sebastiano. *Regole generali di architettura sopra le cinque maniere de gli edifici*. Book IV. Venetia, 1537.

Shaw, Henry. *Details of Elizabethan Architecture*. London: W. Pickering, 1839.

Sitwell, Sacheverell. *British Architects and Craftsmen: A Survey of Taste, Design and Style . . . 1600 to 1830*. London: B. T. Batsford, 1945.

Smith, John. *Curonicon Basticum—Commerciale or Memoirs of Wool*. 1747.

Spiker, Samuel Heinrich. *Travels Through England, Wales and Scotland in the Year 1816*. 2 Vols. Trans. from the German. London: J. D. Dewick, 1820.

Steegman, John. *The Rule of Taste from George I to George IV*. London: Macmillan & Co., 1936.

Steele, Sir Richard and others. *The Spectator*. 4 Vols. London: J. M. Dent & Sons, 1930–34.

Storer, James. *A Description of Fonthill Abbey, Wiltshire. Illustrated by Views*. London, 1812.

Stroud, Dorothy. *Henry Holland, His Life and Architecture*. London: Country Life, 1966.

Stutchbury, Howard Edward. *The Architecture of Colen Campbell*. Cambridge, Mass.: Harvard University Press, 1967.

Summerson, Sir John Newenham. *Heavenly Mansions and Other Essays on Architecture*. New York: Scribner, 1950.

——. *Concerning Architecture: Essays on Architectural Writers and Writing Presented to Nikolaus Pevsner*. London, 1968.

——. *The Country Seat—Studies in the History of the British Country House.* Harmondsworth: Penguin Press, 1970.

Sweetman, George. *History of Wincanton.* London: Henry Williams; Wincanton: George Sweetman, 1903.

Tipping, Henry Avary. *English Homes, Early Georgian Period 1714–1760.* London: Country Life, 1921.

——. *English Homes, Late Georgian Period 1760–1820.* London: Country Life, 1921.

——. *The Story of Montacute and Its House.* London: Country Life, 1933.

Toynbee, Paget Jackson, ed. *Strawberry Hill Accounts.* Oxford: Clarendon Press, 1927.

Turnor, Reginald. *Nineteenth Century Architecture in Britain.* London: B. T. Batsford, 1950.

Vardy, John, ed. *Some Designs of Mr Inigo Jones and Mr William Kent.* London, 1744.

Vitruvius, Marcus Pollio. *Ten Books of Architecture,* trans. by Morris Hicky Morgan, 1914; rpt. New York: Dover Publications, 1960.

Voltaire, François Marie Arouet de. *Oeuvres completes.* Paris, 1785.

Vries, Androuet Vedreman de. *Pictores, Statuarii, Architecti.* Antwerp, 1563.

——. *Variae Architecturae Formae.* Antwerp, 1563.

Walpole, Horace. *Catalogues of the Collections of Pictures of the Duke of Devonshire, General Guise, and the Late Sir Paul Methuen.* Twickenham: Strawberry Hill Press, 1760.

——. *Description of Strawberry Hill.* Twickenham: Strawberry Hill Press, 1774.

——. *The Castle of Otranto: A Gothic Story.* 6th ed. London, 1791.

——. *Anecdotes of Painting in England with some Accounts of the Principal Artists.* Ed. Ralph H. Wornum. London: Chatto & Windus, 1876.

——. *The Letters of Horace Walpole.* 8 Vols. Ed. Paget Jackson Toynbee. Oxford, 1903–5.

Ware, Isaac. *A Complete Body of Architecture.* London, 1768.

Warner, Richard Rev. *Walks Through Some of the Western Counties of England.* Bath, 1800.

Warton, Thomas. *Observations on the Fairy Queen of Spenser.* 2nd ed. London, 1762.

Warton, Rev. T., Rev. J. Bentham, Captain Grose, and Rev. J. Milner. *Essays on Gothic Architecture.* London, 1800.

Wasserman, Earl Reeves. *Aspects of the Eighteenth Century.* Baltimore: Johns Hopkins Press, 1965.

Watts, William. *The Seats of the Nobility and Gentry in a Collection of the Most Interesting and Picturesque Views etc.* 4 Vols. London, 1819.

Whiffen, Marcus. *Thomas Archer.* London: Art & Technics, 1950.

——. *An Introduction to Elizabethan and Jacobean Architecture.* London: Art & Technics, 1952.

Whinney, Margaret. *Renaissance Architecture in England.* London: Longmans, Green & Co., 1952.

Whinney, Margaret and Oliver Millar, *English Art 1625–1714.* Oxford: Clarendon Press, 1957.

Witham, Rev. George. *The History of Lacock Abbey or, Locus Beatae Mariae from Dugdale Stevens etc. with Additions on the Present State of the Abbey.* Lacock, 1806.

Wittkower, Rudolf. *Architectural Principles in the Age of Humanism.* 1962; rpt. New York: Random Press, 1965.

Secondary Sources: Periodicals

Anon. 'Corsham Court, Wiltshire, the Residence of Lord and Lady Methuen,' *The Antique Collector,* July–Aug. 1948, pp. 117–24.

Anon. 'Rococo Gothic Walpole, Bentley and Strawberry Hill,' *Architectural Review,* 98, December, 1945, pp. 151–54.

Bowden, Peter J. 'The Wool Supply and the Woollen Industry.' *Economic History Review,* 2nd Ser., 9, No.1 (1956), pp. 44–58.

Boyer, Abel, ed. 'Obituary Notice of Thomas Coke.' *The Political State of Great Britain,* 33 (January–June 1727), p. 528.

Brockman, H. A. N. 'Fonthill Abbey.' *Architectural Review,* 95 (1944), pp. 149–56.

Anon. 'Bridge Foundations: New Westminster Bridge,' *The Builder* 23 August 1856, p. 454.

Clapham, A. 'The Survival of the Gothic in the Seventeenth Century.' *Archaeological Journal,* 106 (1949), supplement.

Cornforth, John. 'An Early Country House Enthusiast,' *Country Life,* 8 March 1962, pp. 526–28.

Anon. 'Ven House, Somerset.' *Country Life,* 24 June 1911, pp. 924–34.

Denvir, B. 'Visiting Country Houses 200 Years Ago.' *Country Life,* 25 October 1956, pp. 934–36.

Anon. 'Obituary Notice of John Adey Repton.' *The Gentleman's Magazine,* 3rd Series, 10 (1866), pp. 107–10.

Girouard, Mark. 'New Light on Longleat—Allen Maynard: A French Sculptor in England in the 16th Century.' *Country Life,* 20 September 1956, pp. 594–97.

——. 'The Development of Longleat House Between 1546 and 1572.' *Archaeological Journal,* 116 (1959), pp. 200–22.

——. 'Elizabethan Architecture and the Gothic Tradition.' *Jour. of Soc. of Architectural Historians of Great Britain,* 6 (1963), pp. 23–29.

Harris, John. 'Somerset House, London.' *Country Life*, 23 November 1967, pp. 1340–43.

Hibbard, G. R., 'The Country House Poem of the Seventeenth Century,' *Jour. of Warburg and Courtauld Institute*, 19 (1956), pp. 159–74.

Honour, Hugh. 'A House of the Gothic Revival, Lee Priory Near Canterbury by James Wyatt,' *Country Life*, 30 May 1952, pp. 1665–66.

Hudson, T. P. 'Moor Park, Leoni and Sir James Thornhill,' *Burlington Magazine*, 113 (1971), pp. 657–61.

Hughes, H. C. 'Humphry Repton.' *RIBA Journal*, 3rd Series, 35 (1928), p. 35.

Hussey, Christopher Edward Clive. 'Crowcombe,' *Country Life*, 22 April 1933, pp. 414–19; 29 April 1933, pp. 442–47.

——. 'Wiltshire Clothiers' Houses.' *Country Life*, 19 November 1943, pp. 904–7.

——. 'Stowe, Buckinghamshire: The Connection of Georgian Landscape with Whig Politics.' *Country Life*, 12 September 1947, pp. 526–29.

——. 'Burghley House, Northhants.' *Country Life*, 3 December 1953, pp. 1828–32; 10 December 1953, pp. 1962–65; 17 December 1953, pp. 2038–41; 24 December 1953, pp. 2104–7; 31 December 1953, pp. 2164–67.

——. 'Luscombe Castle, Devon.' *Country Life*, 23 February 1956, pp. 336–39.

——. 'Wilbury Park, Wiltshire.' *Country Life*, 3 December 1959, pp. 1014–18; 10 December 1959, 1148–52.

Jackson, John Edward. 'Wulfhall and the Seymours.' *Wiltshire Archaeological and Natural History Magazine*, 15 (1875), pp. 140–207.

Kaufmann, Emil. 'At a 17th Century Crossroads: Algarotti vs. Lodoli,' *Jour. Soc. Architectural Historians*, 4 (1944), pp. 23–29.

Lee, Sidney, ed. 'Sir Paul Methuen.' *Dictionary of National Biography*, 37 (1894), pp. 312–13.

Lewis, W. S. 'The Genesis of Strawberry Hill,' *Metropolitan Museum Studies*, 5 (1934–36), pp. 57–92.

Little, Bryan. 'Ston Easton Park, Somerset.' *Country Life*, 23 March 1945, pp. 508–11; 30 March 1945, pp. 552–55; 6 April 1945, pp. 596–99.

Mahon, Denis. 'Guercino's Paintings of Semiramis.' *Art Bulletin*, 31 (1949), pp. 217–23.

——. 'Notes on The Dutch Gift to Charles II.' *Burlington Magazine*, 91 (1949), pp. 303–5; 92 (1950), pp. 12–18.

Maty, Dr. 'Horace Walpole's Marginal Notes, Written in Dr Maty's Miscellaneous Works and Memoirs of the Earl of Chesterfield.' *Philobiblon Society*, Volume 11, 1854.

Moir, Ester. 'Touring Country Houses in the Eighteenth Century.' *Country Life*, 22 October 1958, pp. 586–88.

Nicolson, Benedict. 'The Sanford Collection.' *Burlington Magazine*, 97 (1955), pp. 207–14.

Oswald, Arthur. 'Montacute Re-visited.' *Country Life*, 20 October 1955, pp. 850–53.

——. 'The Hall, Bradford-on-Avon.' *Country Life*, 11 October 1962, pp. 840–43; 18 October 1962, pp. 900–4; 25 October 1962, pp. 1020–23.

Pevsner, Nikolaus. 'The Genesis of the Picturesque.' *Architectural Review*, 96, November 1944, pp. 139–46.

——. 'Double Profile—A Reconstruction of the Elizabethan Style as seen at Wollaton.' *Architectural Review*, 107, March 1950, pp. 147–53.

Phillips, John Goldsmith, James Parker, Edith A. Standen. 'The Tapestry Room from Croome Court.' *The Metropolitan Museum of Art Bulletin*, 18, No. 3 (Nov. 1959), pp. 77–112.

Piper, John. 'Decrepit Glory: A Tour of Hafod.' *Architectural Review*, 87 (June 1940), pp. 207–10.

Smith, H. Clifford. 'Henry Keene: A Georgian Architect.' *Country Life*, 30 March 1945, pp. 556–57.

Stewart, Donald R. 'James Essex.' *Architectural Review*, 108 (1950), pp. 317–21.

Summerson, Sir John Newenham. 'A Repton Portfolio.' *RIBA Journal*, 3rd Series, 40 (1933), p. 313.

——. 'Records of an Iron Age.' *The Official Architect*, 5 May 1945, p. 235.

——. ed. 'The Book of Architecture of John Thorpe in Sir John Soane's Museum.' *Walpole Society*, 40 (1964–66).

——. 'Three Elizabethan Architects.' *Bulletin of the John Rylands Library*, 25 (1957).

——. 'The Classical Country House in 18th Century England; Three Cantor Lectures, 1959.' *Journal of the Royal Society of Arts*, No. 5036, 107 (July 1959).

Toynbee, Paget, ed. 'Journal of Visits to Country Houses.' *Walpole Society*, 16 (1927/28).

Vallance, Aymer. 'Art in England During the Elizabethan and Stuart Periods.' *Studio*, 1908, Special Spring No.

Webb, Geoffrey. 'John and William Bastard, of Blandford.' *Burlington Magazine*, 47 (1925), pp. 144–50.

Wilson, Charles. 'Cloth Production and International Competition in the Seventeenth Century.' *Economic History Review*, 2nd Series, December 1960, pp. 209–21.

Woodbridge, Kenneth. 'Henry Hoare's Paradise.' *Art Bulletin*, 47 (March 1965), pp. 83–116.

Subject Index

Plate numbers are printed in bold type. A page number followed by *n* indicates information in a footnote.

Index of Places

Country estates are indexed under their names, e.g. Hartham Hall, and Longleat. Town residences and other buildings will be found under the place in which they are located, e.g. High Wycombe: Guildhall.

1 The South Front, Corsham Court, Wiltshire

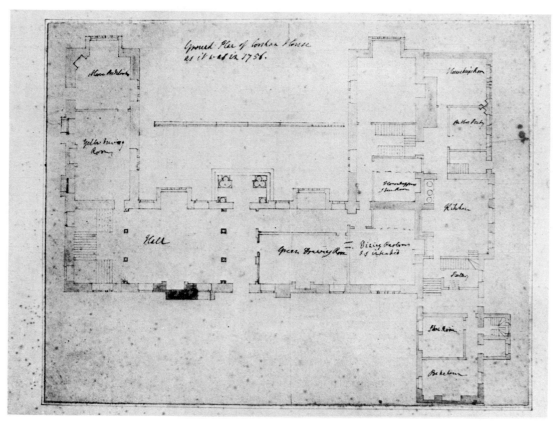

2 The Ground Plan of Corsham House before 1749
(Corsham Archives)

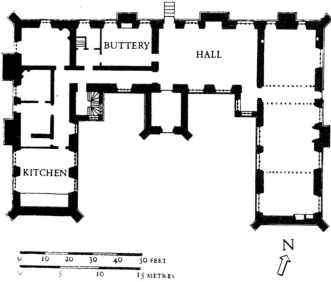

3 The Ground Plan of Barrington Court, Somerset, c. 1530.
From Sir John Summerson *Architecture in Britain* (I11. no. 16
in 1970 ed.) Reproduced by permission of Penguin Books Ltd

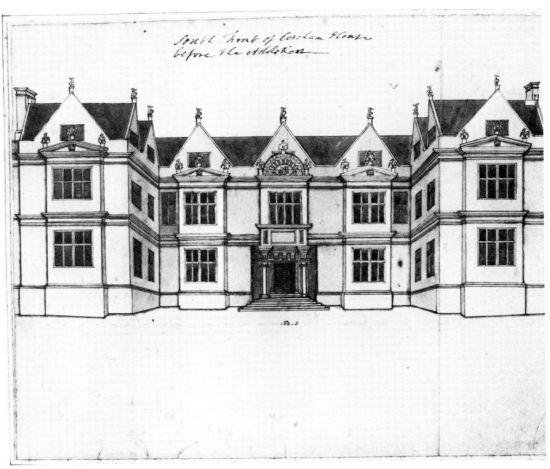

4 The Elizabethan South Front of Corsham House before the alterations under Lancelot Brown (Corsham Archives)

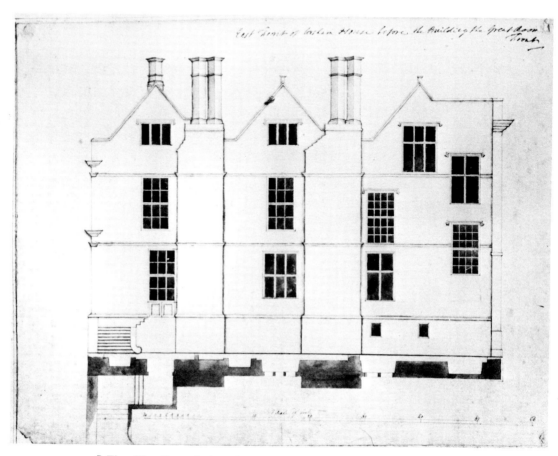

5 The Elevation of the Elizabethan East Front of Corsham House, with the edge of Ireson's facade (1749) appearing on the northeast corner (Corsham Archives)

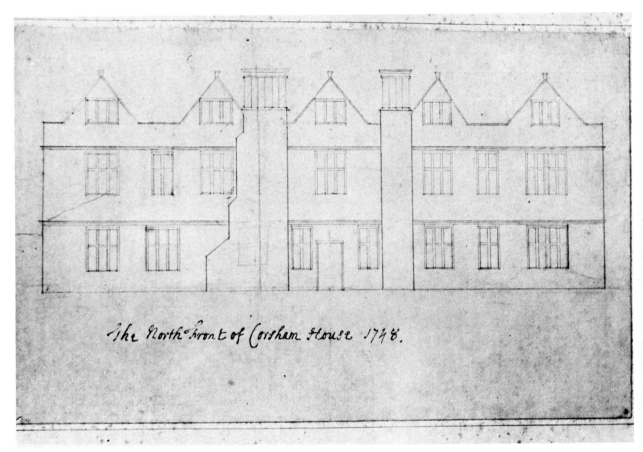

The North front of Corsham House 1748.

6 The Elizabethan North Front of Corsham House, *c.* 1582, before the
addition of Ireson's front of 1749 (Corsham Archives)

10 Detail of the ground-floor Elizabethan bay window in the East wing, Corsham Court

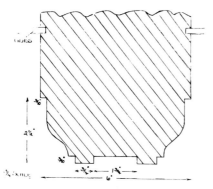

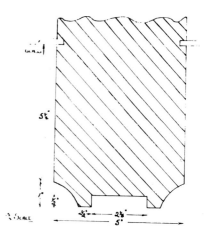

11 Detail of the cross section of an Elizabethan mullion, Corsham Court (*left*) **12** Detail of the cross section of a mullion from the bay windows, Longleat House Wiltshire (*right*). Courtesy the Marquess of Bath

13 The Elizabethan porch on the South Front of Corsham Court

14 Detail of the Doric entablature of the Elizabethan porch, Corsham Court

15 Detail of Plate XI from Jacques Androuet du Cerceau's *Livre d'Architecture* (Paris, 1582)

16 Design A from the remains of dismantled Elizabethan chimney-pieces at Corsham Court

17 Strapwork on the Frieze of the Ionic Order from *Recueil Facades etc., par Joh. Vedreman de Vries* (Bruxelles, 1877), Plate 9

18 Strapwork on the Pedestal of the Ionic Order
from *Recueil Facades etc., par Joh. Vedreman de
Vries* (Bruxelles, 1877), Plate 2

 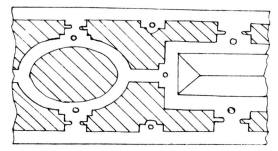

19 Design B from the remains of dismantled Elizabethan chimney-pieces
at Corsham Court (*left*). **20** (*right*) The design from the underside of the
hall-screen entablature, Wollaton Hall, by Robert Smythson, 1580–88
(City of Nottingham National History Museum)

21 'Part of the Screen in the Old Hall, Corsham House', drawn by John Adey Repton. Published by Charles James Richardson, *Observations on the Architecture of England during the reigns of Queen Elizabeth and James I* (London, 1837)

22 The main entrance on the South Front of Corsham Court

23 (OPPOSITE, ABOVE) The Palazzo Chiericati design by Colen Campbell, dedicated to Sir Paul Methuen in 1718. Colen Campbell, *Vitruvius Britannicus*, II, Plate 80

24 (OPPOSITE, BELOW) The North Front of Corsham House, *c.* 1781. An engraving by Thomas Hearne (1744–1817), published by W. Watts. Kemp's Row, Chelsea, 1 May 1784

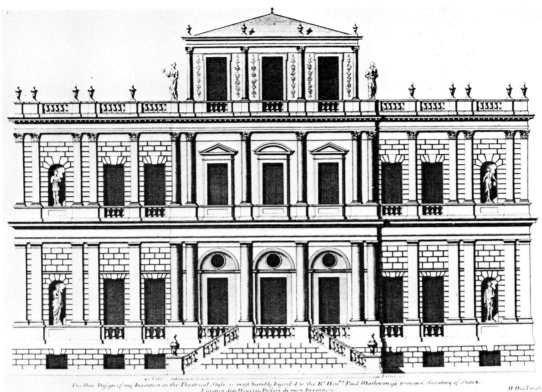

This New Design of my Invention in the Theatrical Style is most humbly Inscrib'd to the R.t Hon.ble Paul Methuen Esq.r proposed Secretary of State.

Elevation d'un Nouveau Desseen de mon Invention

H. Hulsbergh sc.

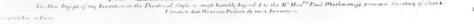

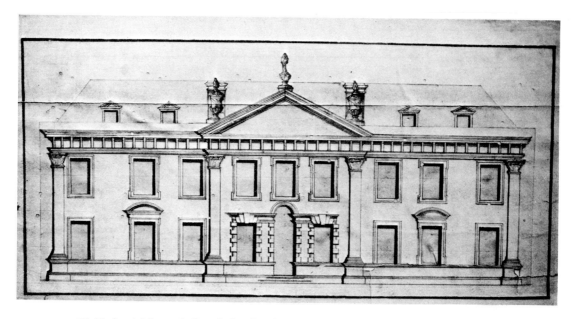

25 Nathaniel Ireson's first design for the North Front of Corsham House, *c.* 1747. (Corsham Archives)

26 A design for the North Front of Corsham House, *c.* 1749, attributed to Nathaniel Ireson (Corsham Archives)

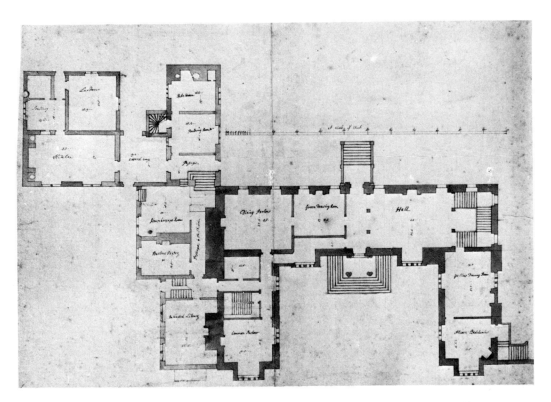

27 A Plan of Corsham House showing Ireson's North Front erected in 1749, with details of the proposed extension to the West wing by Henry Keene, 1759, the location of the new library and domestic premises (Corsham Archives)

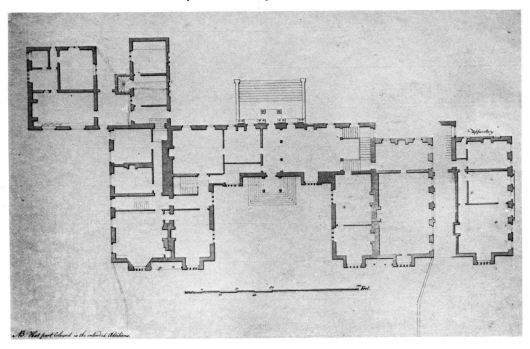

28 Henry Keene's second plan for the alterations at Corsham Court, 1759 (Corsham Archives)

29 Henry Keene's first design for the side elevation of the proposed East Front of Corsham Court, 1759 (Corsham Archives)

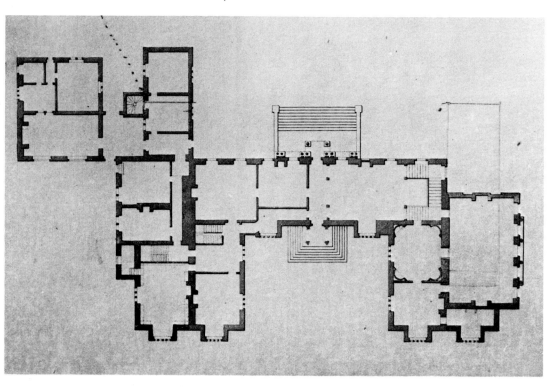

30 Henry Keene's third plan for the alterations at Corsham Court, 1759 (Corsham Archives)

31 Henry Keene's first elevation for the third plan of the
proposed East Front of Corsham Court, 1759 (Corsham Archives)

32 Henry Keene's second elevation for the third plan of the
proposed East Front of Corsham Court, 1759 (Corsham Archives)

33 Henry Keene's elevation of the north end of the picture
gallery for the second elevation of the third plan for the proposed
East Front, Corsham Court 1759 (Corsham Archives)

34 Henry Keene's first design for remodelling the South Front of Corsham Court, 1759 (Corsham Archives)

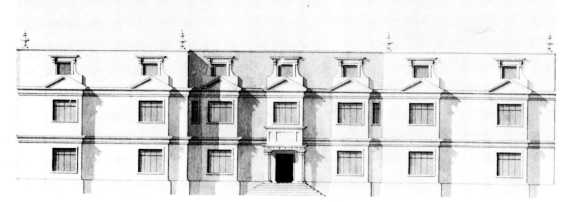

35 Henry Keene's second design for remodelling the South Front of Corsham Court, 1759 (Corsham Archives)

36 Henry Keene's third design for remodelling the South Front of Corsham Court, 1759 (Corsham Archives)

37 Detail of Henry Keene's design, 1759, for the proposed remodelling of the North Front of Corsham Court, erected in 1749 (Corsham Archives)

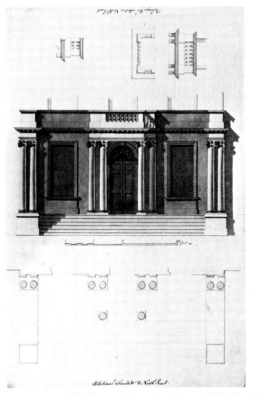

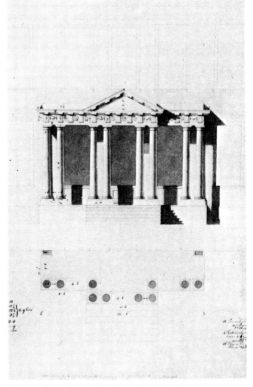

38 Henry Keene's design (*left*) for the proposed porch to be added to the North Front of Corsham Court, 1759. (Corsham Archives). 39 An unidentified design (*right*) for a Doric porch by Henry Keene, Victoria & Albert Museum E898–1921 (Crown Copyright, Victoria & Albert Museum)

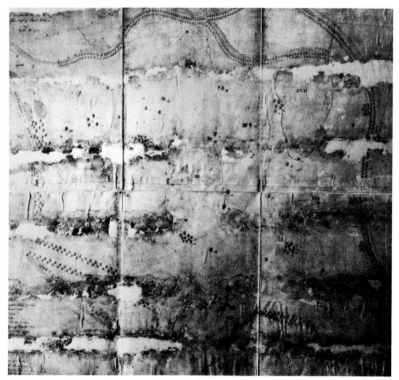

40 Lancelot Brown's map for the alterations of the grounds and park at Corsham Court, 1761 (Corsham Archives)

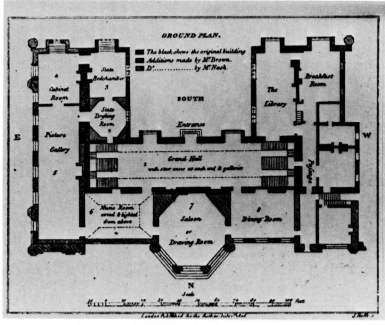

41 The Plan of Corsham Court published by John Britton, *An Historical Account of Corsham House* (London, 1806)

42 A view of the north end of the Picture Gallery, Corsham Court, designed by Lancelot Brown, 1760–63 (*Country Life*)

43 The West Wing, Corsham Court, showing Lancelot Brown's Bath stone facing of the former structure, the Muniment Room, and the Butler's Pantry, late 1759 to 1763 (crenellation added by John Nash)

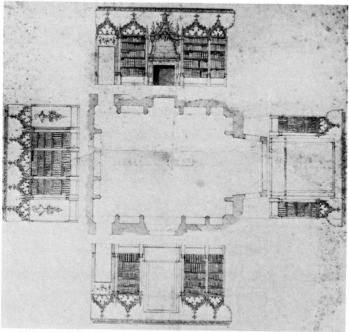

44 An unidentified design for the Rococo-Gothic Library, Corsham Court, *c.* 1759 (Corsham Archives)

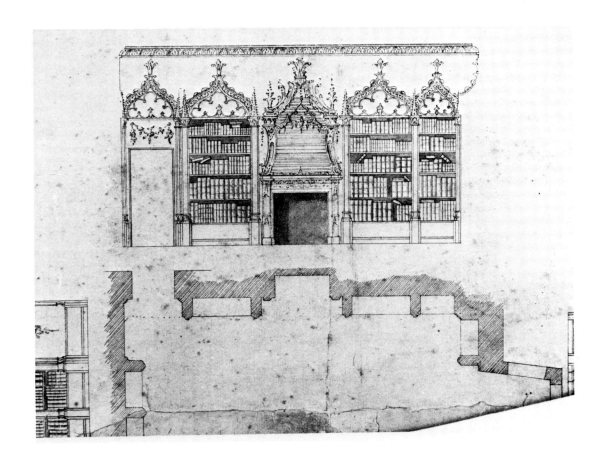

45 Detail of the east wall of the design for the Rococo-Gothic Libary at Corsham Court, *c.* 1759.

46 An unidentified design for a Rococo-Gothic Pavilion or Chapel by Henry Keene, V & A, E901–1921 (Crown Copyright Victoria & Albert Museum)

47 The Library, Strawberry Hill, designed by Horace Walpole, Richard Bentley, and John Chute, 1753–54. A watercolour by John Carter, 1788, from Walpole's extra-illustrated copy of the 1784 *Description*. From Wilmarth Sheldon Lewis: *Horace Walpole*, The A. W. Mellon Lectures in the Fine Arts, Bollingen Series XXV, 9, published by Princeton University Press

48 (OPPOSITE, ABOVE) The Breakfast Room, Corsham Court, converted by John Nash, 1797, from the former Library designed by Lancelot Brown, 1760–63. The ceiling and cornice by Thomas Stocking of Bristol, and the chimney-piece by Prince Hoare of Bath (now removed). (*Country Life*)

49 (OPPOSITE, BELOW) Detail of the Gothic cornice of the Breakfast Room, Corsham Court, executed by Thomas Stocking of Bristol, 1761–62 (*Country Life*)

50 Lancelot Brown's Palladian East Front, Corsham Court, and his lake formed
c. 1761, later filled in by Humphry Repton, 1797–99. An aquatint published by
Archibald Robertson, *A Topographical Survey of the Great Road from London to
Bath and Bristol.* 2 vols. (London, 1792)

51 (*left*) The Alcove or State Bedroom, Corsham Court, interior decoration designed by Lancelot Brown, 1763–64. The ceiling by Thomas Stocking, and the doors by John Hobcraft (National Monuments Record *Crown Copyright*) 52 (*right*) Detail of the door-jamb and dado moulding in the State Bedroom, Corsham Court, designed by Lancelot Brown

53 The Cabinet Room, Corsham Court, designed by Lancelot Brown, 1760–63. The ceiling executed by Thomas Stocking, the marble chimney-piece by Peter Scheemaker, 1764 (National Monuments Record *Crown Copyright*)

54 (OPPOSITE, ABOVE) The sculptured white marble chimney-piece of the Picture Gallery, Corsham Court, supplied by Scheemaker, December, 1764

55 (OPPOSITE, BELOW) The chimney-piece in the Cabinet Room, Corsham Court, showing the frieze after the Choragic Monument of Lysicrates.

56 The Gothic Bath House, Corsham Court, erected
by Lancelot Brown, *c.* 1761–63, and remodelled by
John Nash, 1799

57 Detail of the archways of the Bath House, Corsham Court

A Summer House at Chelsea.

58 A design for a Summer House at Chelsea, attributed
to John or Robert Smythson (RIBA London)

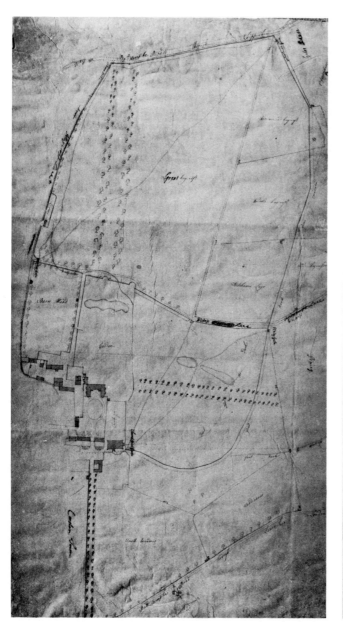

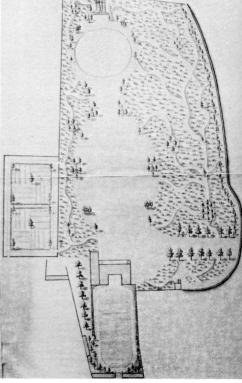

59 (*left*) A map of Corsham House and Grounds, *c.* 1745. (Corsham Archives). 60 (*right*) Greening's 'small' design for the Pleasure Garden, Corsham House, *c.* 1747–49 (Corsham Archives)

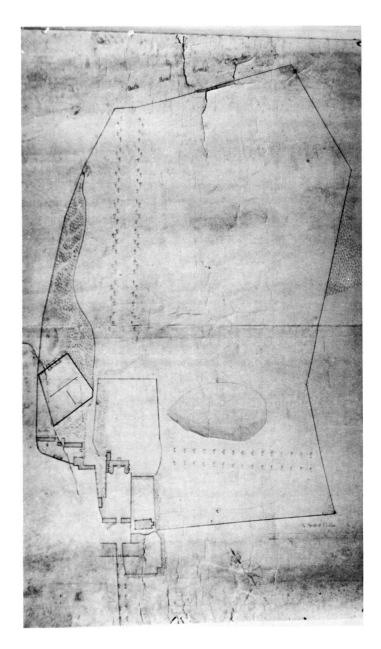

61 Oram's plan for remodelling the gardens and park, Corsham
Court, after 1749. (Corsham Archives)

62 The East Front, Corsham Court, erected by Lancelot Brown. 1762–67, remodelled by John Nash, 1797–1800, with the edge of Thomas Bellamy's North Front, 1846–49, appearing on the northeast corner

63 A watercolour submitted by James Wyatt of his projected design for the North Front and remodelling Brown's East Front of Corsham Court, 1796 (Corsham Archives)

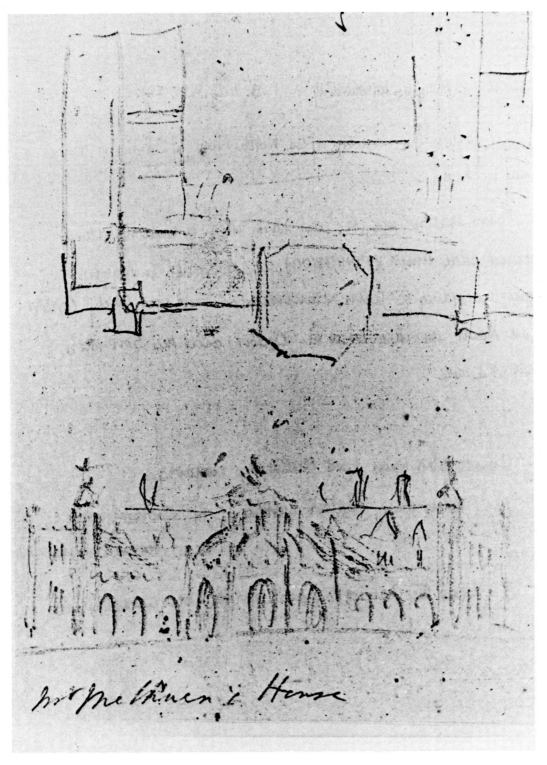

64 'Mr Methuen's House,' a rough sketch made on a letter addressed to
Humphry Repton (Corsham Archives)

65 A view of the North front, Corsham Court, erected by John Nash, from a watercolour by John Buckler, *c.* 1809 (Wiltshire Archaeological & Natural History Society)

67 (OPPOSITE) The Oriel window inserted into the East Front, Corsham Court, by John Nash

66 The first design for the North Front, Corsham Court, drawn to scale and coloured by John Adey Repton (Yale Center for British Art, Paul Mellon collection)

68 The New Library, Corsham Court, designed by John Nash *c.* 1796–97, with a chimney-piece by Prince Hoare of Bath *c.* 1763 (transferred to the Breakfast Room in 1964). (*Country Life*)

69 An illustration of the proposed design for the picture gallery Attingham Park, Shropshire, by John Nash, *c.* 1810. A watercolour attributed to Auguste Charles Pugin by Sir George Trevelyan (National Trust)

70 An engraving of the Grand Hall, Corsham Court, designed by
John Nash, *c*. 1796–97, demolished, 1846. Published by J. P.
Neale, 1 January 1826

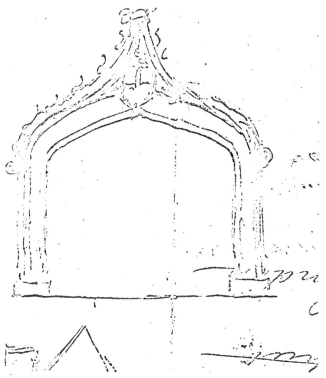

71 A sketch for the chimney-piece in the Grand Hall, Corsham
Court, *c.* 1800, probably made by John Nash (Corsham Archives)

72 The green-and-white marble Gothic chimney-piece designed
by John Nash for the Salon, and supplied by Thomas King of
Bath, 1801, now in Bellamy's Dining Room

73 The Gothic Dairy, Corsham Court, designed by John Nash, 1798

75 (OPPOSITE) The North side of the Elizabethan stable-block, Corsham
Court, gothicised by John Nash, *c.* 1799

74 A detail of the Tudor arches inserted into Lancelot Brown's Bath House by John Nash, *c.* 1799

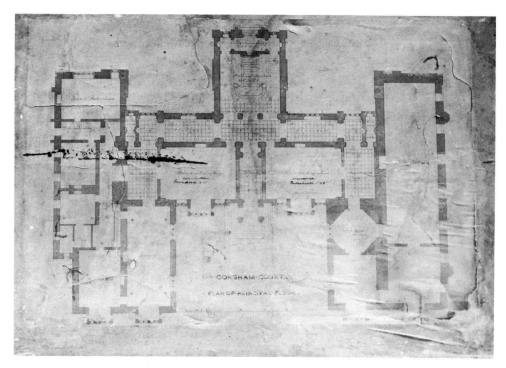

76 The first design for remodelling the ground floor of Corsham Court, 1846, by Thomas Bellamy (Corsham Archives)

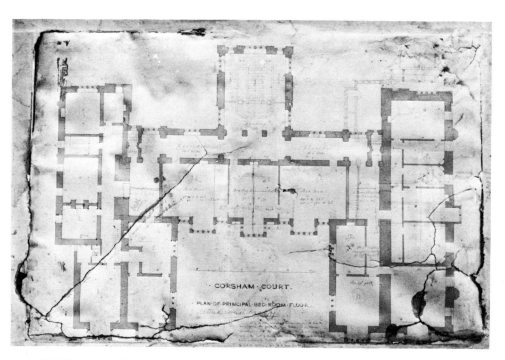

77 The first design for remodelling the first floor of Corsham Court, 1846 by Thomas Bellamy (Corsham Archives)

78 A watercolour view of the north and east fronts, Corsham Court, of Thomas Bellamy's first design 1846 (Corsham Archives)

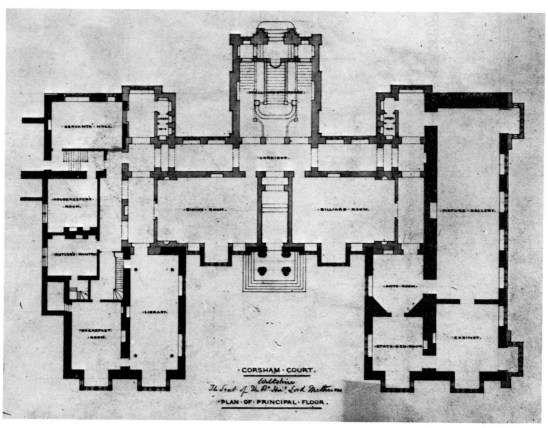

79 The second design for the ground floor of Corsham Court, 1846, by
Thomas Bellamy (RIBA, London)

80 A watercolour view of the north and east fronts of Corsham Court after the second design by Thomas Bellamy, 1846 (RIBA, London)

81 The northeast corner of Corsham Court showing Thomas Bellamy's extension (1846–49) on the North Front, and John Nash's remodelled East Front, 1797–1803

82 Detail of the finials and balustrade of the North Tower, Corsham Court, by Thomas Bellamy, 1846–49

83 A watercolour by Charles James Richardson of the library porch, Montacute House, Somerset, begun 1587 (Victoria & Albert Museum, 3304/4 *Crown Copyright*)

84 A watercolour view of the Staircase Hall, Corsham Court, by Thomas Bellamy, 1846 (RIBA, London)

85 Detail of the right-hand triple archway leading from the Staircase Hall, with a view of the Dining Room doorway, designed by Thomas Bellamy, 1846–9

86 The North Corridor, Corsham Court, from the west end, showing the archways leading to the Staircase Hall, and the niche in the Elizabethan East wall at the end of the corridor, by Thomas Bellamy. Photograph *c.* 1880 by Wilkinson of Trowbridge

87 The Dining Room, Corsham Court, inserted by Thomas Bellamy into the former Grand Hall by John Nash in the original Elizabethan centre section of the house (*Country Life*)

88 The Elizabethan Revival chimney-piece in the West Corridor, Corsham Court, designed by Thomas Bellamy, 1846–49

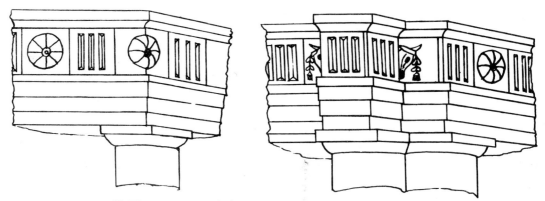

89 The treatment of the corner metope as recommended by Vitruvius (*left*). The corner metope of the Elizabethan south porch of Corsham Court (*right*).

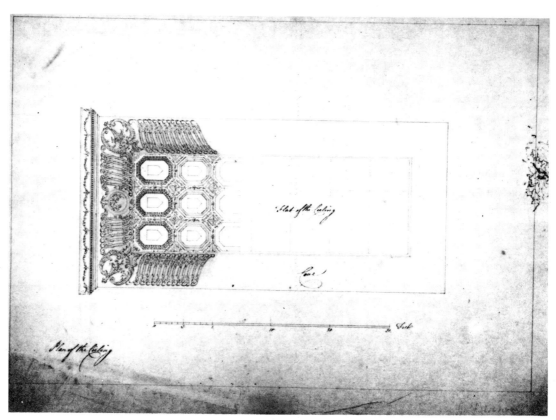

90 Lancelot Brown's design adopted for the Picture Gallery ceiling at Corsham (Reproduced from *Capability Brown* by Dorothy Stroud (Faber & Faber), courtesy J. R. Chichester-Constable)